DISCOURSE TO LADY LAVINIA

HIS DAUGHTER

*Concerning the Manner in Which She Should Conduct Herself
When Going to Court as Lady-in-Waiting to the Most Serene Infanta,
Lady Caterina, Duchess of Savoy*

THE
OTHER VOICE
IN
EARLY MODERN
EUROPE

A Series Edited by Margaret L. King and Albert Rabil Jr.

RECENT BOOKS IN THE SERIES

Annibal Guasco

DISCOURSE TO LADY LAVINIA HIS DAUGHTER

*Concerning the Manner in Which She Should
Conduct Herself When Going to Court
as Lady-in-Waiting to the Most Serene Infanta,
Lady Caterina, Duchess of Savoy*

꒱

*Edited, Translated,
and with an Introduction by Peggy Osborn*

THE UNIVERSITY OF CHICAGO PRESS
Chicago & London

Annibal Guasco, 1540–1619

Peggy Osborn is senior lecturer (retired) in Italian Renaissance literature at the University of Bristol. She is the author of *G. B. Giraldi's Altile: The Birth of a New Dramatic Genre in Renaissance Ferrara*.

The University of Chicago Press, Chicago 60637
The University of Chicago Press, Ltd., London
© 2003 by The University of Chicago
All rights reserved. Published 2003
Printed in the United States of America
12 11 10 09 08 07 06 05 04 03   1 2 3 4 5

ISBN: 0-226-31053-1 (cloth)
ISBN : 0-226-31055-8 (paper)

Library of Congress Cataloging-in-Publication Data
Guasco, Annibale, d. 1619
    Discourse to Lady Lavinia, his daughter : concerning the manner in which she should conduct herself when going to court as lady-in-waiting to the Most Serene Infanta, Lady Caterina, Duchess of Savoy / Annibal Guasco ; edited, translated, and with an introduction by Peggy Osborn.
        p.   cm. — (The other voice in early modern Europe)
    Includes bibliographical references and index.
    ISBN 0-226-31053-1 (cloth : alk. paper) — ISBN 0-226-31055-8 (pbk. : alk. paper)
        1. Conduct of life—Early works to 1900.   2. Women—Conduct of life.   3. Courtesy.   4. Courts and courtiers.   5. Guasco, Lavinia, b. 1574.   6. Ladies-in-waiting—Italy.
    I. Osborn, Peggy.   II. Title.   III. Series.

BJ1584 .G8313 2003
170'.8352—dc21

                                                                          2002153738

CONTENTS

ACKNOWLEDGMENTS

I express my very warmest thanks to my former colleague Mary Morrison for the numerous discussions we have had during the preparation of this edition, to Laura and Giulio Lepscky for their help with obscure sixteenth-century terminology, and especially to Laura for reading and commenting so constructively on my introduction. I also record my thanks to Letizia Panizza for all her advice and unfailing enthusiasm for this project and for organizing the conference at which I first learned of "The Other Voice" series, to Albert Rabil, the series editor, for his encouragement, support, and long patience from across the Atlantic, to Brian Richardson for his invaluable insights into Renaissance publishing, and to Glenise Morgan for her able word processing. In addition, I thank the Marciana Library in Venice for kindly granting permission and arranging for a microfilm to be made for me of their copy of the 1607 edition of Guasco's *Letters*.

Peggy Osborn

THE OTHER VOICE IN EARLY MODERN EUROPE: INTRODUCTION TO THE SERIES

Margaret L. King and Albert Rabil Jr.

THE OLD VOICE AND THE OTHER VOICE

In western Europe and the United States, women are nearing equality in the professions, in business, and in politics. Most enjoy access to education, reproductive rights, and autonomy in financial affairs. Issues vital to women are on the public agenda: equal pay, child care, domestic abuse, breast cancer research, and curricular revision with an eye to the inclusion of women.

These recent achievements have their origins in things women (and some male supporters) said for the first time about six hundred years ago. Theirs is the "other voice," in contradistinction to the "first voice," the voice of the educated men who created Western culture. Coincident with a general reshaping of European culture in the period 1300–1700 (called the Renaissance or early modern period), questions of female equality and opportunity were raised that still resound and are still unresolved.

The other voice emerged against the backdrop of a three-thousand-year history of the derogation of women rooted in the civilizations related to Western culture: Hebrew, Greek, Roman, and Christian. Negative attitudes toward women inherited from these traditions pervaded the intellectual, medical, legal, religious, and social systems that developed during the European Middle Ages.

The following pages describe the traditional, overwhelmingly male views of women's nature inherited by early modern Europeans and the new tradition that the "other voice" called into being to begin to challenge reigning assumptions. This review should serve as a framework for understanding the texts published in the series "The Other Voice in Early Modern Europe." Introductions specific to each text and author follow this essay in all the volumes of the series.

TRADITIONAL VIEWS OF WOMEN, 500 B.C.E. – 1500 C.E.

Embedded in the philosophical and medical theories of the ancient Greeks were perceptions of the female as inferior to the male in both mind and body. Similarly, the structure of civil legislation inherited from the ancient Romans was biased against women, and the views on women developed by Christian thinkers out of the Hebrew Bible and the Christian New Testament were negative and disabling. Literary works composed in the vernacular of ordinary people, and widely recited or read, conveyed these negative assumptions. The social networks within which most women lived—those of the family and the institutions of the Roman Catholic Church—were shaped by this negative tradition and sharply limited the areas in which women might act in and upon the world.

GREEK PHILOSOPHY AND FEMALE NATURE. Greek biology assumed that women were inferior to men and defined them as merely childbearers and housekeepers. This view was authoritatively expressed in the works of the philosopher Aristotle.

Aristotle thought in dualities. He considered action superior to inaction, form (the inner design or structure of any object) superior to matter, completion to incompletion, possession to deprivation. In each of these dualities, he associated the male principle with the superior quality and the female with the inferior. "The male principle in nature," he argued, "is associated with active, formative and perfected characteristics, while the female is passive, material and deprived, desiring the male in order to become complete."[1] Men are always identified with virile qualities, such as judgment, courage, and stamina, and women with their opposites—irrationality, cowardice, and weakness.

The masculine principle was considered superior even in the womb. The man's semen, Aristotle believed, created the form of a new human creature, while the female body contributed only matter. (The existence of the ovum, and with it the other facts of human embryology, was not established until the seventeenth century.) Although the later Greek physician Galen believed there was a female component in generation, contributed by "female semen," the followers of both Aristotle and Galen saw the male role in human generation as more active and more important.

In the Aristotelian view, the male principle sought always to reproduce itself. The creation of a female was always a mistake, therefore, resulting

---

1. Aristotle, *Physics* 1.9.192a20–24, in *The Complete Works of Aristotle,* ed. Jonathan Barnes, rev. Oxford trans., 2 vols. (Princeton, N.J., 1984), 1:328.

from an imperfect act of generation. Every female born was considered a "defective" or "mutilated" male (as Aristotle's terminology has variously been translated), a "monstrosity" of nature.[2]

For Greek theorists, the biology of males and females was the key to their psychology. The female was softer and more docile, more apt to be despondent, querulous, and deceitful. Being incomplete, moreover, she craved sexual fulfillment in intercourse with a male. The male was intellectual, active, and in control of his passions.

These psychological polarities derived from the theory that the universe consisted of four elements (earth, fire, air, and water), expressed in human bodies as four "humors" (black bile, yellow bile, blood, and phlegm) considered respectively dry, hot, damp, and cold and corresponding to mental states ("melancholic," "choleric," "sanguine," "phlegmatic"). In this scheme the male, sharing the principles of earth and fire, was dry and hot; the female, sharing the principles of air and water, was cold and damp.

Female psychology was further affected by her dominant organ, the uterus (womb), *hystera* in Greek. The passions generated by the womb made women lustful, deceitful, talkative, irrational, indeed—when these affects were in excess—"hysterical."

Aristotle's biology also had social and political consequences. If the male principle was superior and the female inferior, then in the household, as in the state, men should rule and women must be subordinate. That hierarchy did not rule out the companionship of husband and wife, whose cooperation was necessary for the welfare of children and the preservation of property. Such mutuality supported male preeminence.

Aristotle's teacher Plato suggested a different possibility: that men and women might possess the same virtues. The setting for this proposal is the imaginary and ideal Republic that Plato sketches in a dialogue of that name. Here, for a privileged elite capable of leading wisely, all distinctions of class and wealth dissolve, as, consequently, do those of gender. Without households or property, as Plato constructs his ideal society, there is no need for the subordination of women. Women may therefore be educated to the same level as men to assume leadership. Plato's Republic remained imaginary, however. In real societies, the subordination of women remained the norm and the prescription.

The views of women inherited from the Greek philosophical tradition became the basis for medieval thought. In the thirteenth century, the supreme Scholastic philosopher Thomas Aquinas, among others, still echoed Aristotle's

2. Aristotle, *Generation of Animals* 2.3.737a27–28, in *The Complete Works*, 1:1144.

views of human reproduction, of male and female personalities, and of the preeminent male role in the social hierarchy.

ROMAN LAW AND THE FEMALE CONDITION. Roman law, like Greek philosophy, underlay medieval thought and shaped medieval society. The ancient belief that adult property-owning men should administer households and make decisions affecting the community at large is the very fulcrum of Roman law.

About 450 B.C.E., during Rome's republican era, the community's customary law was recorded (legendarily) on twelve tablets erected in the city's central forum. It was later elaborated by professional jurists whose activity increased in the imperial era, when much new legislation was passed, especially on issues affecting family and inheritance.. This growing, changing body of laws was eventually codified in the *Corpus of Civil Law* under the direction of the emperor Justinian, generations after the empire ceased to be ruled from Rome. That *Corpus*, read and commented on by medieval scholars from the eleventh century on, inspired the legal systems of most of the cities and kingdoms of Europe.

Laws regarding dowries, divorce, and inheritance pertain primarily to women. Since those laws aimed to maintain and preserve property, the women concerned were those from the property-owning minority. Their subordination to male family members points to the even greater subordination of lower-class and slave women, about whom the laws speak little.

In the early republic, the *paterfamilias*, or "father of the family," possessed *patria potestas*, "paternal power." The term *pater*, "father," in both these cases does not necessarily mean biological father but denotes the head of a household. The father was the person who owned the household's property and, indeed, its human members. The *paterfamilias* had absolute power—including the power, rarely exercised, of life or death—over his wife, his children, and his slaves, as much as his cattle.

Male children could be "emancipated," an act that granted legal autonomy and the right to own property. Those over fourteen could be emancipated by a special grant from the father or automatically by their father's death. But females could never be emancipated; instead, they passed from the authority of their father to that of a husband or, if widowed or orphaned while still unmarried, to a guardian or tutor.

Marriage in its traditional form placed the woman under her husband's authority, or *manus*. He could divorce her on grounds of adultery, drinking wine, or stealing from the household, but she could not divorce him. She could neither possess property in her own right nor bequeath any to her children upon her death. When her husband died, the household property passed not to her but to his male heirs. And when her father died, she had no claim to any family inheritance, which was directed to her brothers or more remote male relatives. The effect of these laws was to exclude women from civil society, itself based on property ownership.

In the later republican and imperial periods, these rules were significantly modified. Women rarely married according to the traditional form. The practice of "free" marriage allowed a woman to remain under her father's authority, to possess property given her by her father (most frequently the "dowry," recoverable from the husband's household on his death), and to inherit from her father. She could also bequeath property to her own children and divorce her husband, just as he could divorce her.

Despite this greater freedom, women still suffered enormous disability under Roman law. Heirs could belong only to the father's side, never the mother's. Moreover, although she could bequeath her property to her children, she could not establish a line of succession in doing so. A woman was "the beginning and end of her own family," said the jurist Ulpian. Moreover, women could play no public role. They could not hold public office, represent anyone in a legal case, or even witness a will. Women had only a private existence and no public personality.

The dowry system, the guardian, women's limited ability to transmit wealth, and total political disability are all features of Roman law adopted by the medieval communities of western Europe, although modified according to local customary laws..

CHRISTIAN DOCTRINE AND WOMEN'S PLACE. The Hebrew Bible and the Christian New Testament authorized later writers to limit women to the realm of the family and to burden them with the guilt of original sin. The passages most fruitful for this purpose were the creation narratives in Genesis and sentences from the Epistles defining women's role within the Christian family and community.

Each of the first two chapters of Genesis contains a creation narrative. In the first "God created man in his own image, in the image of God he created him; male and female he created them" (Gen. 1:27). In the second, God created Eve from Adam's rib (2:21–23). Christian theologians relied principally on Genesis 2 for their understanding of the relation between man and woman, interpreting the creation of Eve from Adam as proof of her subordination to him.

The creation story in Genesis 2 leads to that of the temptations in Genesis 3: of Eve by the wily serpent and of Adam by Eve. As read by Christian theologians from Tertullian to Thomas Aquinas, the narrative made Eve responsible for the Fall and its consequences. She instigated the act; she deceived her husband; she suffered the greater punishment. Her disobedience made it necessary for Jesus to be incarnated and to die on the cross. From the pulpit, moralists and preachers for centuries conveyed to women the guilt that they bore for original sin.

The Epistles offered advice to early Christians on building communities of the faithful. Among the matters to be regulated was the place of women. Paul offered views favorable to women in Gal. 3:28: "There is neither Jew nor Greek, there is neither slave nor free, there is neither male nor female; for you are all one in Christ Jesus." Paul also referred to women as his coworkers and placed them on a par with himself and his male coworkers (Phil. 4:2–3; Rom. 16:1–3; 1 Cor. 16:19). Elsewhere Paul limited women's possibilities: "But I want you to understand that the head of every man is Christ, the head of a woman is her husband, and the head of Christ is God" (1 Cor. 11:3).

Biblical passages by later writers (though attributed to Paul) enjoined women to forgo jewels, expensive clothes, and elaborate coiffures; and they forbade women to "teach or have authority over men," telling them to "learn in silence with all submissiveness" as is proper for one responsible for sin, consoling them, however, with the thought that they will be saved through childbearing (1 Tim. 2:9–15). Other texts among the later Epistles defined women as the weaker sex and emphasized their subordination to their husbands (1 Pet. 3:7; Col. 3:18; Eph. 5:22–23).

These passages from the New Testament became the arsenal employed by theologians of the early church to transmit negative attitudes toward women to medieval Christian culture—above all, Tertullian (*On the Apparel of Women*), Jerome (*Against Jovinian*), and Augustine (*The Literal Meaning of Genesis*).

THE IMAGE OF WOMEN IN MEDIEVAL LITERATURE. The philosophical, legal, and religious traditions born in antiquity formed the basis of the medieval intellectual synthesis wrought by trained thinkers, mostly clerics, writing in Latin and based largely in universities. The vernacular literary tradition that developed alongside the learned tradition also spoke about female nature and women's roles. Medieval stories, poems, and epics also portrayed women negatively—as lustful and deceitful—while praising good housekeepers and loyal wives as replicas of the Virgin Mary or the female saints and martyrs.

There is an exception in the movement of "courtly love" that evolved in southern France from the twelfth century. Courtly love was the erotic love between a nobleman and noblewoman, the latter usually superior in social rank. It was always adulterous. From the conventions of courtly love derive modern Western notions of romantic love. The tradition has had an impact disproportionate to its size, for it affected only a tiny elite, and very few women. The exaltation of the female lover probably does not reflect a higher evaluation of women or a step toward their sexual liberation. More likely it gives expression to the social and sexual tensions besetting the knightly class at a specific historical juncture.

The literary fashion of courtly love was on the wane by the thirteenth century, when the widely read *Romance of the Rose* was composed in French by two authors of significantly different dispositions. Guillaume de Lorris composed the initial four thousand verses about 1235, and Jean de Meun added about seventeen thousand verses—more than four times the original—about 1265.

The fragment composed by Guillaume de Lorris stands squarely in the tradition of courtly love. Here the poet, in a dream, is admitted into a walled garden where he finds a magic fountain in which a rosebush is reflected. He longs to pick one rose, but the thorns prevent his doing so, even as he is wounded by arrows from the god of love, whose commands he agrees to obey. The rest of this part of the poem recounts the poet's unsuccessful efforts to pluck the rose.

The longer part of the *Romance* by Jean de Meun also describes a dream. But here allegorical characters give long didactic speeches, providing a social satire on a variety of themes, some pertaining to women. Love is an anxious and tormented state, the poem explains: women are greedy and manipulative, marriage is miserable, beautiful women are lustful, ugly ones cease to please, and a chaste woman is as rare as a black swan.

Shortly after Jean de Meun completed *The Romance of the Rose*, Mathéolus penned his *Lamentations*, a long Latin diatribe against marriage translated into French about a century later. The *Lamentations* sum up medieval attitudes toward women and provoked the important response by Christine de Pizan in her *Book of the City of Ladies*.

In 1355 Giovanni Boccaccio wrote *Il Corbaccio*, another antifeminist manifesto, though ironically by an author whose other works pioneered new directions in Renaissance thought. The former husband of his lover appears to Boccaccio, condemning his unmoderated lust and detailing the defects of women. Boccaccio concedes at the end "how much men naturally surpass women in nobility" and is cured of his desires.[3]

---

3. Giovanni Boccaccio, *The Corbaccio; or, The Labyrinth of Love*, trans. and ed. Anthony K. Cassell, rev. ed. (Binghamton, N.Y., 1993), 71.

WOMEN'S ROLES: THE FAMILY. The negative perceptions of women expressed in the intellectual tradition are also implicit in the actual roles that women played in European society. Assigned to subordinate positions in the household and the church, they were barred from significant participation in public life.

Medieval European households, like those in antiquity and in non-Western civilizations, were headed by males. It was the male serf (or peasant), feudal lord, town merchant, or citizen who was polled or taxed or succeeded to an inheritance or had any acknowledged public role, although his wife or widow could stand as a temporary surrogate. From about 1100, the position of property-holding males was further enhanced: inheritance was confined to the male, or agnate, line—with depressing consequences for women.

A wife never fully belonged to her husband's family, nor was she a daughter to her father's family. She left her father's house young to marry whomever her parents chose. Her dowry was managed by her husband, and at her death it normally passed to her children by him.

A married woman's life was occupied nearly constantly with cycles of pregnancy, childbearing, and lactation. Women bore children through all the years of their fertility, and many died in childbirth. They were also responsible for raising young children up to six or seven. In the propertied classes that responsibility was shared, since it was common for a wet nurse to take over breast-feeding, and servants performed other chores.

Women trained their daughters in the household duties appropriate to their status, nearly always tasks associated with textiles: spinning, weaving, sewing, embroidering. Their sons were sent out of the house as apprentices or students, or their training was assumed by fathers in later childhood and adolescence. On the death of her husband, a woman's children became the responsibility of his family. She generally did not take "his" children with her to a new marriage or back to her father's house, except sometimes in the artisan classes.

Women also worked. Rural peasants performed farm chores, merchant wives often practiced their husbands' trades, the unmarried daughters of the urban poor worked as servants or prostitutes. All wives produced or embellished textiles and did the housekeeping, while wealthy ones managed servants. These labors were unpaid or poorly paid but often contributed substantially to family wealth.

WOMEN'S ROLES: THE CHURCH. Membership in a household, whether a father's or a husband's, meant for women a lifelong subordination to others.

In western Europe, the Roman Catholic Church offered an alternative to the career of wife and mother. A woman could enter a convent, parallel in function to the monasteries for men that evolved in the early Christian centuries.

In the convent, a woman pledged herself to a celibate life, lived according to strict community rules, and worshiped daily. Often the convent offered training in Latin, allowing some women to become considerable scholars and authors as well as scribes, artists, and musicians. For women who chose the conventual life, the benefits could be enormous, but for numerous others placed in convents by paternal choice, the life could be restrictive and burdensome.

The conventual life declined as an alternative for women as the modern age approached. Reformed monastic institutions resisted responsibility for related female orders. The church increasingly restricted female institutional life by insisting on closer male supervision.

Women often sought other options. Some joined the communities of laywomen that sprang up spontaneously in the thirteenth century in the urban zones of western Europe, especially in Flanders and Italy. Some joined the heretical movements that flourished in late medieval Christendom, whose anticlerical and often antifamily positions particularly appealed to women. In these communities, some women were acclaimed as "holy women" or "saints," whereas others often were condemned as frauds or heretics.

In all, though the options offered to women by the church were sometimes less than satisfactory, they were sometimes richly rewarding. After 1520 the convent remained an option only in Roman Catholic territories. Protestantism engendered an ideal of marriage as a heroic endeavor and appeared to place husband and wife on a more equal footing. Sermons and treatises, however, still called for female subordination and obedience.

THE OTHER VOICE, 1300 – 1700

When the modern era opened, European culture was so firmly structured by a framework of negative attitudes toward women that to dismantle it was a monumental labor. The process began as part of a larger cultural movement that entailed the critical reexamination of ideas inherited from the ancient and medieval past. The humanists launched that critical reexamination.

THE HUMANIST FOUNDATION. Originating in Italy in the fourteenth century, humanism quickly became the dominant intellectual movement in

Europe. Spreading in the sixteenth century from Italy to the rest of Europe, it fueled the literary, scientific, and philosophical movements of the era and laid the basis for the eighteenth-century Enlightenment.

Humanists regarded the Scholastic philosophy of medieval universities as out of touch with the realities of urban life. They found in the rhetorical discourse of classical Rome a language adapted to civic life and public speech. They learned to read, speak, and write classical Latin and, eventually, classical Greek. They founded schools to teach others to do so, establishing the pattern for elementary and secondary education for the next three hundred years.

In the service of complex government bureaucracies, humanists employed their skills to write eloquent letters, deliver public orations, and formulate public policy. They developed new scripts for copying manuscripts and used the new printing press to disseminate texts, for which they created methods of critical editing.

Humanism was a movement led by males who accepted the evaluation of women in ancient texts and generally shared the misogynist perceptions of their culture. (Female humanists, as we will see, did not.) Yet humanism also opened the door to a reevaluation of the nature and capacity of women. By calling authors, texts, and ideas into question, it made possible the fundamental rereading of the whole intellectual tradition that was required in order to free women from cultural prejudice and social subordination.

A DIFFERENT CITY. The other voice first appeared when, after so many centuries, the accumulation of misogynist concepts evoked a response from a capable female defender: Christine de Pizan (1365–1431). Introducing her *Book of the City of Ladies* (1405), she described how she was affected by reading Mathéolus's *Lamentations:* "Just the sight of this book . . . made me wonder how it happened that so many different men . . . are so inclined to express both in speaking and in their treatises and writings so many wicked insults about women and their behavior."[4] These statements impelled her to detest herself "and the entire feminine sex, as though we were monstrosities in nature."[5]

The rest of *The Book of the City of Ladies* presents a justification of the female sex and a vision of an ideal community of women. A pioneer, she has received the message of female inferiority and rejected it. From the fourteenth

4. Christine de Pizan, *The Book of the City of Ladies,* trans. Earl Jeffrey Richards, foreword by Marina Warner (New York, 1982), 1.1.1, pp. 3–4.
5. Ibid., 1.1.1–2, p. 5.

to the seventeenth century, a huge body of literature accumulated that responded to the dominant tradition.

The result was a literary explosion consisting of works by both men and women, in Latin and in the vernaculars: works enumerating the achievements of notable women; works rebutting the main accusations made against women; works arguing for the equal education of men and women; works defining and redefining women's proper role in the family, at court, in public; works describing women's lives and experiences. Recent monographs and articles have begun to hint at the great range of this movement, involving probably several thousand titles. The protofeminism of these "other voices" constitutes a significant fraction of the literary product of the early modern era.

THE CATALOGS. About 1365 the same Boccaccio whose *Corbaccio* rehearses the usual charges against female nature wrote another work, *Concerning Famous Women*. A humanist treatise drawing on classical texts, it praised 106 notable women, ninety-eight of them from pagan Greek and Roman antiquity, one (Eve) from the Bible, and seven from the medieval religious and cultural tradition; his book helped make all readers aware of a sex normally condemned or forgotten. Boccaccio's outlook nevertheless was unfriendly to women, for it singled out for praise those women who possessed the traditional virtues of chastity, silence, and obedience. Women who were active in the public realm—for example, rulers and warriors—were depicted as usually being lascivious and as suffering terrible punishments for entering the masculine sphere. Women were his subject, but Boccaccio's standard remained male.

Christine de Pizan's *Book of the City of Ladies* contains a second catalog, one responding specifically to Boccaccio's. Whereas Boccaccio portrays female virtue as exceptional, she depicts it as universal. Many women in history were leaders, or remained chaste despite the lascivious approaches of men, or were visionaries and brave martyrs.

The work of Boccaccio inspired a series of catalogs of illustrious women of the biblical, classical, Christian, and local pasts, among them Filippo da Bergamo's *Of Illustrious Women*, Pierre de Brantôme's *Lives of Illustrious Women*, Pierre Le Moyne's *Gallerie of Heroic Women*, and Pietro Paolo de Ribera's *Immortal Triumphs and Heroic Enterprises of 845 Women*. Whatever their embedded prejudices, these works drove home to the public the possibility of female excellence.

THE DEBATE. At the same time, many questions remained: Could a woman be virtuous? Could she perform noteworthy deeds? Was she even, strictly speaking, of the same human species as men? These questions were debated over four centuries, in French, German, Italian, Spanish, and English, by authors male and female, among Catholics, Protestants, and Jews, in ponderous volumes and breezy pamphlets. The whole literary genre has been called the *querelle des femmes*, the "woman question."

The opening volley of this battle occurred in the first years of the fifteenth century, in a literary debate sparked by Christine de Pizan. She exchanged letters critical of Jean de Meun's contribution to *The Romance of the Rose* with two French royal secretaries, Jean de Montreuil and Gontier Col. When the matter became public, Jean Gerson, one of Europe's leading theologians, supported de Pizan's arguments against de Meun, for the moment silencing the opposition.

The debate resurfaced repeatedly over the next two hundred years. *The Triumph of Women* (1438) by Juan Rodríguez de la Camara (or Juan Rodríguez del Padron) struck a new note by presenting arguments for the superiority of women to men. *The Champion of Women* (1440–42) by Martin Le Franc addresses once again the negative views of women presented in *The Romance of the Rose* and offers counterevidence of female virtue and achievement.

A cameo of the debate on women is included in *The Courtier,* one of the most widely read books of the era, published by the Italian Baldassare Castiglione in 1528 and immediately translated into other European vernaculars. *The Courtier* depicts a series of evenings at the court of the duke of Urbino in which many men and some women of the highest social stratum amuse themselves by discussing a range of literary and social issues. The "woman question" is a pervasive theme throughout, and the third of its four books is devoted entirely to that issue.

In a verbal duel, Gasparo Pallavicino and Giuliano de' Medici present the main claims of the two traditions. Gasparo argues the innate inferiority of women and their inclination to vice. Only in bearing children do they profit the world. Giuliano counters that women share the same spiritual and mental capacities as men and may excel in wisdom and action. Men and women are of the same essence: just as no stone can be more perfectly a stone than another, so no human being can be more perfectly human than others, whether male or female. It was an astonishing assertion, boldly made to an audience as large as all Europe.

THE TREATISES. Humanism provided the materials for a positive counterconcept to the misogyny embedded in Scholastic philosophy and law and inherited from the Greek, Roman, and Christian pasts. A series of humanist treatises on marriage and family, on education and deportment, and on the nature of women helped construct these new perspectives.

The works by Francesco Barbaro and Leon Battista Alberti—*On Marriage* (1415) and *On the Family* (1434–37)—far from defending female equality, reasserted women's responsibility for rearing children and managing the housekeeping while being obedient, chaste, and silent. Nevertheless, they served the cause of reexamining the issue of women's nature by placing domestic issues at the center of scholarly concern and reopening the pertinent classical texts. In addition, Barbaro emphasized the companionate nature of marriage and the importance of a wife's spiritual and mental qualities for the well-being of the family.

These themes reappear in later humanist works on marriage and the education of women by Juan Luis Vives and Erasmus. Both were moderately sympathetic to the condition of women without reaching beyond the usual masculine prescriptions for female behavior.

An outlook more favorable to women characterizes the nearly unknown work *In Praise of Women* (ca. 1487) by the Italian humanist Bartolommeo Goggio. In addition to providing a catalog of illustrious women, Goggio argued that male and female are the same in essence, but that women (reworking the Adam and Eve narrative from quite a new angle) are actually superior. In the same vein, the Italian humanist Maria Equicola asserted the spiritual equality of men and women in *On Women* (1501). In 1525 Galeazzo Flavio Capra (or Capella) published his work *On the Excellence and Dignity of Women*. This humanist tradition of treatises defending the worthiness of women culminates in the work of Henricus Cornelius Agrippa *On the Nobility and Preeminence of the Female Sex*. No work by a male humanist more succinctly or explicitly presents the case for female dignity.

THE WITCH BOOKS. While humanists grappled with the issues pertaining to women and family, other learned men turned their attention to what they perceived as a very great problem: witches. Witch-hunting manuals, explorations of the witch phenomenon, and even defenses of witches are not at first glance pertinent to the tradition of the other voice. But they do relate in this way: most accused witches were women. The hostility aroused by supposed witch activity is comparable to the hostility aroused by women. The evil deeds the victims of the hunt were charged with were exaggerations of the vices to which, many believed, all women were prone.

The connection between the witch accusation and the hatred of women is explicit in the notorious witch-hunting manual *The Hammer of Witches* (1486) by two Dominican inquisitors, Heinrich Krämer and Jacob Sprenger. Here the inconstancy, deceitfulness, and lustfulness traditionally associated with women are depicted in exaggerated form as the core features of witch behavior. These traits inclined women to make a bargain with the devil—sealed by sexual intercourse—by which they acquired unholy powers. Such bizarre claims, far from being rejected by rational men, were broadcast by intellectuals. The German Ulrich Molitur, the Frenchman Nicolas Rémy, and the Italian Stefano Guazzo all coolly informed the public of sinister orgies and midnight pacts with the devil. The celebrated French jurist, historian, and political philosopher Jean Bodin argued that because women were especially prone to diabolism, regular legal procedures could properly be suspended in order to try those accused of this "exceptional crime."

A few experts such as the physician Johann Weyer, a student of Agrippa's, raised their voices in protest. In 1563 he explained the witch phenomenon thus, without discarding belief in diabolism: the devil deluded foolish old women afflicted by melancholia, causing them to believe they had magical powers. Weyer's rational skepticism, which had good credibility in the community of the learned, worked to revise the conventional views of women and witchcraft.

WOMEN'S WORKS. To the many categories of works produced on the question of women's worth must be added nearly all works written by women. A woman writing was in herself a statement of women's claim to dignity.

Only a few women wrote anything before the dawn of the modern era, for three reasons. First, they rarely received the education that would enable them to write. Second, they were not admitted to the public roles—as administrator, bureaucrat, lawyer or notary, or university professor—in which they might gain knowledge of the kinds of things the literate public thought worth writing about. Third, the culture imposed silence on women, considering speaking out a form of unchastity. Given these conditions, it is remarkable that any women wrote. Those who did before the fourteenth century were almost always nuns or religious women whose isolation made their pronouncements more acceptable.

From the fourteenth century on, the volume of women's writings rose. Women continued to write devotional literature, although not always as cloistered nuns. They also wrote diaries, often intended as keepsakes for their children; books of advice to their sons and daughters; letters to family members and friends; and family memoirs, in a few cases elaborate enough to be considered histories.

A few women wrote works directly concerning the "woman question," and some of these, such as the humanists Isotta Nogarola, Cassandra Fedele, Laura Cereta, and Olympia Morata, were highly trained. A few were professional writers, living by the income of their pens; the very first among them was Christine de Pizan, noteworthy in this context as in so many others. In addition to *The Book of the City of Ladies* and her critiques of *The Romance of the Rose*, she wrote *The Treasure of the City of Ladies* (a guide to social decorum for women), an advice book for her son, much courtly verse, and a full-scale history of the reign of King Charles V of France.

WOMEN PATRONS. Women who did not themselves write but encouraged others to do so boosted the development of an alternative tradition. Highly placed women patrons supported authors, artists, musicians, poets, and learned men. Such patrons, drawn mostly from the Italian elites and the courts of northern Europe, figure disproportionately as the dedicatees of the important works of early feminism.

For a start, it might be noted that the catalogs of Boccaccio and Alvaro de Luna were dedicated to the Florentine noblewoman Andrea Acciaiuoli and to Doña María, first wife of King Juan II of Castile, while the French translation of Boccaccio's work was commissioned by Anne of Brittany, wife of King Charles VIII of France. The humanist treatises of Goggio, Equicola, Vives, and Agrippa were dedicated, respectively, to Eleanora of Aragon, wife of Ercole I d'Este, duke of Ferrara; to Margherita Cantelma of Mantua; to Catherine of Aragon, wife of King Henry VIII of England; and to Margaret, duchess of Austria and regent of the Netherlands. As late as 1696, Mary Astell's *Serious Proposal to the Ladies, for the Advancement of Their True and Greatest Interest* was dedicated to Princess Anne of Denmark.

These authors presumed that their efforts would be welcome to female patrons, or they may have written at the bidding of those patrons. Silent themselves, perhaps even unresponsive, these loftily placed women helped shape the tradition of the other voice.

THE ISSUES. The literary forms and patterns in which the tradition of the other voice presented itself have now been sketched. It remains to highlight the major issues around which this tradition crystallizes. In brief, there are four problems to which our authors return again and again, in plays and catalogs, in verse and letters, in treatises and dialogues, in every language: the problem of chastity, the problem of power, the problem of speech, and the problem of knowledge. Of these the greatest, preconditioning the others, is the problem of chastity.

THE PROBLEM OF CHASTITY. In traditional European culture, as in those of antiquity and others around the globe, chastity was perceived as woman's quintessential virtue—in contrast to courage, or generosity, or leadership, or rationality, seen as virtues characteristic of men. Opponents of women charged them with insatiable lust. Women themselves and their defenders—without disputing the validity of the standard—responded that women were capable of chastity.

The requirement of chastity kept women at home, silenced them, isolated them, left them in ignorance. It was the source of all other impediments. Why was it so important to the society of men, of whom chastity was not required, and who more often than not considered it their right to violate the chastity of any woman they encountered?

Female chastity ensured the continuity of the male-headed household. If a man's wife was not chaste, he could not be sure of the legitimacy of his offspring. If they were not his and they acquired his property, it was not his household, but some other man's, that had endured. If his daughter was not chaste, she could not be transferred to another man's household as his wife, and he was dishonored.

The whole system of the integrity of the household and the transmission of property was bound up in female chastity. Such a requirement pertained only to property-owning classes, of course. Poor women could not expect to maintain their chastity, least of all if they were in contact with high-status men to whom all women but those of their own household were prey.

In Catholic Europe, the requirement of chastity was further buttressed by moral and religious imperatives. Original sin was inextricably linked with the sexual act. Virginity was seen as heroic virtue, far more impressive than, say, the avoidance of idleness or greed. Monasticism, the cultural institution that dominated medieval Europe for centuries, was grounded in the renunciation of the flesh. The Catholic reform of the eleventh century imposed a similar standard on all the clergy and a heightened awareness of sexual requirements on all the laity. Although men were asked to be chaste, female unchastity was much worse: it led to the devil, as Eve had led mankind to sin.

To such requirements, women and their defenders protested their innocence. Furthermore, following the example of holy women who had escaped the requirements of family and sought the religious life, some women began to conceive of female communities as alternatives both to family and to the cloister. Christine de Pizan's city of ladies was such a community. Moderata Fonte and Mary Astell envisioned others. The luxurious salons of the French *précieuses* of the seventeenth century, or the comfortable English drawing rooms of the next, may have been born of the same impulse. Here women not only might escape, if briefly, the subordinate position that life in the family entailed but might also make claims to power, exercise their capacity for speech, and display their knowledge.

THE PROBLEM OF POWER. Women were excluded from power: the whole cultural tradition insisted on it. Only men were citizens, only men bore arms, only men could be chiefs or lords or kings. There were exceptions that did not disprove the rule, when wives or widows or mothers took the place of men, awaiting their return or the maturation of a male heir. A woman who attempted to rule in her own right was perceived as an anomaly, a monster, at once a deformed woman and an insufficient male, sexually confused and consequently unsafe.

The association of such images with women who held or sought power explains some otherwise odd features of early modern culture. Queen Elizabeth I of England, one of the few women to hold full regal authority in European history, played with such male/female images—positive ones, of course—in representing herself to her subjects. She was a prince, and manly, even though she was female. She was also (she claimed) virginal, a condition absolutely essential if she was to avoid the attacks of her opponents. Catherine de' Medici, who ruled France as widow and regent for her sons, also adopted such imagery in defining her position. She chose as one symbol the figure of Artemisia, an androgynous ancient warrior-heroine who combined a female persona with masculine powers.

Power in a woman, without such sexual imagery, seems to have been indigestible by the culture. A rare note was struck by the Englishman Sir Thomas Elyot in his *Defence of Good Women* (1540), justifying both women's participation in civic life and their prowess in arms. The old tune was sung by the Scots reformer John Knox in his *First Blast of the Trumpet against the Monstrous Regiment of Women* (1558); for him rule by women, defects in nature, was a hideous contradiction in terms.

The confused sexuality of the imagery of female potency was not reserved for rulers. Any woman who excelled was likely to be called an Amazon, recalling the self-mutilated warrior women of antiquity who repudiated all men, gave up their sons, and raised only their daughters. She was often said to have "exceeded her sex" or to have possessed "masculine virtue"—as the very fact of conspicuous excellence conferred masculinity even on the female subject. The catalogs of notable women often showed those female heroes dressed in armor, armed to the teeth, like men. Amazonian heroines romp through the epics of the age—Ariosto's *Orlando Furioso* (1532) and Spenser's *Faerie Queene* (1590–1609). Excellence in a woman was perceived as a claim for power, and power was reserved for the masculine realm. A woman who possessed either one was masculinized and lost title to her own female identity.

THE PROBLEM OF SPEECH. Just as power had a sexual dimension when it was claimed by women, so did speech. A good woman spoke little. Excessive speech was an indication of unchastity. By speech, women seduced men. Eve had lured Adam into sin by her speech. Accused witches were commonly accused of having spoken abusively, or irrationally, or simply too much. As enlightened a figure as Francesco Barbaro insisted on silence in a woman, which he linked to her perfect unanimity with her husband's will and her unblemished virtue (her chastity). Another Italian humanist, Leonardo Bruni, in advising a noblewoman on her studies, barred her not from speech but from public speaking. That was reserved for men.

Related to the problem of speech was that of costume—another, if silent, form of self-expression. Assigned the task of pleasing men as their primary occupation, elite women often tended toward elaborate costume, hairdressing, and the use of cosmetics. Clergy and secular moralists alike condemned these practices. The appropriate function of costume and adornment was to announce the status of a woman's husband or father. Any further indulgence in adornment was akin to unchastity.

THE PROBLEM OF KNOWLEDGE. When the Italian noblewoman Isotta Nogarola had begun to attain a reputation as a humanist, she was accused of incest—a telling instance of the association of learning in women with unchastity. That chilling association inclined any woman who was educated to deny that she was or to make exaggerated claims of heroic chastity.

If educated women were pursued with suspicions of sexual misconduct, women seeking an education faced an even more daunting obstacle: the assumption that women were by nature incapable of learning, that reasoning was a particularly masculine ability. Just as they proclaimed their chastity, women and their defenders insisted on their capacity for learning. The major work by a male writer on female education—that by Juan Luis Vives, *On the Education of a Christian Woman* (1523)—granted female capacity for intellection but still argued that a woman's whole education was to be shaped around the requirement of chastity and a future within the household. Female writers of the following generations—Marie de Gournay in France, Anna Maria van Schurman in Holland, Mary Astell in England—began to envision other possibilities.

The pioneers of female education were the Italian women humanists who managed to attain a literacy in Latin and a knowledge of classical and Christian literature equivalent to that of prominent men. Their works implicitly and explicitly raise questions about women's social roles, defining problems that beset women attempting to break out of the cultural limits that had bound them. Like Christine de Pizan, who achieved an advanced education through her father's tutoring and her own devices, their bold questioning makes clear the importance of training. Only when women were educated to the same standard as male leaders would they be able to raise that other voice and insist on their dignity as human beings morally, intellectually, and legally equal to men.

THE OTHER VOICE. The other voice, a voice of protest, was mostly female, but it was also male. It spoke in the vernaculars and in Latin, in treatises and dialogues, in plays and poetry, in letters and diaries, and in pamphlets. It battered at the wall of prejudice that encircled women and raised a banner announcing its claims. The female was equal (or even superior) to the male in essential nature—moral, spiritual, intellectual. Women were capable of higher education, of holding positions of power and influence in the public realm, and of speaking and writing persuasively. The last bastion of masculine supremacy, centered on the notions of a woman's primary domestic responsibility and the requirement of female chastity, was not as yet assaulted—although visions of productive female communities as alternatives to the family indicated an awareness of the problem.

During the period 1300–1700, the other voice remained only a voice, and one only dimly heard. It did not result—yet—in an alteration of social patterns. Indeed, to this day they have not entirely been altered. Yet the call for justice issued as long as six centuries ago by those writing in the tradition of the other voice must be recognized as the source and origin of the mature feminist tradition and of the realignment of social institutions accomplished in the modern age.

We thank the volume editors in this series, who responded with many suggestions to an earlier draft of this introduction, making it a collaborative enterprise. Many of their suggestions and criticisms have resulted in revisions of this introduction, though we remain responsible for the final product.

PROJECTED TITLES IN THE SERIES

Isabella Andreini, *Mirtilla*, edited and translated by Laura Stortoni

Tullia d'Aragona, *Complete Poems and Letters*, edited and translated by Julia Hairston

Tullia d'Aragona, *The Wretch, Otherwise Known as Guerrino*, edited and translated by Julia Hairston and John McLucas

Giuseppa Eleonora Barbapiccola and Diamante Medaglia Faini, *The Education of Women*, edited and translated by Rebecca Messbarger

Francesco Barbaro et al., *On Marriage and the Family*, edited and translated by Margaret L. King

Laura Battiferra, *Selected Poetry, Prose, and Letters*, edited and translated by Victoria Kirkham

Giulia Bigolina, *Urania*, edited and translated by Valeria Finucci

Francesco Buoninsegni and Arcangela Tarabotti, *Menippean Satire: "Against Feminine Extravagance" and "Antisatire,"* edited and translated by Elissa Weaver

Elisabetta Caminer Turra, *Writings on and about Women*, edited and translated by Catherine Sama

Maddalena Campiglia, *Flori*, edited and translated by Virginia Cox with Lisa Sampson

Rosalba Carriera, *Letters, Diaries, and Art*, edited and translated by Shearer West

Madame du Chatelet, *Selected Works*, edited by Judith Zinsser

Gabrielle de Coignard, *Spiritual Sonnets*, edited and translated by Melanie E. Gregg

Vittoria Colonna, *Sonnets for Michelangelo*, edited and translated by Abigail Brundin

Vittoria Colonna, Chiara Matraini, and Lucrezia Marinella, *Marian Writings*, edited and translated by Susan Haskins

Marie Dentière, *Epistles*, edited and translated by Mary B. McKinley

Marie-Catherine Desjardins (Madame de Villedieu), *Memoirs of the Life of Henriette-Sylvie de Molière*, edited and translated by Donna Kuizenga

Princess Elizabeth of Bohemia, *Correspondence with Descartes*, edited and translated by Lisa Shapiro

Isabella d'Este, *Selected Letters*, edited and translated by Deanna Shemek

Fairy-Tales by Seventeenth-Century French Women Writers, edited and translated by Lewis Seifert and Domna C. Stanton

Moderata Fonte, *Floridoro*, edited and translated by Valeria Finucci

Moderata Fonte and Lucrezia Marinella, *Religious Narratives*, edited and translated by Virginia Cox

Francisca de los Apostoles, *Visions on Trial: The Inquisitional Trial of Francisca de los Apostoles*, edited and translated by Gillian T. W. Ahlgren

Catharina Regina von Greiffenberg, *Meditations on the Life of Christ*, edited and translated by Lynne Tatlock

In Praise of Women: Italian Fifteenth-Century Defenses of Women, edited and translated by Daniel Bornstein

Louise Labé, *Complete Works*, edited and translated by Annie Finch and Deborah Baker

Madame de Maintenon, *Lectures and Dramatic Dialogues*, edited and translated by John Conley, S.J.

Lucrezia Marinella, *L'Enrico, or Byzantium Conquered*, edited and translated by Virginia Cox

Lucrezia Marinella, *Happy Arcadia*, edited and translated by Susan Haskins and Letizia Panizza

Chiara Matraini, *Selected Poetry and Prose*, edited and translated by Elaine MacLachlan

Isotta Nogarola, *Selected Letters*, edited and translated by Margaret L. King and Diana Robin

Eleonora Petersen von Merlau, *Autobiography* (1718), edited and translated by Barbara Becker-Cantarino

Alessandro Piccolomini, *Rethinking Marriage in Sixteenth-Century Italy*, edited and translated by Letizia Panizza

Christine de Pizan et al., *Debate over the "Romance of the Rose,"* edited and translated by Tom Conley with Elisabeth Hodges

Christine de Pizan, *Life of Charles V*, edited and translated by Charity Cannon Willard

Christine de Pizan, *The Long Road of Learning*, edited and translated by Andrea Tarnowski

Madeleine and Catherine des Roches, *Selected Letters, Dialogues, and Poems*, edited and translated by Anne Larsen

Oliva Sabuco, *The New Philosophy: True Medicine*, edited and translated by Gianna Pomata

Margherita Sarrocchi, *La Scanderbeide*, edited and translated by Rinaldina Russell

Madeleine de Scudéry, *Orations and Rhetorical Dialogues*, edited and translated by Jane Donawerth with Julie Strongson

Justine Siegemund, *The Court Midwife of the Electorate of Brandenburg* (1690), edited and translated by Lynne Tatlock

Gabrielle Suchon, *"On Philosophy" and "On Morality,"* edited and translated by Domna Stanton with Rebecca Wilkin

Sara Copio Sullam, *Sara Copio Sullam: Jewish Poet and Intellectual in Early Seventeenth-Century Venice*, edited and translated by Don Harrán

Arcangela Tarabotti, *Convent Life as Inferno: A Report*, introduction and notes by Francesca Medioli, translated by Letizia Panizza

Arcangela Tarabotti, *Paternal Tyranny*, edited and translated by Letizia Panizza

Laura Terracina, *Works*, edited and translated by Michael Sherberg

Katharina Schütz Zell, *Selected Writings*, edited and translated by Elsie McKee

THE "DISCOURSE": CONTEXT AND HISTORICAL BACKGROUND

Se quando nasce una figliuola il padre,
La ponesse col figlio a un'opra eguale,
Non saria nelle imprese alte, e leggiadre
Al frate inferior né diseguale,
O la ponesse in fra l'armate squadre
Seco, o a imparar qualche arte liberale,
Ma perché in altri affari viene allevata,
Per l'educazione poco è stimata.

(If, when a daughter is born, her father were to give her the same opportunities as he gives his son, she would not prove unequal in talent to her brother in any lofty or glorious undertaking, whether she be placed alongside her brother in a squad of armed soldiers, or whether she be set to learn some liberal art, but because she is given a different sort of education, she is regarded as being of inferior ability.)
—Moderata Fonte, *Tredici canti del Floridoro* (Venice, 1581), Cantos 4–5[1]

AN EXCEPTIONAL FATHER-DAUGHTER RELATIONSHIP IN LATE SIXTEENTH-CENTURY ITALY

Readers of the present series may be surprised to discover, when they come to this particular volume, that the voice addressing us here is neither that of a woman nor in any obvious sense a defense of the female sex. Instead, what we hear is a paternal and patriarchal voice. The work's "otherness," and hence its reason for being included in this series, lies in the fact that Guasco has planned a professional career for his young daughter and mapped out an appropriate educational program to equip her for this. One could well assume that she was an only child, fulfilling the role of substitute

1. For further information on Fonte, see Virginia Cox's introduction to her edition and translation of *The Worth of Women*, published in this series in 1997. Valeria Finucci published a modern edition of the *Tredici Canti* in 1995 (Bologna).

son to Guasco, but this is not the case: Lavinia is in fact one of a large family of siblings of both sexes, of which she is not even the eldest, but due to her exceptional abilities and the deep affection her father always felt for her, she was singled out and privileged over the rest of them to receive what appears to have been a unique education. Unlike most young girls of the time, who were brought up to be pious, chaste, and domesticated in preparation either for marriage or for the cloister, Lavinia was instructed from her earliest infancy in the skills required of a lady-in-waiting at court and is on the very point of embarking on this career as her father concludes the work of advice he has written for her. Although she is only eleven years old, her accomplishments are such that her father is confident she will shine in her new environment. Empowered by her education, she will be a means of forging a link for this patrician family with one of the most important power bases in Italy, as well as earning honor for herself not in the subordinate role of a wife but in her own professional right.

Although virtually disregarded down the centuries, Guasco's *Discourse* represents a landmark in the history of women's education in that it is based on the assumption that, because this young girl possessed outstanding abilities, not only should she be given every opportunity and encouragement to develop them to their fullest potential, but that she should also receive a training to equip her for a career appropriate to her sex where they could be put to good use. Seen against the backdrop of an age when girls were educated for a life of self-effacement and narrow domesticity, this is an astonishingly far-sighted view.

THE AUTHOR

Annibale (or Annibal, as he more frequently terms himself) Guasco was born on March 19, 1540, and died at the age of seventy-nine in what was then regarded as extreme old age [*vecchissimo*] on February 4, 1619. His wife was Laura Bellone, daughter of Luigi Bellone who was a patrician of Alessandria and vice-president of the Senate of Milan. She outlived her husband by five years, dying on February 15, 1624. Their union produced three sons, Francesco, Cesare, and Baldassare, three daughters, Lavinia, Caterina, and Veronica, and at least four other children, all of whom died in infancy.

From contemporary accounts Guasco comes across as a man of the highest integrity, an outstanding citizen and the most loyal of friends; to know him, we are told, was to respect and love him.[2] He was a member of several literary academies, and in 1596 he was unanimously elected president of the

2. For one contemporary account, see Girolamo Ghilini's *Teatro d'Huomini letterati* (Venice, 1647), 14–15.

Accademia degli Immobili, which had been founded in Alessandria in 1562. His numerous letters show that his friends and correspondents included some of the most influential figures of contemporary Italy—heads of state, princes of the Church, nobles, writers, and diplomats. He was an ardent patriot, and in 1598 was sent as his country's ambassador to swear an oath of fealty to the governor of Milan in the name of the king of Spain. From his *Discourse* and letters he shows himself to be an affectionate and considerate husband and a proud and devoted father and grandfather. He makes no effort to conceal the fact that Lavinia, who was born in 1574, the eldest of the three daughters who survived childhood, is his favorite child, the apple of his eye; indeed he makes a virtue of his great love for her, claiming that no father ever loved a daughter more deeply. His pride in her achievements is immense.

Guasco's writings consist of a collection of spiritual compositions (1599); a volume of madrigals, the *Tela Cangiante*, published in 1605; an ottava rima version of the *Decameron* tale of Ghismonda and Tancredi (4.1); a discourse on the government of Alessandria; three volumes of letters and poems; and the current work, which Lavinia published in 1586.[3]

Guasco's funeral oration was recited by the doctor and celebrated orator Nicolao Dal Pozzo, and he was buried in the church of Santo Stefano di Borgoglio in his native Alessandria. He bequeathed his library to the Serviti Fathers of this same church.

His heir, Francesco, who graduated in jurisprudence from the University of Pavia, was elected mayor of Tortona, where he was highly esteemed, and he later became a senator in Milan. He married Clara Luce Stageno. Lavinia's two sisters, Caterina and Veronica, both entered convents at an early age.

LAVINIA GUASCA

Lavinia was the eldest of Guasco's three surviving daughters. She was born on the feast of Saint Anthony (June 13), 1574, in her parental home in Alessandria. While her two sisters were sent to be educated as boarders in the Alessandrian convent of Santa Marguerita, Lavinia was kept at home and educated partly by her father and partly by a whole series of hired tutors, always under her father's strict supervision. Guasco appears to have decided from Lavinia's earliest infancy that in view of her precocious intelligence and

---

3. Guasco's ottava rima version of the *Decameron* tale of Ghismonda and Tancredi was first published in Pavia in 1583, together with the text of the novella, under the title, *La Ghismonda del Boccaccio composta in ottava rima dal sig. Annibal Guasco;* it was republished by Domenico Maria Manni in Milan in 1820. It is significant that out of Boccaccio's one hundred stories, it is this particular tale that Guasco should have selected to render into verse. Doubtless he was attracted to it due to its depiction of a father's singular love for his daughter.

musical talents, she should be groomed for a court career, and the news in 1584 that the new young duke of Savoy, Carlo Emanuele, was to marry the infanta Caterina of Spain and that his bride would be arriving in Turin the following year gave Guasco exactly the opportunity he was seeking for a placement for his daughter. His negotiations were successful, and Lavinia was summoned to court at the age of eleven to begin her service as lady-in-waiting to the duchess. Her departure from home took place at the end of 1585 or the beginning of 1586, certainly in the depths of that winter and well before March 1586, when we find her ensconced in the palace and about to publish her manuscript of the *Discourse.* For her court career and married life thereafter, see my appendix.

HISTORICAL BACKGROUND: A CONJUGAL UNION BETWEEN THE KINGDOM OF SPAIN AND THE DUCHY OF SAVOY IN THE LATE SIXTEENTH CENTURY

Lavinia's employer, the infanta Caterina (or Catalina, as she was known in Spain) Michaela of Austria, who was born in October 1567, was the second daughter of Philip II of Spain by his third wife, Elisabeth of Valois, the daughter of King Henri II. Just over a year after giving birth to Caterina, her mother died, and in 1570 Philip married again for the fourth time, to the daughter of the emperor Maximilian, Anne of Austria, who became a virtual mother to Caterina and her elder sister Isabella Clara Eugenia. Philip was devoted to the two little girls, who brought him much happiness. He played a large part in their education, wrote them numerous affectionate letters when he was absent from them, and later even discussed affairs of state with them. Their childhood appears to have been a happy time for the two little infantas. In the autumn of 1583, the marriage of Caterina to the new young duke of Savoy, Carlo Emanuele I, was arranged, and the contract was signed the following summer.[4] This was not an ambitious match for an infanta of Spain, but one intended to underscore the continued alliance between the Habsburgs and the House of Savoy. Carlo Emanuele had succeeded to the duchy of Savoy in 1580 on the death of his father, Emanuele Filiberto.

After three decades of exile in France, the previous duke, Emanuele Filiberto (1528–80), had regained Piedmont in 1559 under the terms of the treaty of Cateau-Cambrésis, as his reward for leading the Spanish troops to victory in the battle of Saint-Quentin (1557). A ruler of great political

4. The marriage contract was signed on August 23, 1584, between Carlo Emanuele and Baron Sfondrato.

acumen and foresight, he had decided to move his capital to the Alpine-protected Turin from Chambéry, which was constantly threatened by French occupation, and to make Italian the official language of his duchy. The French troops that had been occupying Turin finally left in 1563, and the duke, with the help of his architect, Francesco Paciotto, set about transforming this city, already the seat of Savoyard administration in Piedmont, from a modest garrison town of some forty thousand inhabitants into a national capital. Precariously placed as Turin was between the two mighty European rivals, France and Spain, the duke's first concern was to fortify it securely and surround it with a huge zone of ducal property. Paciotto built a pentagonal fortress, the Cittadella (1564–68), to serve as a statement of his employer's power and authority, and started work on enlarging the ducal palace. Few of the Savoyard nobility had followed Emanuele Filiberto over the Alps, so he had to set about rekindling the loyalties of the local nobility after an absence of a quarter century from Turin. In 1578 the duke transferred the Holy Shroud from Chambéry to Turin. The Shroud, which was the personal property of the Sabaudian dynasty, was one of the most venerated relics of Christendom, and at once made the court of Turin an important focus for pilgrimage.

In 1580, Emanuele Filiberto was succeeded by his eighteen-year-old son and only legitimate offspring, Carlo Emanuele, later surnamed "the Great" (1562–1630). The new young duke was a good musician and an archaeologist and, from his mother, Marguerite de Valois, sister of Henri II, had inherited a great love of literature and the sciences. Marguerite, who had also died in 1580, was a highly educated woman who had brought many intellectuals and writers to her court and had educated her son herself up to the age of twelve. Carlo Emanuele and his architect, Ascanio Vitozzi, set out together to redesign Turin as a true capital city, with wide streets and piazzas intended to provide a backdrop for elaborate ceremonies and spectacles that would impress and entertain the duke's subjects and glorify his regime. A new rectilinear layout was planned for the city's architectural development that would symbolize the order, discipline, and decorum of a centralized state under princely authority. The court doubled in size during the early years of the duke's reign, with 250–300 permanent officers. A large gallery wing known as *il teatro* was added to the palace compound, consisting of thirty-two arcaded bays at ground level and an equal number of windows above, commanding a panoramic view of the hills and river Po on the one side while flanking the city square on the other. This housed the duke's art collection, which included works by leading Italian painters (some of which he had himself commissioned), his archive, and his extensive library and was said to be the finest gallery in Europe after the Louvre. Vitozzi created a new piazza in front of the palace and laid out an elaborate garden, the Reggio Parco, with woods, lawns, fountains, grottoes, statues, temples, and even an enclosure for wild animals. When not away fighting, the duke organized endless feasts for his subjects' entertainment, and he quickly earned a reputation for magnanimity, liberality, and grandiose schemes. He was highly expert in every aspect of soldiering and was a tireless soldier, who could ride for twenty-four hours without food or sleep.

In January 1585, King Philip II of Spain, his family, and his entire court set off from Madrid for Saragossa, where Caterina's wedding to the duke of Savoy was to be celebrated.[5] The royal party made a triumphant entry into Saragossa on February 24. Meanwhile, Carlo Emanuele had sailed from Villafranca to Barcelona and continued on to Saragossa, where he arrived on March 10. Philip received him with great cordiality, and the wedding was celebrated in Saragossa Cathedral by Cardinal Granvelle on the following day, March 11, 1585. The bridegroom was dressed in a yellow suit bordered with pearls under a black cloak, and the bride wore a red gown embroidered with gold, pearls, and precious stones. Philip himself joined in the dancing after the nuptial ceremony, and later conferred the Order of the Golden Fleece on his son-in-law. He gave Caterina a dowry of 500,000 scudi. From Saragossa the whole royal party journeyed slowly to Barcelona, whence the duke and his new duchess set sail for Nice on June 13 in a fleet of forty galleys commanded by the admiral Gian Andrea Doria.[6] The leave-taking on the quayside lasted two hours, as Caterina was weeping so much at parting from her father and sister. The ducal pair arrived in Nice on June 18 and proceeded by land to Turin, which they reached on August 10, to tremendous celebrations. In a letter to the marquis d'Este, the duke wrote that the qualities of his bride far exceeded his hopes and his expectations, and Caterina for her part

5. For a long time it was believed that the portrait titled *A Lady in a Fur Wrap*, which is in the Stirling Maxwell Collection belonging to Glasgow Museums and Art Galleries, was the work of Sofonisba Anguissola and represented the Infanta Caterina's wedding portrait. However, the currently accepted view now is that the portrait is by El Greco, and was painted in the late 1570s. Since the infanta would only have been an adolescent at that time and her marriage had not even been arranged, this would preclude it being a wedding portrait of her. Moreover, it has been pointed out that the lady depicted lacks the reserve, stiffness, and formal court attire that usually characterize such dynastic portraits. (See J. Alvarez Lopera, *Lady in a Fur Wrap*, entry 27 in *El Greco: Identity and Transformation—Crete-Italy-Spain*, exhibition catalog, ed. J. Alvarez Lopera [Milan, 1999].)

6. The Doria family were Genoa's leading citizens and its virtual rulers. Gian Andrea Doria (1539–1606) was the great-nephew and heir of Andrea Doria, who had served Charles V as admiral of his fleet and frequently entertained the emperor in his palace in Genoa. Gian Andrea succeeded him as a naval commander.

was delighted with her new life and with the informality of the Sabaudian court after the rigid etiquette of the court of Spain, even though her Spanish chamberlain complained that her household was meager and her attendants too few in number. She soon proved herself to be a worthy confidante and adviser to her husband and an able ruler during his long absences campaigning, and he consulted her on all political problems. What had begun as a marriage of diplomacy and *raison d'état* was transformed into a true love match, as is testified by the letters, totaling nearly seven thousand in number, which the ducal pair exchanged during their frequent separations. The Venetian ambassador, Fantino Corraro, wrote of the infanta's constantly cheerful though grave mien, her affability, her readiness to bestow favors, her physical beauty, and the great trust placed in her by the duke, concluding, "I really do not believe that any wife ever took such delight in her husband, or that one could find a more united and harmonious pair."[7]

One of the infanta's major contributions to the Duchy of Savoy lay in reorganizing and promoting the rapidly expanding court of Turin, which in the early years of her husband's reign doubled in size, housing 250–300 permanent officers, and which by the time of her death had acquired an almost royal status. In a recent essay, the historian Robert Oresko commented: "Although Catalina Michaela's presence in Turin was relatively brief—she died in 1597 after twelve years of marriage and pregnancies—her influence in shaping the structure of her husband's court was longer lasting. Her experience of life at the court of her father propelled her to sharpen definitions of etiquette and precedence at Turin and by the time of Carlo Emanuele's death, the court of the Duke of Savoy possessed clear structures of both hierarchy and administration."[8]

---

7. Further, on the trust placed in Caterina by the Duke: "This princess . . . was moreover very benign when giving audiences, very gracious in her replies and very ready to bestow favors, and where physical gifts were concerned, of more than normal beauty, due to which and to her other qualities, she came to be greatly loved and heeded by His Highness the Duke, who wished her to possess, as indeed she did possess, every supreme authority" (*Relazione di Savoia di Fantino Corraro*, 1598, in *Relazioni degli Ambasciatori veneti al senato durante il secolo decimosesto, raccolte ed illustrate da Eugenio Albéri* [Florence, 1863], 15:378,. my translation).

8. Robert Oresko, "The Duchy of Savoy and the Kingdom of Sardinia: The Sabaudian Court, 1563–c. 1750," in *The Princely Courts of Europe: Ritual, Politics and Culture under the Ancient Regime, 1500–1750*, ed. John Adamson (London, 1999), 238.

Mary Hollingsworth, in her book *Patronage in Sixteenth-Century Italy* (London, 1996), comments as follows on the court of Spain, in which Caterina spent the first eighteen years of her life:

Philip II was conscious of the importance of extravagant display as a means of exhibiting his immense power and prestige. One of the outstanding patrons of the sixteenth century, he set out to create a court that would visibly demonstrate his position as the pre-

In April 1586, Caterina's first child, a son and heir, Filippo Emanuele, was born. Philip was overjoyed when he received the news of the birth. She bore her husband nine more children over the next eleven years, and died in Turin on December 7, 1597, while giving birth prematurely to a baby girl, due largely to the shock of receiving an unfounded rumor that her husband had been killed in battle. Both Philip and Carlo Emanuele were inconsolable. It was said of Philip: "Never before or again would they see him express such grief as now, not in the death of his sons nor in that of his wife nor at the loss of the Armada."[9] The duchess was survived by five sons and four daughters. The duke, her husband, lived until 1630 but never remarried. During this exceptionally long reign of fifty years he rebuilt and transformed his capital into a major European city, brilliantly continuing the initiative begun by his father.

Back in 1586, however, a post at the court of Turin would doubtless have been an exciting and rewarding experience for any young girl, especially one endowed with Lavinia's talents, presided over as it was by a warm-hearted, lively, and highly intelligent nineteen-year-old duchess and a gifted and ambitious young duke. Whereas under Emanuele Filiberto and his wife, Marguerite de Valois, the court of Turin had been under the sway of France, now with the arrival of the infanta and her entourage it became predominantly Spanish in language and customs, and Guasco speaks eloquently in the *Discourse* of the dignified charm and wit of the newly arrived Spanish ladies-in-waiting, clearly regarding them as excellent role models for his daughter. Moreover, Lavinia's life at court would have been filled with a succession of colorful and impressively staged events, as Symcox comments: "The court under the rule of Carlo Emanuele was the focus of a highly elaborate ceremonial life, with grand festivities staged to celebrate ducal coronations,

---

mier prince of Europe. He abandoned the tradition of peripatetic courts, establishing his administration in Madrid which, though an unprepossessing town, was located in the center of his kingdom. His presence was visible in the Alcazar, which he remodeled as the royal palace with great state rooms and, separated from the bustle of court life, his own private apartments. His main project was the Escorial (1563–84), a vast complex outside Madrid that comprised a royal palace, a grand ceremonial staircase, a monastery and a church, San Lorenzo, containing the family mausoleum. The Escorial was never his official residence, the court remaining based at the Alcazar. Sumptuously decorated, these palaces contained his magnificent collection of tapestries, painting and sculpture. (319–20)

9. See Fray Jerónimo de Sepúlveda, *Historia,* in *Documentos para la Historia del Monasterio de San Lorenzo el Real,* ed. E. J. Zarco Cuevas (Madrid, 1924), 4:182, translated and quoted by Henry Kamen in his book, *Philip of Spain* (New Haven, Conn., and London, 1997), 312.

birthdays, weddings and funerals, or to mark important public events like the conclusion of peace treaties. These ceremonies were designed to convey a powerful political message, magnifying the achievements of the ruler and the dynasty through every available means—carousels and knightly exercises; parades of troops; firework displays; sumptuous costumes; music and dancing."[10] It is not surprising that, despite the language barrier that confronted her, little Lavinia appears to have quickly found her feet in such a lively and eventful setting or that her mistress was prepared to give her the time and encouragement she needed to develop the various skills she had brought with her that would serve to enhance the court. After the rigorous and Spartan educational regime to which Lavinia had been subjected at home throughout her early childhood, the Sabaudian court must indeed have seemed to her, as she touchingly describes it to her father in her foreword, like a paradise presided over by an angel from heaven.

THE GENRE: THE COURTLY CODE FOR WOMEN

In contrast to the large number of moralists who pontificated on a woman's role as wife and mother during the Renaissance, surprisingly few writers addressed the question of the conduct and decorum appropriate to a woman at court, despite the proliferation at this time of French and Italian courts and the consequent increase in the number of women entering court service. Does this perhaps reflect a certain unease and uncertainty on what advice to offer this emerging category of women who, even after marriage, would be answerable primarily to a powerful female figure rather than to their husbands?

The earliest writer to touch on the question is Christine de Pizan who, although of Italian birth, had grown up in France and wrote in French. In her *Livre des trois vertus*, also called *Le tresor de la cité des dames*, written in 1405 and published in 1497, Christine offers advice to every category of women from princesses to prostitutes. The first section of the second part is dedicated to "Celles qui demeurent a court de Princepce ou haulte dame" [Those who dwell at the court of a princess or noble lady]. Her advice, which is mainly aimed at the older court attendant, is to love and fear God, to love your mis-

10. See Geoffrey Symcox, "From Commune to Capital: The Transformation of Turin from the Sixteenth to the Eighteenth Centuries," in *Royal and Republican Sovereignty in Early Modern Europe*, ed. Robert Oresko, G. C. Gibbs, and H. M. Scott, eds. (Cambridge, 1997), 248–49. For further information on the development of Turin under Carlo Emanuele and his father, see Martha D. Pollack, *Turin, 1564–1600* (Chicago and London, 1983).

tress, to avoid overfamiliarity with men, which can lead to idle gossip, to shun envy even when another is favored above yourself, and never to slander or defame the other court ladies, above all your mistress.[11]

The first writer to devote an entire work to the topic of the woman at court is Anne de France, duchess of Bourbon and daughter of Louis XI, in whose library at the Château de Moulins there were two copies of Christine's book. She wrote her *Enseignements* as a birthday gift for her daughter Susanne around 1504. Recently widowed, Anne writes out of concern for her fatherless child and for what will become of Susanne should she also lose her mother while still unmarried. If this should come about, Anne advises Susanne to enter the service of some great lady, reliable, sensible, and of good repute. Once at court, she should be gentle, friendly, humble and truthful to all, never meddling in other people's business or getting embroiled in court affairs, since this is unbecoming in a young girl. She should honor those esteemed for their wisdom and, remembering that speech is God's noblest gift to human beings, control her tongue, taking care not to become heated in her conversation or overhasty in her replies but, instead, speaking courteously, amiably, and chastely. She should avoid boisterous behavior and teasing or mocking others. She should carry out her religious observances at all times with true devotion. Her dress should be fashionable but not extravagant and suitably warm in winter. Anticipating that Susanne will marry and have female attendants of her own, her mother also includes some advice for her on running a court and on directing and ruling her ladies-in-waiting. Like Guasco, Anne is writing as a loving parent who wishes to offer a young daughter the best guidance she can on avoiding the snares and pitfalls of court life. Her precepts are clear and to the point but lack the perceptive explanations and comments on human psychology that Guasco includes to convince Lavinia of the soundness of his advice. Anne's work was published before 1521.[12]

In 1528, Castiglione published his *Courtier*, far and away the most widely read and influential work on courtly conduct ever to appear in Western literature. In book 3, which is devoted to discussing the court lady or *donna di palazzo*, Castiglione addresses the questions of how far her behavior should differ from that of the male courtier and of what her principal role at court should be. In contrast with the former's virile and bellicose skills, the court lady should aim to develop her social talents and feminine charms to the

---

11. See Christine de Pizan, *The Treasure of the City of Ladies; or, The Book of the Three Virtues*, trans. Sarah Lawson (New York, 1985), pt. 2, chap. 5 (118–21).

12. Anne de France, *Les Enseignements d'Anne de France duchesse de Bourbonnais et d'Auvergne a sa fille Susanne de Bourbon* (Lyon, n.d.).

fullest extent by being graceful, unaffected, well-mannered, modest, and serene, as well as circumspect and prudent. She should be prepared to dance and perform music in public but only when pressed to do so and with a certain bashfulness. Her principal contribution to court life will be her ability to engage her male counterparts, and all who come to court, in congenial and appropriate conversation, entertaining them with a delightful vivacity and a sound spectator knowledge of all the arts and sports practiced by the male courtier. If bawdiness or boorishness should break out in a gathering at which she is present, she must strike a difficult balance between appearing, on the one hand, too straight-laced, and on the other, too free and easy. Her role is essentially a decorative and inspirational one: she is there to enhance the life of the courtiers, to applaud their feats, to entertain and charm them with her conversational and hostessing skills but, at the same time, like the ladies present throughout the four nights of Castiglione's dialogue, to remain a silent spectator during any serious intellectual discussion on the part of the men. Nevertheless, her silence does not necessarily imply an ignorance of the topics under discussion for, as Castiglione clearly spells out, her social conversation must be based on a real understanding of whatever subject she is addressing.[13]

In 1528, the same year in which *The Courtier* appeared, Agostino Nifo published his *De re aulica*, book 2 of which was concerned with women at court.[14] In 1564 Lodovico Domenichi translated this section of Nifo's text as a single work under the title of *The Court Lady* (*La donna di corte*), without any acknowledgment that this was a mere borrowing, with a few embellishments.[15] Here the traditional misogynistic view of woman as an imperfect and "imbecile" creature resurfaces: incapable of maturing into adulthood or of exercising prudence or wit, she is no more suited to court life than a child would be. The only courtly virtue within her competence, and that poses no threat to her chastity, is affability, which is natural to her since it arises out of her instinct to please. However, this quality will be based on an artless simplicity entirely unlike the essential courtly virtue of urbanity with which her male counterpart delights and entertains his lord during his leisure hours, with its vital components of prudence and reason. But just as the prince needs his following of courtiers, so too his wife must have her retinue of ladies, and Nifo/Domenichi grudgingly concede, therefore, that the presence of ladies

13. See the *Discourse*, n. 63.

14. Agostino Nifo, *De re aulica ad Phausinam libri duo* (Naples, 1534).

15. Lodovico Domenichi, *La donna di corte, discorso di Lodovico Domenichi: Nel quale si ragiona dell'affabilità e honesta creanza da doversi usare per gentildonna d'honore* (Lucca, 1564).

at court is unavoidable, even though they can never attain to more than half the degree of courtiership of their male counterparts.

In their endeavors to define and codify the type of behavior appropriate to a lady at court, these writers are clearly addressing an important contemporary issue. They were all too aware that, with her arrival at court, woman had emerged at last from her enclosed voiceless and purely domestic sphere into a public and articulate one, and no matter how condescending their attitudes may seem today, they were being forced to accept that from now on there could be no denying her a place in this sophisticated mixed society, nor a voice, however limited, in its discussions and entertainments.

Castiglione had said nothing regarding the manner in which his *donna di palazzo* was to acquire her musical skills or her wide-ranging knowledge of the topics that she was to discuss with the male courtiers and with the people who came to visit the court, but in 1574 we do find one important comment regarding the education of girls destined for life at court: Guasco's good friend and neighbor, Stefano Guazzo, in book 3 of his *Civil conversatione*, draws a clear line of distinction between such girls and those who will remain all their lives in a purely domestic sphere and states that if the former are to gain the favor of their mistresses, "it behoveth them to learne to reade, to write, to discourse, to sing, to play on Instruments, to daunce, and to be able to perfourme all that which belongeth to a Courtier to doe," and so they should be educated accordingly.[16] These sensible and realistic comments, written in the very year in which Lavinia was born, would most certainly have been known to her father and, indeed, may even have sown in his mind the first seeds of the system of education he was shortly to devise for his baby daughter. They show, too, that by the last third of the century, the well-born daughters of northern Italian families were being sent to court in sufficient numbers for Guazzo to make a distinct category of them and of their special pedagogical requirements.

GUASCO'S "DISCOURSE": CONTENT AND ANALYSIS

A Preliminary Note on the Use of the Term "Virtù"

The term *virtù* is used recurrently by Guasco throughout the *Discourse* to denote Lavinia's learned attainments; it is usually used in the plural but is used once or twice in the singular. In the latter case I have rendered it by its En-

---

16. *The Civile Conversation of M. Steeven Guazzo*, bks. 1–3 trans. George Pettie (Anno 1581), bk. 4 trans. Bartholomew Young (Anno 1586) (London, 1925), 78.

glish equivalent of virtuosity, but there is, unfortunately, no plural term in English that carries the same moral overtones as the Italian plural, *le virtù*, and this should be borne in mind when reading this translation, where I have had to translate it with the uncolored designation of skills or attainments. As F. H. Jacobs remarks in her book *Defining the Renaissance Virtuosa*, the liberal arts and the moral virtues were so closely connected in the Renaissance that their identities became fused, and the *Discourse* is a good illustration of this, for example, when Guasco refers to *virtù* as a worthy and lofty thing approved by God.[17]

Guasco is not using the term in connection with his daughter inadvertently. Normally, as its etymology from the Latin *vir* suggests, it would only have been applied to male attributes, such as the virile courage with which Machiavelli's prince overcomes adverse fortune, but by the end of the sixteenth century there was some acceptance that the term *virtuosa* could be applied to very exceptional women. In 1582, Torquato Tasso had published his *Discorso della virtù feminile, e donnesca*, in which he had claimed that there is a special category of heroic women of noble lineage who aspire to the virile virtues of their glorious male forebears, unlike the private gentlewoman whose virtues are the lesser ones of chastity, obedience, and parsimony. Such exceptional women transcend their female condition and become worthy to rank beside men for their achievements: "Coming back to the *virtù* of ladies such as these, I say that in heroic ladies it is heroic *virtù* rivalling the heroic *virtù* of a man . . . nor is there any difference to be found between their deeds and offices and those of heroic men."[18]

As far as Castiglione is concerned, this same term is used recurrently throughout the *Courtier* in a general sense of outstanding ability in all spheres of life. See, for instance, the section in book 3 where the Magnifico says, "Therefore if you study ancient and modern history . . . you will find that women as well as men have constantly given proof of their worth [*la virtù*]; and also that there have been some women who have waged wars and won glorious victories, governed kingdoms with the greatest prudence and justice, and done all that men have done. As for learning, cannot you recall reading of many women who knew philosophy, of others who have been consummate poets, others who have prosecuted, accused and defended before judges with great eloquence?"[19] From this passage it can be seen that

17. Fredrika H. Jacobs, *Defining the Renaissance Virtuosa: Women Artists and the Language of Art History and Criticism* (Cambridge, 1997); see chap. 7, "Femmina Masculo e Masculo Femmina," 157–64.

18. Torquato Tasso, *Discorso della virtù feminile e donnesca* (Venice, 1582), 7; my translation.

19. Baldassarre Castiglione, *The Book of the Courtier*, ed. George Bull (Baltimore, 1967), 219. All subsequent references are to this edition unless stated otherwise.

there is a precedent in Castiglione for applying the term in its widest sense to women as well as to men, though generally speaking he prefers to designate his court lady's accomplishments as *ottime condizioni* (finest accomplishments), or *esercizi*. Rather than use blander terms such as these, it seems probable that Guasco deliberately chose to refer to his daughter's attainments as her *virtù* throughout the *Discourse* in order to convey the message to the contemporary reader that she is an exceptional young woman who has *virilmente*, or with the courage of a man, acquired professional skills for which she stands to gain public recognition. By applying the term *virtù* to her skills, Guasco seems to be stating that the conventional social rules and decorum governing and restricting the conduct of young girls at that time do not apply to a girl like Lavinia and that her brilliance merits public recognition notwithstanding her sex.

Lavinia's Foreword

This foreword is of the very greatest importance, since it is the only place in Guasco's text where we hear Lavinia's voice speaking directly. Written in response to her father's request that on arriving at the court of Turin she should set to work to copy out by hand the only existing manuscript of his *Discourse*, which is now in her possession, and send it home to him, Lavinia has very sensibly decided instead to get the work printed. She diplomatically points out to her father that in this way his wish can be fulfilled all the sooner, and his precepts can be shared with the other ladies at court. In any case, it seems highly probable that Guasco was intending to publish his *Discourse* at some point and, thus, project to the wider public the images of both himself and his daughter that he had so carefully crafted in his text. This would help to account for his insistence that Lavinia must make a copy of his manuscript and send it home to him. It is also possible that he had actually urged her instead to publish the work in Turin herself if her ducal employers were prepared to back the enterprise. And the facts that the Bevilacqua publishing firm had been established in Turin in 1572 by special invitation of Duke Emanuele Filiberto and had since then maintained close associations with the Sabaudian dynasty, that the title page of the *Discourse* bears the Savoy coat of arms, and that the duchess's name features prominently in the title of the work would all seem to suggest that Lavinia's employers had indeed had a hand in the publication of the *Discourse*.

She also sets her father's mind at rest regarding the maintenance of her skills, something about which he had expressed so much concern in the *Discourse*, and reassures him as to her happiness in the palace. Last, she avails herself of the opportunity to praise her mistress, likening her both to a mother figure and to a celestial being, and hinting that she herself has already been singled out by this exalted lady for special favors. Lavinia's tone as she addresses her father is both respectful and affectionate, expressing the deference to his wishes proper to an obedient daughter and at the same time justifying her practical and enterprising solution to the problem of duplicating his manuscript. Her one short intervention in the *Discourse* reveals Lavinia to us as a young girl of great self-possession and maturity, delighted with her new life at court and confident enough to write her own personal preface to her father's work, clearly stating her position.

"Discourse," Part 1: The Education of a Renaissance Child Prodigy

Guasco's *Discourse* is intended as a parting gift to guide and direct his small daughter in her new life at the court of Turin, for which she is on the point of setting out. It consists of two parts. In his main section, Guasco looks forward to all that her new role is likely to involve in terms of duties, relationships, and responsibilities and offers Lavinia the best advice and guidelines he can in dealing with these. He refers to his *Discourse* as a *regola* or rule book, which Lavinia will have on hand at court to refer to and consult in all eventualities. Such prescriptive writings for women were a recurrent feature of Renaissance literature, but the *Discourse* stands out from the rest by virtue of its nondescending and highly personal tone and the great sense of immediacy it conveys.

However, before he embarks on his advice manual, Guasco writes a long introductory section in which he invites his daughter to cast a backward look at the first eleven years of her life, in a spirit of pious gratitude to God and to her parents for all the benefits she has received in her short life and especially for the outstanding talents and educational opportunities that have enabled her to obtain her post at court. As a result of this section, we can build up some kind of picture of the intensive program of studies Guasco had specifically devised for Lavinia. Writing in solemn, almost prayerful, tones, though with great tenderness, solicitude, and at times a vein of wry humor, combined with innumerable rhetorical questions and frequent invocation, Guasco eloquently reminds his daughter of all the gifts she has received direct from the Almighty to date, namely, her birth into a Christian and well-born family, her robust health, and her precocious intelligence. He then proceeds to recapitulate in exclamatory mode all that he himself has done to develop and foster her gifts at enormous expense and inconvenience to himself, guided, as he believes, by the hand of God. The ensuing account both of Guasco's educational methods and of the curriculum of studies he had devised for Lavinia is an extraordinary one, almost certainly unique in Italian Renaissance literature for its clear-cut underlying objectives, its directness of tone, and its detail. Lavinia's achievements were phenomenal for an eleven-year-old if we are to believe the testimony of her father and of those who had vouched for her to the duke and his new duchess, but they had not been acquired without immense effort, even suffering, and Guasco is at pains to remind his daughter of all this so as to make her value them the more.[20] His account may also well be intended as a promotional exercise, to present Lavinia to all those at court, from the duchess down, who might happen to read his *Discourse,* as the highly accomplished young woman she was, with Guasco himself as the hand that had perfected her.

We learn that Lavinia's education had begun at the earliest possible age, before she had even learned to speak properly. Under Guasco's personal tutelage, she was reading as fluently as her father by the age of four, and probably at about this time Guasco took the bold and highly inconvenient decision to move his large household to the university city of Pavia, where he tells us the available teaching talent was vastly superior to that to be found in his native city of Alessandria. Since none of the other children of the household were troubling to take advantage of their opportunities, Guasco soon began to focus all his attention on Lavinia alone. He recalls to her mind how, "for your benefit and honor" [*per beneficio and honor tuo*] he had hired every teacher of good repute in the whole of Pavia, three and four in the same subject, all of whom came to the house and competed together in a spirit of loving and solicitous rivalry to insure that little Lavinia made as much progress in their disciplines in a few days as another girl would have made in several months. In between their visits, Guasco reminds her of how he himself had been forever at her side, urging and goading her on to retain all she had been taught, often when she least welcomed it, in short, behaving, as he says with great complacency, like the most importunate and tyrannical father that ever lived. And on top of all that, Guasco informs us that every member of his domestic staff was carefully selected on the basis of possessing sufficient education to be able to help Lavinia with her lessons in the absence of her tutors. Guasco

20. On the matter of those who had vouched for her to the duke and his new duchess, Guasco was extremely fortunate in having two highly placed friends who could act as go-betweens for him in his negotiations with the palace regarding Lavinia's placement, i.e., Baron Sfondrato, ambassador to Philip II of Spain at the court of Savoy, a distant relative of Guasco's, and Lady Sanchia di Guzman, the infanta's head lady-in-waiting. Without their assistance in vouching for Lavinia's skills to the duke and duchess it is unlikely that a mere patrician like Guasco could have pulled off the tremendous coup of a court post for his daughter.

gives us no explicit details as to Lavinia's education in the liberal arts, but he does make specific reference to the additional subjects he himself had decided it would be necessary for her to learn to insure her success in a career at court.

Adopting a stance of "let's pretend," Guasco next asks Lavinia to imagine that she is only now embarking on her education, as he says was the case with many young girls of her age, and that all the toil and effort still lie before her. By holding up to her each of the skills he had had her taught and in which she now possessed a considerable degree of competence, and by asking her to reflect on the enormous input of time and effort they had involved and on how impossible the task would be were she only now embarking on these various disciplines, Guasco hopes to bring home to her the extent of her obligation to God, who had enabled her, through her father, to acquire them all so early in life. He imagines he can see his small daughter standing before him protesting plaintively, "My noble father, how do you expect me to be able to do so many things at the same time?" And yet with the help of God and of her father, acting under His guidance, she had done so and mastered them all. The terms *maraviglia* (marvel) and *maraviglioso* (wonderful) recur throughout this part of the *Discourse*, underscoring the main thrust of Guasco's argument that Lavinia's prodigious educational progress and her unimpaired health are little short of a divine miracle. He also uses the image found at the beginning of the *Decameron* for her hard-won achievements, of the weary traveler who, after scaling terrible peaks and forbidding precipices, finally reaches a beautiful flowery plain and looks back marveling, to see what heights and obstacles he has overcome on his journey, an image with which Lavinia would doubtless have been familiar.[21]

Lavinia's specific training for her career at court lay in two main areas of study, namely, music and calligraphy. Her father reminds her that she has now mastered all the principles of singing and can sight-read a part from any songbook placed in front of her, including the highly complicated songs that were being written in the late sixteenth century by contemporary composers. She has also learned to play the viola da gamba and can use it to accompany any song or part, as well as the clavichord, on which she can play a range of fashionable musical compositions and, if so required, continue playing and extemporizing for two hours or more at a stretch, with continual variations. In addition, she has mastered the art of counterpoint and has learned how to notate, under the guidance of not one but four music masters who have been coming to the house on a daily basis to teach her, all four

---

21. For the passage at the beginning of the *Decameron*, see n. 15 in the *Discourse*.

competing with one another to help her master these difficult skills. Meanwhile, seemingly determined to push Lavinia to her very limit, her father has for the past five years, from when she was only six years old, been himself teaching her the difficult calligraphic skill of chancery cursive, despite knowing nothing whatsoever of this skill himself and readily admitting he was no more use in helping her form these letters than a dumb man would have been. Lavinia's only aid here was the manual *Il perfetto cancelleresco corsivo* [Perfect chancery cursive], newly published by the great Renaissance calligrapher, Giovanni Francesco Cresci, whose illustrations and instructions Guasco tells us had made their task feasible.[22] (See figs. 1 and 2 for examples of Cresci's

---

22. Giovan Francesco Cresci, who describes himself as a Milanese gentleman in the titles of his writings, held the post of scriptor to the Vatican Library from 1556 and of scriptor to the Sistine Chapel from 1560. He introduced many innovations that greatly facilitated the art of calligraphy, making the letters faster and easier to form. In 1570 he published *Il perfetto scrittore* in Rome, in which he states that for many years he has been seeking to rediscover a way of writing the chancery cursive style more attractively and easily than the hand at present in use and informs the reader that he is currently working on a book that he hopes soon to publish, which will contain his new rules. He defines this script as the type of hand appropriate to good secretaries. In 1579 this work did indeed appear in Rome under the title of *Il perfetto cancellaresco corsivo di Giovan Francesco Cresci*. In it Cresci included innumerable illustrations of the various types of chancery cursive in vogue at that time, explaining to which situations each was best suited. In his introduction Cresci also makes some interesting comments on the office of secretary, declaring that it is one held in great esteem in courts:

> And as everyone knows, it is appropriate in those charged with so honorable a duty not only to be loyal, agreeable, shrewd, diligent, versed in several languages and experienced in learning and science, so as to be able effectively to convey the concepts of their minds, but also, in their handwriting, to be profuse and above all to possess a most beautiful chancery hand. . . . This aspect of writing well is as necessary as all the rest, because it is not desirable that when he [the secretary] comes to write a letter, or anything else, that must end up in the hands of a king, an emperor, or some other great prince, even though it may be perfect in all other respects, it should be lacking and defective in its handwriting, because he has written it in indistinct, shaky, uneven and ill-formed characters. For when this happens, not only does it wrong the personage to whom he has written in so hideous a hand, but it also greatly detracts from the dignity of that gentleman on whose behalf he is writing, and dulls the reputation of the secretary himself, and of his learning and composition.
>
> (My translation; introduction unpaginated)

In contrast, Cresci asserts, when the recipient opens the letter and sees that it is written in a beautiful, elegant hand, he will read it eagerly and feel predisposed to concur with whatever it contains. In a typically Renaissance analogy, Cresci compares a letter written in a graceful hand to a precious gem mounted in a beautiful golden setting by a skillful goldsmith.

In *Schooling in Renaissance Italy: Literacy and Learning, 1300–1600* (Baltimore and London, 1989), Paul Grendler describes how the student setting out to master chancery cursive must first learn to prepare his quill pen by trimming off the feathers and cutting the quill to make a point suitable for broad or for narrow strokes; he must then choose the right kind of paper and thin his ink correctly. Normally, the writing master would put his hand over the child's hand initially and guide it through the correct motions, but since Guasco knew nothing of calligraphy, Lavinia

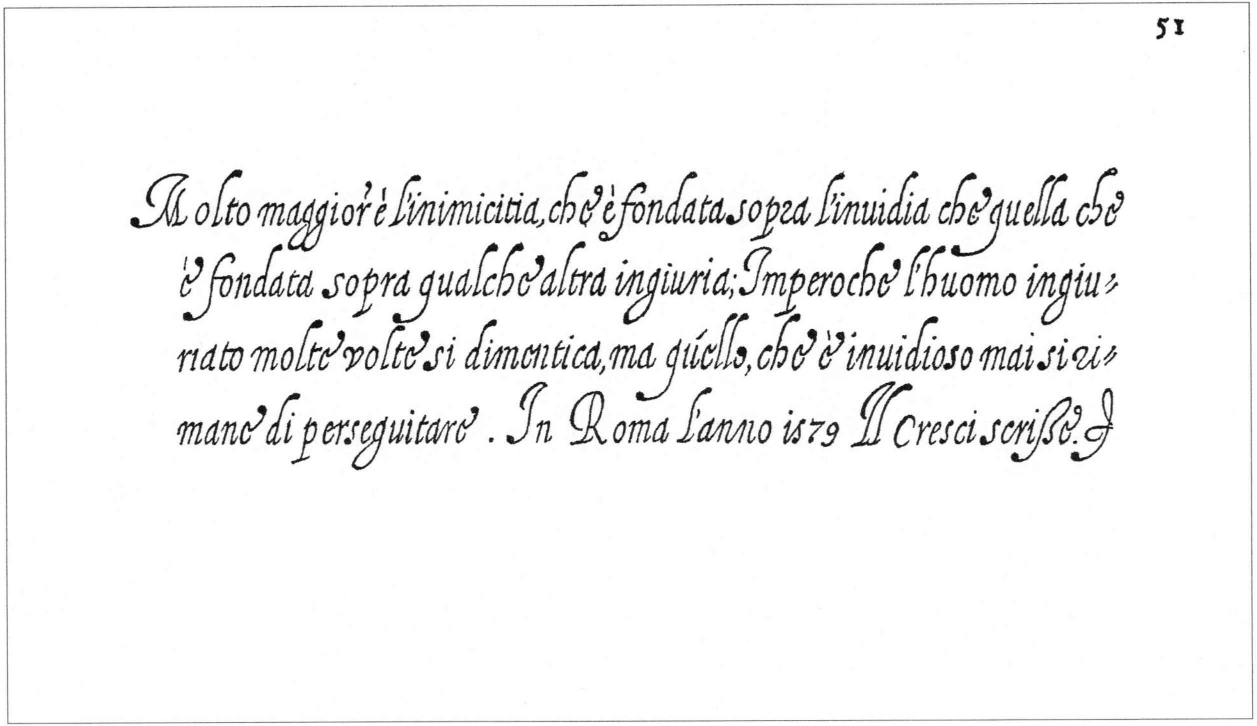
51

Molto maggior'è l'inimicitia, che è fondata sopra l'inuidia che quella che
è fondata sopra qualche altra ingiuria; Imperoche l'huomo ingiu-
riato molte volte si dimentica, ma quello, che è inuidioso mai si ri-
mane di perseguitare. In Roma l'anno 1579 Il Cresci scrisse.

Figure 1. Translation: "Far greater is the enmity that is based on envy than one that is founded on any other injury; for a man will often forget an injury, but he who is envious will never cease his harassing." (From *Il perfetto cancellaresco corsivo di Giovan Francesco Cresci* [Rome, 1579].)

Figure 2. Translation: "The duty of a wise man is to remember the benefits he has received, forget the injuries he has suffered, hold onto what is his without coveting what is another's, encourage the good, feign with the bad, be grave with his elders and sociable with his youngers, do good to those who are present and speak well of those who are absent, place little value on the adversities of fortune and much on any small losses of honor, jeopardize many things for a certainty and never jeopardize a certainty for many doubtful things, and be of service to everyone, and offend no one." (From *Il perfetto cancellaresco corsivo di Giovan Francesco Cresci* [Rome, 1579].)

chancery cursive script taken from *Il perfetto cancelleresco corsivo*.) According to Guasco's testimony, acquiring this skill was a task that required an immense labor, taking up hours of time each day, winter and summer alike, and entailing great vexation and many tears on Lavinia's part and a long penance on the part of her father. Why was Guasco so anxious to see his daughter master a skill that was so time consuming and difficult, and for which there appear to have been no tutors available in Pavia? In fact he had a very good reason for doing so, to which he frankly admits in the second part of his *Discourse*, namely, that so rare a skill would doubtless give her a special advantage over the other ladies-in-waiting when she arrived at court and, hopefully, lead her to be chosen for the prestigious post of secretary to her mistress the infanta. With this end in view, he informs her that he has bought some manuals on the art of letter-writing for her to take with her to court and encourages her by reminding her of how, when she was only eight years old, she had already mastered this skill sufficiently for him to have preserved a sample of her handwriting for posterity.

We also learn from this section that Guasco had had his daughter instructed in the use of the abacus and that after she became eight years old he had banished all childish games from her leisure hours, setting her instead to learn chess, backgammon, and similar skillful board games that would prove useful at court and at which she was soon beating her father. Clearly, Guasco had given considerable thought to all the skills that would best enhance a young lady-in-waiting and had spared no pains to adorn his daughter with these.

Why had Guasco put his daughter, and indeed himself, under such pressure to achieve so much in so short a time and while Lavinia was still so very young, at the risk of both their healths? No doubt his parental pride in her brilliant precocity played a part in all this, but the vital constraint would probably have been the fact that a high-born girl at this time, not destined for the convent, was normally expected to be married off by the age of twenty at the latest, and once she became a wife, her new domestic cares, duties and likely frequent pregnancies would, of course, rule out any serious court career.[23] Clearly, if she was to make any contribution to public life in

would presumably have been obliged to learn the skill through tracing and copying the examples in Cresci's manual. According to contemporary testimony, it was possible for a pupil under an outstanding writing master to become proficient in chancery cursive in three to six months but under an indifferent one it would take two to three years of hard work and consistent practice. Given that Lavinia had no teacher at all but only a writing manual from which to work, it is hardly surprising that the task of acquiring this skill became for her the painful and laborious process stretching over several years that Guasco describes so graphically in his *Discourse*.

23. For a further discussion of the topic of typical marriage age for Renaissance girls, see James S. Grubb, "Age at Marriage," in his *Provincial Families of the Renaissance* (Baltimore and London, 1996), 4–6.

her own right, it had to be before she reached her late teens. By sending Lavinia off to become a lady-in-waiting at the age of eleven (which was probably considered a normal age at this period), Guasco was ensuring that she could, and did, enjoy a career of six to seven years at the court of Turin, long enough for her to be able to establish a reputation for her virtuosity with her mistress and her fellow court attendants. In his letters, Guasco refers to Lavinia's close friend at court, Orintia Langosca, as being of the same age as Lavinia herself, and in the *Discourse* he implies that there may even be younger girls than herself there. In some ways the palace would have functioned rather like a top finishing school for these young girls, enabling them to acquire polish, self-possession, and prestigious contacts. Guasco refers later in his letters to the match that he arranged for Lavinia at the age of eighteen as his final act of parental responsibility.

Guasco concludes this introductory section to his *Discourse* by summarizing for Lavinia in a series of terse, tense, and highly emotional sentences all that he and her mother have done for her in order to prepare her for this crucial moment in her life and for the great opportunity that now lies before her, reiterating his confidence that she will bring benefit to her employer and honor to herself in her new life. He ends with the solemn statement: "Nothing more remains for us to do, all our duties toward you are now fulfilled." Then, using the humanistic device of the writer offering his work to his patron or dedicatee as the most precious of all gifts, he announces to his daughter that he has one last present to bestow on her before she departs, a thing more rich and rare than all he has ever given her up till now, a priceless jewel which she must keep with her always, so as constantly to recall her father's great love and tenderness toward her. Guasco imagines he sees little Lavinia standing before him gazing expectantly at his hands, all agog to discover what he is about to give her, while he playfully keeps her in suspense, telling her that it is no precious stone, nor does it come from the bowels of the earth, but from the depth of her father's heart. Finally he tells her that she will find it in the paper he is holding out to her, on which he has written for her "a rule book to govern your conduct," to which she can turn in all eventualities while she is away from home and hear her father's voice addressing and advising her from its pages. Thus equipped, Guasco can confidently consign his young daughter to the care of another, assuring her that the prayers of her parents both to God and to her guardian angel for her well-being will accompany her. In this way, Guasco uses the precious jewel device to link the introductory, retrospective, section of his *Discourse* to its main, prescriptive, component.

This first section of the *Discourse* presents a curious contrast: on the one hand it conveys, in an agreeable and convincing manner, the sincere and deep love Guasco clearly feels for his daughter and his desire to see her flourish and earn prestige at court, while on the other it charts the insensitive and oppressive manner in which he had exploited her talents, her youth, and her duty of filial obedience in order to make her meet his extraordinarily demanding educational objectives. Today's reader will be astonished and probably shocked by the frankness, and indeed pride, with which Guasco boasts of how he had goaded and urged Lavinia on, almost past the limits of human endurance, throughout her childhood years, debarring her from all childish play and leaving her, as he says, barely time to take breath, let alone to rest or relax, and of how he had weighed every ounce of her time to insure she never wasted so much as one jot of it. He complacently admits that her health could have been permanently impaired, and even her very life threatened, by the long and intensive hours of study he had imposed on her, holding up her survival and continued robustness as proof that God had favored their endeavors. In contrast, probably a contemporary reader's main reaction to Guasco's *Discourse*, unlike ours, would have been one of amazement that so much expense and effort had been invested in a daughter's education. And what might Lavinia's own feelings have been regarding her training? Despite all the deprivations and weary toil it had entailed for her, she would have been sustained to some extent by the sense of being enormously privileged over and above the rest of her sex, combined with the reassurance of knowing she was her father's favorite child, source of his greatest pride, and destined for a shining public career. In no way were her talents to be allowed to go to waste. We should recall that it was Lavinia herself who published the *Discourse* and who, in her foreword, expresses only eagerness to satisfy her father's wishes, delight at having been enabled, due to her skills, to obtain her post at court, and a desire to share with others the content of her father's work. Moreover, however harsh, idiosyncratic, and pressurized Guasco's methods of fast-track education seem in the light of today's standards, they must be read in the context of a period when there was little awareness of the nature of childhood and when children were simply regarded as the property of their parents.[24] Certainly Lavinia must have been a child of great resilience, as well as of precocious intelligence, to have survived those early years deprived of play and relaxation without, apparently, rebelling or suffering any mental or psychological ill-effects and to have gone on to be a success at court. We are almost inclined to endorse the view that Guasco seems

---

24. On the subject of childhood and attitudes toward children in the Renaissance, see Philippe Ariès, *Centuries of Childhood* (Harmondsworth, 1973); and Linda A. Pollock, *Forgotten Children: Parent-Child Relations from 1500 to 1900* (Cambridge, 1983).

to be intending to promote, that he is recounting the unfolding of a miraculous happening; while the extraordinarily opportune arrival in Turin of the infanta of Spain as the bride of Carlo Emanuele at the precise moment when Guasco was casting around for a suitable and not too distant Catholic court to which to send Lavinia, coupled with the new duchess's agreement to waive a part of the fees normally payable by parents for this privilege, are cited by him as the crowning proofs that his plans for his daughter were the express inspiration and intention of the Lord.

"Discourse," Part 2: How to Succeed at Court

The second, and major, part of Guasco's *Discourse* follows more conventional lines, falling into the category of the many moral and prescriptive works written for women during the fifteenth and sixteenth centuries. However, it stands out from the general run of these by virtue of the highly personal, solicitous, and practical tones in which Guasco addresses his young daughter, his perceptive explanations for the directives he gives her, and the fact that he is offering her guidance for a public and professional role and not for a merely domestic one. The *Discourse* must also, of course, be seen as stemming partly from Guasco's desire to continue to exercise his paternal authority and control over his daughter to some degree even after she has left home and passed under the jurisdiction of her new mistress. In a letter concerning a poetic composition that he had written for a friend and that little Lavinia, aged only seven at the time, had copied out for him in her beautiful hand, he brackets her and his poem together, describing her as "my composition as well" [*componimento mio anch'essa*], a Pygmalion-like attitude that tells us a great deal about his attitude toward her.[25]

This part of the *Discourse* is subdivided into eight sections, each with its own heading, and each focusing on a different aspect of Lavinia's new life. The first two sections deal with Lavinia's spiritual and moral obligations both as a Christian and as a well-brought-up and pure young girl; Guasco then considers her role as a lady-in-waiting and the problem of maintaining her skills alongside her new duties at court and advises her on how she should care for her physical health and her belongings, maintain social relations with her fellow courtiers, and treat her domestic staff. Although Guasco uses no paragraph divisions in the *Discourse*, as if to stress both its hurried and impromptu nature and its urgency, but writes in one continuous flow from start

---

25. See Guasco's letter to S. Domenico Chiariti in *Lettere: Di nuovo aggiuntavi in questa nostra seconda impressione la seconda parte delle Lettere dell'istesso Auttore* (Treviso, 1603), 35.

to finish without a spatial pause, each of these eight divisions forms a distinct entity in the work with a tone and stylistic devices appropriate to its content. These will now be considered briefly one by one.

The first section consists of a homily to Lavinia on the fundamental importance of her Christian faith and the duties it entails, which must take precedence over all else. To convey to her the vital need for daily prayer, Guasco uses the homely image of the fodder every traveler must pause to give his horse, since in the end this represents not time lost but time gained on his journey. The role model Guasco offers his daughter here is no shadowy figure from history or scripture but her own mother, whose prayers Guasco claims always to have been the very bedrock of their family's prosperity. He uses moving, biblical-style language to enumerate all that God will both do and be for Lavinia in her new life so far from home in return for her chaste daily prayers. Introducing a typically Renaissance metaphor from painting such as we find in Castiglione, Guasco tells her that, while he has only been able to sketch out the picture of her new life at court in his *Discourse,* God the supreme artist [*ottimo dipintore*] will color in all the details for her, provided she serves him faithfully. He concludes by commanding Lavinia, with the voice of stern parental authority, to obey him in all this or God's vengeance will strike them both; then, with a rapid change of tone, typical of certain key passages in his *Discourse,* he reassures her, telling her that he knows she will do so and that God will duly reward her. Thus an image of God emerges from this section as the ultimate patriarchal figure, punishing or rewarding in proportion to the devoutness of each individual.

The second section of the *Discourse* concerns the topic regarded as of paramount importance by Renaissance moralists, that is, the preservation of a woman's purity and chastity (see "The Other Voice in Early Modern Europe: Introduction to the Series," xxiv–xxv). Guasco makes it very clear to Lavinia that her chastity is the basis of all her other virtues, but his strictures are succinct, and he refrains from citing any of the long catalogs of exempla of famous chaste women usually included by such writers. He uses metaphors from jewelry and clothing to help Lavinia envisage chastity as a woman's one essential adornment, without which she can be neither comely nor a true member of her sex, and which, once blemished, can never again be washed clean. He then adduces the conventional example of the ermine, reputed to choose death rather than allow its pure white coat to become sullied. He also stresses the fragility of a woman's honor, which can be despoiled by the slightest breath of scandal. Once again, it is Lavinia's mother who should serve as her role model here, together with other female forebears on both sides of the family. Never averse to using moral blackmail on his daugh-

ter, Guasco threatens that should Lavinia fall short of these ladies' high standards, she will no longer deserve to be regarded as a legitimate offspring of
the Guasco lineage nor to serve a mistress who lays as much store by the principles of morality and chastity as does the infanta. By offering Lavinia examples of chaste women from her own immediate circle, rather than the conventional ones of history and legend, Guasco is able to lay greater moral
pressure on her to preserve her honor and purity.

In sections 3 and 4 of the *Discourse*, Guasco moves on to address the
specific requirements of Lavinia's new professional role as a lady-in-waiting
and the problem of how to maintain her skills once she arrives at court.
In her offices toward her mistress, Guasco borrows imagery typically applied by moralists to the duty of a young wife toward her husband: as a
chameleon adapts its colors to its circumstances, so Lavinia must adapt all
her wishes to those of her employer and, like a readily grafted young
plant, accommodate her habits to the demands of her new and very different way of life, putting childishness behind her. The reward of devoted
service will be her mistress's ever-increasing love toward her. Coming
down to specifics, Guasco offers advice to his daughter on the importance
of serving her mistress to the very best of her abilities at all times, even
endeavoring to anticipate her wishes and putting the infanta's ease before
her own personal comfort. Lavinia's deportment and conduct should con-
sistently demonstrate her dutiful affection for her employer, and she should
never indulge in flighty or indecorous behavior. Under no circumstances
must she ever speak disrespectfully of her or allow others to do so in her
presence. Guasco also addresses in this section the pitfalls that sooner or
later all courtiers had to confront of requesting favors from the prince
they served for friends and relations. Guasco is here propounding an ideal
of service founded on devotion, vigilance, and self-effacement: the only
desire of an exemplary female court attendant should be the well-being of
her mistress.

Guasco then goes on to develop these points by instructing Lavinia in
how best to demonstrate both her love for her mistress and her deference to
her wishes in her day-to-day service as her lady-in-waiting. She should study
her mistress's humor and note what things please her best both in her other
attendants and in Lavinia in particular; her affection and respect for her mistress should manifest itself in her facial expression, which should be one of
loving solicitude, never of grumpiness or melancholy, and in her gestures and
movements, which should be respectful and properly controlled; her attendance on her mistress should be prompt and diligent; and like Castiglione's
ideal courtier, Lavinia should endeavor to characterize all her actions with a

grace and charm that will appear entirely natural and spontaneous, no matter how much study and effort these qualities may have involved, since they are of the utmost importance in eliciting a response of favor from others. One of the first difficult lessons Lavinia must learn in her new role is that of humility: when another is preferred to her, rather than taking offense, she should honor that person as superior to her in merit, and redouble her own efforts to please; if, on the other hand, she should be favored or singled out by her mistress, she should not react with overfamiliarity toward her or with boastfulness but humbly and respectfully, showing she truly appreciates her mistress's bounty toward her but regards it as stemming from the latter's goodness rather than from her own deserts. Echoing Castiglione's advice to his courtier, Guasco goes on to say that rarely, if ever, should Lavinia request any favor for herself and only for someone else if they truly deserve it and if it is something honest, easily granted, and opportunely requested, for should her mistress deny her request, or only grant it with reluctance, future relations between them could be impaired.

This section underscores the almost god-like status and paramount will of court rulers at this period—*semidei in terra* [demigods on earth] as Guasco terms them—and of the crucial importance for the courtier of earning and retaining his prince's favor or, in the court lady's case, that of his consort, who of course frequently ruled the court and entire state for long periods during her husband's absence on military campaigns. All the potential benefits of court life hinged on this vital relationship, which could clearly never be guaranteed but only striven for through a service comprised of the qualities listed here by Guasco: solicitude [*sollecitudine*], diligence [*diligenza*], reverence [*reverenza*], humility [*humiltà*], and adorned with the pleasing quality of grace [*gratia*]. For those courtiers fortunate enough to win the favor of their prince, there was still what Guasco terms the "mortal poison" of the envy of their fellows to be overcome. Success could all too easily be its own undoing, and Lavinia's exceptional talents and skills clearly set her especially at risk here.

In section 4 of the *Discourse*, Guasco addresses a theme that deeply concerns him, namely, how Lavinia is to combine the maintenance of her many skills with all her new duties at court. It is clearly Guasco's greatest dread that she may fail to put the necessary practice into these once her father is no longer at her side to urge her on and when she has so much else to distract her and that, consequently, she will begin to lose what has been gained with so much effort. His anxiety is understandable: Lavinia has been given a reduced-fees position in the infanta's entourage on the understanding that she possesses certain desirable accomplishments that will contribute to the enhancement of the court of Turin and to her mistress's pleasure, and should she be found wanting in these, either now or in the future, it would discredit those in high positions who had vouched for her and lead to a scandal both for her and for her next of kin. Moreover, all in the family have had to make sacrifices to facilitate the huge financial outlay that her move to court has entailed, and the one reward they look for now is the prestige they expect her skills to earn for her in her career as a lady-in-waiting.

This section consists of a long series of persuasive arguments, totaling sixteen in all, and each more urgent and compelling than the one before (*potentissime* as Guasco describes them), aimed to convince Lavinia of the vital importance of maintaining her skills. Building on his graphic introductory section in which he had reminded Lavinia of all the effort, toil, and suffering she had had to endure in the acquisition of these same skills, Guasco now holds up the two alternatives facing her in her new career, either to throw them away through neglect or to maintain and improve on them and turn them to good account. He argues that her targets have now been met and that the goals of honor and glory that her family and friends so much desire for her now lie within her reach; however, should she take the shameful course of failing to preserve and cultivate them, she will be guilty henceforth not only of breaking the Fifth Commandment, namely, her duty to honor her parents but, even worse, of sinning against God Himself, who will one day require her to give account of the gifts with which He had endowed her. To reinforce his message and remind Lavinia of the taxing program of education she had undergone to reach this point, Guasco uses a vocabulary of terms throughout this section that denote exhaustion and extreme physical suffering, such as *intolerabili fatiche* (unbearable labors), *sudore* (sweat), *pena* (pang), *supplicio* (torture), *stento* (toil), and *tormento* (anguish), offsetting these with positive terms underlining her present level of achievement and high hopes for the future: *honor*, *felicità* (happiness), *gloria*, *laude* (praise), *fama* (renown), and *dilettatione* (delight). The adverb *virilmente*, with its masculine connotations, is contrasted with *vilmente* and *impietà* to summarize the two options that now lie before her either of manly courage or of cowardice. The repeated command, *"Fallo,"* "Do it," referring to the maintenance of Lavinia's skills, thunders through this section, sternly insistent. No child of eleven could have failed to feel the impact of all this rhetoric. Finally, Guasco succinctly reiterates all his arguments and gives his daughter some practical advice on how to put what little spare time she is likely to have in the palace to the best possible use in keeping up her skills, using the analogy of a piece of iron that will quickly rust if left in disuse but that can be preserved in good condition by just a little regular use. It is small wonder that Lavinia avails herself of her foreword to the published edition of the *Discourse* to reassure her father with childish eagerness that she is obeying him in this matter and even being allowed time and given encouragement by her mistress to practice her skills.

Taken together, these two sections, 3 and 4, vividly convey the difficult balancing act that a young court attendant needed to sustain in order to succeed in her career: she must learn, on the one hand, to subordinate all her desires to those of her mistress, to exercise humility, and to defer to all around her, while on the other hand she must promote herself and her own interests whenever possible through whatever talents she possesses, cultivate a grace and charm of manner that will earn her general favor, and play her part in the complicated patronage network of a Renaissance court through learning the difficult and potentially dangerous art of requesting favors and pressing petitions.

In the next section Guasco turns from sternness to solicitude, as he offers advice to his daughter on preserving her health in her new life at court. This advice has mainly to do with the management of her diet, her attire, and her personal appearance. He contrasts the rich diet that will await her in the palace with the frugal one to which she has been accustomed at home and warns her against the danger of overindulging at mealtimes, but he is also concerned that she should not follow the habit of the Spanish ladies-in-waiting and drink only water: she should continue to drink a moderate daily quantity of wine for its nutritional value. Guasco associates mental alertness, vigilance, and the preserving of a good singing voice with these two aspects of her diet. He then stresses the importance of cleanliness, especially where her hair, hands, and teeth are concerned, features that the Spanish ladies regard as of paramount importance to a woman's beauty. This leads Guasco on to discuss the use of cosmetics, a practice that, like almost all Renaissance moralists, he heavily condemns, on the grounds that it both endangers a woman's health and offends God by seeking to distort her natural appearance. Lavinia should apply nothing but fresh water to her face. Equally, she should not attempt to dye her hair blond or dress it in overelaborate and time-consuming styles but aim always to create the impression of a simple, unstudied grace [*un' artificiosa negligenza*] that conceals whatever effort has gone into it. Here again we find strong resonances from *The Courtier*, with its emphasis on the natural coloring, unadorned hair, and seemingly uncontrived elegance of a lovely woman. Guasco reminds Lavinia that she must also pay heed to the decorum of a lady-in-waiting, and he gives her a highly practical illustration of this: since she will have to serve her mistress at table, as is the court custom, she must at all costs avoid spilling any of the dishes down her skirt, for grease-stained garments are more appropriate to a kitchen maid than to a court lady.

The care of her clothes and other possessions is understandably a topic that concerns Guasco very closely in view of the enormous expense they have entailed as well as the numerous trips that he claims he has had to make to Milan and other such centers to buy them. With his customary specificity Guasco here includes a list itemizing the main purchases he has had to make for Lavinia, which include such costly items as a canopy bed, wall hangings, rugs, musical instruments, dresses of gold and silver, and precious jewelry. No other Italian Renaissance text that has so far come to light better illustrates the practicalities and expenses of sending a daughter to court than Guasco's. A strong sense of immediacy also emerges from this section, for most of the purchases Guasco refers to here must have been made within the last few months before Lavinia's leave-taking, since obviously he would not have wanted to buy a wardrobe for his growing daughter too much in advance of her departure from home.

He reminds her that while equipping her for court has been his responsibility, caring for all her new possessions will be Lavinia's, so in section 6 Guasco offers her some simple practical advice on how best to do this, such as repairing tears in garments as soon as they occur, keeping her clothes safe from dust, mud, mice, and moths, and making an inventory of all she has with her as a safeguard against theft. Traditionally, moralists had always ascribed the storing and preserving of all the household goods to the female, while the man's task was to go out and obtain them (as has been the case here with Guasco). The final challenge with which Guasco presents his daughter in this section is to arrange all the contents of her chamber in such a way that instead of cluttering it they will adorn it, in preparation for the day when she will have a whole house of her own to organize. To inspire her and show her what can be achieved in a small space, he borrows verbatim an account he had found in Speroni of a room belonging to a cloth merchant on the Rialto in Venice: despite being crammed with bales of cloth, bed, desk, innumerable musical instruments, stove, and utensils, this merchant had succeeded in creating a tiny *locus amenus* out of it, with the help of a well and of citrus trees in tubs and by cleverly ordering all its contents so as to create a generally decorative effect. Guasco playfully reminds his daughter that it will be far easier for her to arrange her room attractively than it was for that merchant, since unlike him she will not have all those haversacks to deal with; moreover she has a servant to assist her and, being a woman, she is naturally more inclined anyway toward such matters.

Section 7, which is more than twice the length of any of Guasco's other subdivisions, addresses the highly complex topic of Lavinia's social relations with the rest of the court, one about which he remarks that he could easily write a whole book Since he cannot do this, Guasco is giving her three invaluable works to take with her to court, all of which are still regarded today as the great fundamental handbooks of social and courtly behavior during the Renaissance, namely, Castiglione's *Cortegiano*, Della Casa's *Galateo*, and the *Civil conversatione* of Guasco's close friend and neighbor Stefano Guazzo.[26] Guasco urges Lavinia to read all these with the greatest attention if she wishes to avoid committing serious errors in her social conduct and conversation. Much of what Guasco has to say in this section relates to verbal communication, "how to rule your tongue" as he calls it. As Anna Bryson pointed out in her recent work, *From Courtesy to Civility*, the sixteenth century saw a new interest arising in the social implications of language and in discourse and conversation as important means of exemplifying ideals of conduct and courtly values.[27] In a simile symptomatic of the attitude of his age, Guasco tells his daughter that just as the ring of a piece of metal will reveal whether it is true or base, so her speech will manifest the quality of her personality. In marked contrast to the view of the majority of prescriptive writers of the time, who regarded any utterance by a woman outside the privacy of her home as a violation of her chastity, and who endlessly exhorted her to preserve an eloquent silence in public, Guasco here offers Lavinia every encouragement to become a successful and witty conversationalist at court, no doubt bearing in mind Castiglione's significant statement that the court lady's most important attribute should be "a certain pleasing affability whereby she will know how to entertain graciously every kind of man with charming and honest conversation."[28] Unlike that sophisticated lady, however, Lavinia has as yet no experience of any but a familial and domestic society, and so she must be discreet and guarded in her utterances. Moreover, since the predominant language of the court is now Spanish, she has a language barrier to overcome, for clearly there simply had not been time for Guasco to have her taught the Spanish language before she set off. Thus part of this section is devoted to reminding Lavinia of all the reasons why she must strive to acquire this new language as quickly as possible, since linguistic fluency is essential both in carrying out her daily court duties and in forging good relations with

26. Castiglione's *Courtier* was first published in Venice in 1528 (in English, 1561); Giovanni della Casa published his *Galateo* in Venice in 1558; Stefano Guazzo's *Civil Conversatione* was first published in Venice in 1574 (in English, 1581).

27. Anna Bryson, *From Courtesy to Civility: Changing Codes of Conduct in Early Modern England* (Oxford, 1998).

28. See Castiglione, *The Book of the Courtier*, 212.

her mistress and the ladies of her entourage. It is also vital that she should learn to write Spanish competently, for if she does so there is a hope that her mistress may decide to choose her as her personal secretary "in view of the excellence of your handwriting." This is a bold statement, and one that reveals Guasco's most cherished ambition for his outstanding young daughter, for it was generally accepted that the post of secretary to a ruler, or to a ruler's consort such as the new duchess of Savoy, who acted as head of state during her husband's frequent absences on military campaigns, carried enormous prestige and brought prince and subject to into a very close and special relationship.

Just as Castiglione had urged his court lady to spice her conversation with a "quick and vivacious spirit" when entertaining the male courtiers, so Guasco stresses the importance of wit in a courtly society, complimenting the Spanish court ladies for their verbal adroitness. Since in the past Lavinia's wit and repartee have astonished her family, Guasco expresses every confidence that she will succeed in this capacity at court. To illustrate how banter and jest should be properly used so as not to cause hurt feelings, Guasco introduces the easily remembered simile of the harmless and pleasant nips of Lavinia's small pet dog that gently graze the skin without ever piercing it. Guasco's positive and encouraging attitude toward his small daughter's witty capabilities is in sharp contrast with the highly chauvinistic stance adopted by Lodovico Domenichi some twenty years earlier in his *La Donna di corte* (mentioned above in the section titled "The Courtly Code for Women"). Here, this writer who, ironically, had earlier written in praise of women in his treatise *La Nobiltà delle donne* (1558), declares wit to be entirely outside a woman's competence due to the state of childishness in which she remains throughout her life and, in any case, incompatible with her chastity, so not even to be attempted by her; for these two reasons, therefore, no woman can ever become a true courtier. Although such a narrow view of the lady at court differs fundamentally from that of Castiglione and Guasco, all three writers are then clearly in agreement that wit, or *urbanità* as Domenichi terms it, is the very essence of courtiership, a vital means of contributing to the life of the enclosed community of the court.

Guasco devotes much of this long section to alerting Lavinia to the many different ways in which speech can be misused through idle gossip, backbiting, indiscreet remarks, and calumny. In order to impress on her mind that sooner or later such talk will out, he recounts the fable to her of King Midas and his barber. He also points out that you can antagonize people through what you fail to say or what you allow others to say in your presence as well as through unguarded facial expressions such as sneers and grimaces, which, as he perceptively remarks, can offend even more than spoken insults, in that they can neither be answered back nor appraised.

To assist Lavinia in her personal relations with her peers at court, Guasco offers her a long series of practical guidelines on preserving friendships, reminding her of the many obligations the relationship imposes. Where the senior court ladies are concerned, Lavinia is duty-bound to obey them with deferential and cheerful compliance, as representatives of her mistress. To supplement her own inexperience through seeking their advice will be doubly beneficial, in that everyone likes to be asked to proffer their advice. Lavinia must at all times remember that she is alone at court with no compatriots to turn to, should she be in need of help: it is essential, therefore, that not only should she antagonize no one in the palace but also that she should earn the good opinion and affection of all, down to its very lowliest inmate. Once again we find Guasco drawing on Castiglione's concept of grace, which he described in *The Courtier* as "the seasoning without which all other attributes and good qualities would be almost worthless"; in similar vein, Guasco exhorts Lavinia to do all she can to cultivate a charming and delightful manner, since this is a gateway into the affections of others, putting them under an obligation to do all they can to further your interests.[29] Like Castiglione's courtier, Lavinia should make good any deficiencies she may have here through observing and copying the graces of others.

This section of the *Discourse* conveys to us something of the atmosphere of an Italian Renaissance court, with its jealousies and bitter rivalries, its joke playing and banter, the vast and diversified throng of people that the palace housed, sometimes in very close quarters, and the wariness that stemmed from knowing that in every word and action one was being closely observed and appraised and continually gaining or losing favor with others—a challenging and daunting environment for anyone, let alone an inexperienced eleven-year-old with a language barrier. Although Guasco is careful to try and convey a picture of the court as an environment where talent, loyal service, and integrity are rewarded, there are moments in the *Discourse* when he hints at a darker side of court life, where no one is safe from the envy and malice of others, and where Lavinia's best safeguard will be humility. However, her surest way forward, as is implicit throughout this section of the *Discourse*, will be by creating a network of ties of affection and obligation for herself in the palace through the many different means Guasco has outlined for her

29. Ibid., p. 65.

here; in this way she will soon be surrounded not by a throng of strangers but by friends and well-wishers prepared to promote her interests.

In the eighth and last section Guasco addresses the important question of fostering good relations with one's domestic servants. Lavinia will be accompanied to court by a reliable domestic staff consisting of a male servant and a maid, carefully selected by her parents to wait on her in her new position. In order to make Lavinia pause and reflect on their situation, Guasco reminds her that she, too, is in the service of another but with the fundamental difference that while courtiers serve in order to win honor, servants do so merely to obtain the small wage they earn and so will always serve grudgingly unless they feel genuine love for their employer. Guasco also underlines the specifics of Lavinia's situation at court, her very young age, which makes a high-handed and peremptory manner toward her servants especially inappropriate, and the fact that it is her parents, not she herself, who are paying their wages, whilst her mistress is supplying their board. In the highly vulnerable position in which she will find herself in the palace, she must be aware that her servants can do her reputation great harm both by speaking ill of her behind her back and by arguing with her or answering her back in public. To guard against such humiliations Lavinia must do all she can to earn their respect, taking especial care to avoid overfamiliarity with her maid with whom she will be sharing a bedchamber. Although other Renaissance writers such as Alberti and Vives had offered many precepts to married women on how to rule their domestic staff, Guasco's advice to his daughter is unique in that it addresses Lavinia's particular situation, attended at court by servants who are only on loan to her and to whom she must give orders without the authority that is conferred by age and married status.

Guasco's parting present to his daughter of this book of precepts written expressly for her constitutes an invaluable vade mecum to help Lavinia steer her way through the innumerable pitfalls of court life. It is a clearly spelled out and very specific work full of thoroughly practical and perceptive advice for her on managing every aspect of life at this very young age in the palace of Turin and, especially, on promoting good relations with her fellow courtiers. But more than this, it is a reminder to Lavinia of her own personal identity and achievements to date and of the values of the family from which she comes, of their supportiveness, their piety, integrity, and respect for excellence, and it is moreover a pledge of their continuing love and pride in her while she is far from home.

Guasco concludes his *Discourse* with a valedictory passage in which he refers in tones of great dramatic immediacy to the perilous journey on which they are all about to embark as he and his wife accompany Lavinia to her new post. He reminds his daughter that her mother is heavily pregnant and close to giving birth, that it is the depths of winter, the weather atrocious, and the roads snowbound, and he prays to God for their safe arrival in Turin. He then reassures Lavinia once again of his confidence in her ability to make a success of her palace career, evincing as a good omen the eagerness she is showing to leave the family home, where she has been brought up with so much loving care, to go to their highnesses the duke and duchess, on the analogy of flames of fire that soar naturally upward from their place of origin, in order to find their own perfection. In token of her gratitude for all that her parents are doing for her, Guasco exhorts Lavinia to reread his *Discourse* at least once a month in order to imprint all his precepts on her mind, imagining as she does so that she can hear her father's voice vigorously intoning in her ears the words he has written for her. He also desires her to make a copy of the work in her own hand to send home to him, an onerous task that Lavinia managed to dodge by publishing it instead. Finally, he gives her a solemn parental benediction, at the same time invoking the blessing of God on her also.

THE CRITICAL FORTUNE OF THE TEXT

The most important contemporary critical reaction and testimonial we have to Guasco's *Discourse* is to be found in a letter addressed to the author by his close friend, the distinguished writer Stefano Guazzo, which appeared in 1603 in a collective edition of Guazzo's letters. He tells Guasco that a mutual friend has given him the work to read, and after a careful and critical perusal of it, Guazzo has nothing but praise for it. Referring to it as "your most godly and moral work of advice," he pronounces everything about it to be admirable, its precepts and concepts, the arrangement of its material, its style, which he regards as exemplary for its clarity, gravity, and elegance, and, above all, the pattern it offers in honest living. It is significant that Stefano Guazzo sees the *Discourse* not just as a work of advice and guidance for a young girl but as a moral comment aimed to rehabilitate court life in general, and he praises Lavinia for having offered it for general consumption by publishing it, instead of keeping it locked away. In Guazzo's eyes, his friend had adroitly concealed his true aim of reforming courts in particular, and society in general, under the guise of instructing a daughter. He likens the work to a river, the fertile waters of which will overflow its banks and carry its benefits through the court to the cities and provinces beyond, so sorely in need of such guidance. Guazzo concludes that, in short, this is a golden book, "*un vol-*

ume d'oro," high praise indeed from the celebrated writer of the *Civil conversatione.*[30]

In 1618, the year before Guasco died, a final volume of his letters was published in Pavia by an editor named Agostino Bordoni. In his dedication to two ecclesiastics, Bordoni proudly explains that this publication is due to his own personal initiative in going in person to visit Guasco in his home to ask him whether he had any copies of new letters in his possession that he would allow Bordoni to publish. He states that his reason for making this request was the great merit of Guasco's writings, both in prose and in verse, as demonstrated by the huge success they had been having "in all the bookshops of Italy," and Bordoni's consequent eagerness to "adorn" his own bookshop with some of them.[31] Clearly, then, Guasco did enjoy a degree of literary fame in Italy, at least in his own lifetime.

Writing within thirty years of Guasco's death, Girolamo Ghilini in his *Teatro d'Huomini letterati*, published in Venice in 1647, describes Guasco as a gifted writer in every branch of belles lettres, both prose and poetry, but so overeager that he rushed precipitously through all the literary genres "like an impetuous torrent" [*a guisa d'impetuosa torrente*] without pausing long enough to perfect himself in any one of them. Had he concentrated his mind on one thing alone, he would doubtless have become a great writer, in view of his learning and intellectual capacity. Ghilini mentions in particular Guasco's verse rendering of Boccaccio's novella and the *Discourse,* which he refers to as an instruction to a court attendant on how to conduct herself well at court.[32]

For the next three centuries, Guasco's *Discourse* appears to have remained more or less in oblivion. Then in 1924 a distant descendant, Francesco Guasco, devoted a section to the writer in the first volume of his *Tavole genealogiche di famiglie nobili Alessandrine e Monferrine.* Possibly family pride comes into play to some extent in Francesco Guasco's assessment of his forebear, but he describes him as one of the best writers flourishing at the turn of the sixteenth century, as well as one of the most outstanding citizens of which Alessandria could ever boast, a man of the highest integrity, an entertaining conversationalist, a loyal friend and patriot, austere in his habits, someone highly regarded by many princes and considered by all who knew him as one

30. See *Lettera del Signor Stefano Guazzo, Gentilhuomo di Casale di Monferrato* (Venice, 1590), 38–39.

31. See Agostino Bordoni's dedicatory introduction, "A gl'Illustrimi Signori I Signori Abbati D. Gregorio et D. Gio. Batt. Sfondrati," to *Lettere del signor Annibal Guasco Alessandrino, con alcune sue Rime secondo le occasioni accompagnate alle lettere,* ed. Agostino Bordoni (Pavia, 1618), 2v. This interesting comment shows the great popularity of letter collections with the contemporary reading public.

32. Ghilini, *Teatro d'Huomini letterati,* 14–15.

of the greatest intellectuals of his age. Francesco Guasco then lists his works, making a special mention of the *Discourse*: "But the work that best vouches for the mind and heart of Annibale Guasco is the one entitled *An Instruction to a Lady-in-Waiting on How to Conduct Herself Well at Court*. This book, addressed by the author to his daughter Lavinia when she was going as lady-in-waiting to the Court of Savoy, reveals in the writer a profound knowledge of men and affairs, and it was always highly esteemed and a work of which even today's women would do well to make a special study."[33]

Whether or not Guasco's *Discourse* did in fact influence for good the mores either of courtiers or of society in general as Guazzo had forecast and as Francesco Guasco appears to suggest, it is impossible to assess today, but certainly it seems likely that the duke read it (and probably his spouse also when her command of Italian became sufficiently good to do so), since a child of eleven, newly arrived at court, would hardly have dared publish her father's work in the Sabaudian capital without first obtaining her mistress's approval of its contents. Lavinia states her intention, moreover, of sharing it with her fellow ladies-in-waiting (see her foreword).

In 1956 Ruth Kelso published her comprehensive work, *Doctrine for the Lady of the Renaissance*. In chapter 7, "The Lady at Court," she devotes a considerable section to Guasco's *Discourse*.[34] Kelso is not, however, aiming to analyze but, rather, as she herself states, to summarize the vast number of texts that have contributed to her work; nevertheless, as well as outlining the general guidance Guasco offers his daughter in the second part of the *Discourse*, she does stress the similarity of his instructions to her regarding her relationship with her mistress to the sort of advice being offered at this time to girls about to marry: she must learn to subdue her will and her every wish to her lady's until she has no other. Kelso's discussion contains several misinterpretations, especially her confusing translation of the recurrent term *virtù* as virtue rather than as virtuosity or, in the plural, skills, the senses in which Guasco mainly uses the term in the *Discourse* (see pp. 12–14 above); also, her statement that the detailed description in the *Discourse* of the merchant's room on the Fondaco dei Tedeschi in Venice (which Guasco had in fact taken verbatim from Speroni) was an account the writer had received in a friend's letter of "the kind of room she (Lavinia) will be assigned in the palace." It is made clear by both Guasco and Speroni that this room description is included

33. Francesco Guasco, *Tavole genealogiche di famiglie nobili alessandrine e monferrine dal secolo IX al XX*, vol. 1, *Famiglia Guasco di Alessandria* (Casale, 1924), table 12; my translation.
34. Ruth Kelso, *Doctrine for the Lady of the Renaissance* (Urbana, Ill., 1956), 222–30.

purely to provide the two young girls in question with an example of how orderliness can still be achieved under even the most cramped of conditions.[35]

NOTE ON THE TEXT

No manuscript of the *Discourse* has come to light, and the text is known only through its first and only edition, published in Turin by the Bevilacqua printing firm in 1586 on Lavinia's instructions. There can be little doubt that this edition is faithful to the author's intentions, since it was published so soon after Guasco had completed his manuscript, and since Lavinia would certainly have been eager to insure it was reproduced to her father's entire satisfaction. It is printed in a beautiful italic script, which was perhaps intended to represent the calligraphic hand in which Guasco had hoped his daughter would herself transcribe it for him. It appears bound with another treatise, the anonymous work, *Il novo cortegiano de vita cauta et morale,* which also offers precepts on life at court.

The original text proceeded from start to finish in an unbroken flow, as if intended to resemble one long, urgent speech. In the interests of clarity and readability I have paragraphed it in my translation, divided it into two sections, and amended Guasco's punctuation according to modern criteria. I have also introduced a framework of headings to mark subdivisions in the text.

35. See *Discourse,* n. 56.

VOLUME EDITOR'S
BIBLIOGRAPHY

PRIMARY SOURCES

Albéri, Eugenio. *Relazioni degli Ambasciatori veneti al senato durante il secolo decimosesto: Raccolte, annotate, ed edite da Eugenio Albéri.* Florence: Società editrice fiorentina, 1863.

Anne de France. *Les Enseignements d'Anne de France duchesse de Bourbonnais et d'Auvergne à sa fille Susanne de Bourbon.* Lyon: Le Prince, n.d.

Boccaccio, Giovanni (1313–75). *Famous Women.* Translated by Virginia Brown. I Tatti Renaissance Library. Cambridge, Mass.: Harvard University Press, 2001.

Castiglione, Baldassare (1478–1529). *The Book of the Courtier.* Translated by George Bull. New York: Penguin, 1967.

Cresci, Giovanni Francesco. *Il Perfetto Scrittore . . . Dove si veggono i veri Caratteri, & le natural forme di tutte quelle sorti di lettere, che a vero scrittore si appartengono: Con alcun'altre da lui nuovamente ritrovate, Et i modi che deve tenere il mastro per ben insegnare* (The perfect writer . . . where can be seen the true characters, and the natural forms of all those sorts of letters, that appertain to a true writer: with some others newly invented by him, and the modes the teacher should adopt in order to instruct well). Venice: Rampazetti, 1569.

———. *Il Perfetto Cancelleresco corsivo, copioso d'ogni maniera di lettere appartenenti a Secretarii, adornato di bellissime & vaghe Inventioni di Caratteri, & collegamenti, nuovamente posti in uso dallo stesso Autore* (The perfect chancery script manual, copious in every type of calligraphy appropriate to secretaries, adorned with most beautiful and delightful inventions of some new characters and links utilized by this same author). Rome: Pietro Spada, 1579.

Dolce, Lodovico. *Dialogo di M. Lodovico della institution delle donne: Secondo li tre stati, che cadono nella vita humana* (Dialogue of M. Lodovico concerning the education of women: according to the three conditions that befall them in this life). Venice: Giolito, 1545.

Domenichi, Lodovico. *La donna di corte, nel quale si ragiona dell'affabilità & honesta creanza da doversi usare per gentildonna d'honore* (The court lady, in which are discussed the affability and good manners appropriate to a lady-in-waiting). Lucca: Busdrago, 1564.

Firenzuola, Agnolo. *Dialogo delle bellezze delle donne* (Dialogue on the beauties of women), in *Prose.* Edited by Bernardo di Giunta. Florence, 1548.

Fonte, Moderata. *The Worth of Women, Wherein Is Clearly Revealed Their Nobility and Their*

Superiority to Men. Edited and translated by Virginia Cox. Chicago and London: University of Chicago Press, 1997.

Ghilini, Girolamo. *Teatro d'Huomini letterati.* Venice: Guerigli, 1647.

Guasco, Annibal. *La Ghismonda del Boccaccio Composta in Ottava Rima.* Pavia: Bartoli, 1583.

———. *Ragionamento a D. Lavinia sua figliuola, della maniera del governarsi ella in corte; andando per Dama alla Serenissima Infante D. Caterina, Duchessa di Savoia.* Turin: Bevilacqua Heir, 1586.

———. *Lettere: Di nuovo aggiuntavi in questa nostra seconda impressione la seconda parte delle Lettere dell'istesso Auttore.* Treviso: Gio. Battista Bertoni, 1603.

———. *Il secondo volume delle lettere del signor Annibal Guasco Alessandrino.* Alessandria: Felice Motti, 1607.

———. *Lettere del signor Annibal Guasco Alessandrino, con alcune sue Rime secondo le occasioni accompagnate alle lettere.* Pavia: Gio. Battista Rossi, 1618.

Guasco, Francesco. *Tavole genealogiche di famiglie nobili Alessandrine e Monferrine dal secolo IX al XX.* Vol. 1, *Famiglia Guasco di Alessandria,* table 12. Casale, 1927.

Guazzo, M. Steeven. *The Civil Conversation.* Bks. 1–3 (1581), translated by George Pettie. Bk. 4 (1586), translated by Bartholomew Young. London: Constable & Co.; New York: Alfred A. Knopf, 1925.

Guazzo, Stefano. *Lettere.* Venice: B. Barezzi, 1590.

Horne, Philip. "The Gentleman at Court," chap. 1 of his introduction to *Selene: An Italian Renaissance Tragedy,* by G. B. Giraldi, xiii–xxii. Edited by Philip Horne. Lewiston: Edwin Mellen Press, 1996.

Sansovino, Francesco. *Del Secretario Libri IV Nel quale si mostra et insegna il modo di scriver lettere acconciamente e con arte, in qualsivoglia soggetto.* Venice: Rampazetto, 1564.

Speroni, Sperone degli Alvarotti. *Dialogo della cura della famiglia.* In *Opere Tratte da' MSS. originali* (1542), edited by Mario Pozzi, 1:75–96. Venice: Domenico Occhi, 1740; Rome: Vecchiarelli, 1989.

Tasso, Torquato. "Malpiglio; or, On the Court," in *Dialogues: A Selection, with the Discourse on the Art of the Dialogue,* 153–91. Translated by Carnes Lord and Dain A. Trafton. Berkeley and London: University of California Press, 1982.

———. *Discorso della virtù feminile, e donnesca.* Venice: B. Giunti & fratelli, 1582.

Vives, Juan Luis. *The Education of a Christian Woman: A Sixteenth-Century Manual.* Edited and translated by Charles Fantazzi. Chicago and London: University of Chicago Press, 2000.

Xenophon. *The Oeconomicus.* In *Xenophon: Memorabilia and Oeconomicus,* 363–525. Translated by E. C. Marchant. Loeb Classical Library. London: Heinemann, 1923.

SECONDARY SOURCES

Anglo, Sydney. "*The Courtier,* the Renaissance and Changing Ideals." In *The Courts of Europe: Politics, Patronage and Royalty, 1400–1800,* edited by A. G. Dickens, 33–53. London: Thames & Hudson, 1977.

Ariès, Philippe. *Centuries of Childhood.* Harmondsworth: Penguin Books, 1973.

Barber, Peter. "Maps and Monarchs in Europe, 1550-1800." In *Royal and Republican Sovereignty in Early Modern Europe: Essays in Memory of Ragnhild Hatton,* edited by Robert Oresko, G. C. Gibbs, and H. M. Scott, 75–124. Cambridge: Cambridge University Press: 1977, .

Biagioli, Mario. *Galileo Courtier: The Practice of Science in the Culture of Absolutism*. Chicago: University of Chicago Press, 1993.

Bruni, Roberto L., and D. Wyn Evans. *Italian Seventeenth-Century Books*. Exeter: Exeter University Library, 1984.

Bryson, Anna. *From Courtesy to Civility: Changing Codes of Conduct in Early Modern England*. Oxford: Clarendon Press, 1998.

Burke, Peter. "The Courtier." In *Renaissance Characters*, edited by Eugenio Garin; translated by Lydia C. Cochrane, 98–122. Chicago and London: University of Chicago Press, 1991

———. *The Fortunes of the "Courtier": The European Reception of Castiglione's "Cortegiano."* Cambridge: Polity Press, 1995.

Clough, Cecil H, ed. *Cultural Aspects of the Italian Renaissance: Essays in Honour of Paul Oskar Kristeller*. Manchester and New York: Manchester University Press, 1976.

Elias, Norbert. *The Civilising Process: The History of Manners*. Oxford: Basil Blackwell, 1983.

Fletcher, Anthony. *Gender, Sex and Subordination in England, 1500–1800*. New Haven, Conn.: Yale University Press, 1995.

Grubb, James S. *Provincial Families of the Renaissance: Private and Public Life in the Veneto*. Baltimore and London: John Hopkins University Press, 1996.

Hollingsworth, Mary. *Patronage in Sixteenth-Century Italy*. London: John Murray, 1996.

Jayawardine, S. A. "The 'Trattato d'abaco' of Piero della Francesca." In *Cultural Aspects of the Italian Renaissance: Essays in Honour of Paul Oskar Kristeller*, edited by Cecil H, Clough, 229–43. Manchester and New York: Manchester University Press, 1976.

Kemp, Walter H. "Some Notes on Music in Castiglione's *Il libro del Cortegiano*." In *Cultural Aspects of the Italian Renaissance: Essays in Honour of Paul Oskar Kristeller*, edited by Cecil H, Clough, 345–69. Manchester and New York: Manchester University Press, 1976.

Kent, F. W. and Patricia Simons, eds., with J. C. Eade. *Patronage, Art and Society in Renaissance Italy*. Canberra: Humanities Research Centre; Oxford: Clarendon Press, 1987.

King, Catherine. *Renaissance Women Patrons: Wives and Widows in Italy, c. 1300–c. 1550*. New York and Manchester: Manchester University Press, 1998; distributed in U.S. by St. Martin's Press.

Oresko, Robert. "The Duchy of Savoy and the Kingdom of Sardinia: The Sabaudian Court, 1563–c.1750." In *The Princely Courts of Europe: Ritual, Politics and Culture under the Ancien Régime, 1500–1750*, edited by John Adamson, 231–53. London: Weidenfeld & Nicolson, 1999.

———. "The House of Savoy in Search for a Royal Crown in the Seventeenth Century." In *Royal and Republican Sovereignty in Early Modern Europe: Essays in Memory of Ragnhild Hatton*, edited by Robert Oresko, G. C. Gibbs, and H. M. Scott, 270–350. Cambridge: Cambridge University Press, 1997.

Oresko, Robert, G. C. Gibbs, and H. M. Scott, eds. *Royal and Republican Sovereignty in Early Modern Europe: Essays in Memory of Ragnhild Hatton*. Cambridge: Cambridge University Press: 1977.

Pollock, Linda A. *Forgotten Children: Parent-Child Relations from 1500 to 1900*. Cambridge: Cambridge University Press, 1983.

Quondam, Amedeo. *Le "carte messaggiere": Retorica e modelli di comunicazione epistolare per un indice dei libri di lettere del Cinquecento*. Rome: Bulzoni, 1981.

Raulich, Italo. *Storia di Carlo Emanuele I, duca di Savoia, Con documenti degli archivi italiani e stranieri.* Milan: Hoepli, 1896–1902.

Raven, James, Helen Small, and Naomi Tadmor, eds. *The Practice and Representation of Reading in England.* Cambridge: Cambridge University Press, 1996.

Symcox, Geoffrey. "From Commune to Capital: The Transformation of Turin from the Sixteenth to the Eighteenth Centuries." In *Royal and Republican Sovereignty in Early Modern Europe: Essays in Memory of Ragnhild Hatton,* edited by Robert Oresko, G. C. Gibbs, and H. M. Scott, 242–69. Cambridge: Cambridge University Press, 1997.

DISCOURSE TO LADY LAVINIA

HIS DAUGHTER

*Concerning the Manner in Which She Should Conduct Herself
When Going to Court as Lady-in-Waiting to the Most Serene Infanta,
Lady Caterina, Duchess of Savoy*

LAVINIA'S
FOREWORD

IN OBEDIENCE TO MY MOST ILLUSTRIOUS FATHER, ANNIBAL GUASCO

When your Lordship commanded me, as I was leaving Alessandria, to copy by hand the discourse that you had written for me, of which I knew you had no other copy, I set to work to do so, but I realized that, due to the many tasks I find I have here, it would drag on too long, and meanwhile your Lordship might perhaps complain that I had failed to comply with your wishes in this respect. There being an abundance of printing firms in this city, I have therefore taken the liberty of having it published, both out of respect for your wishes and in order to share it with these ladies.[1] I beg of you therefore to pardon my presumption, since my intentions were good.

As for the rest, be of good cheer, for I am in Paradise here, serving a heavenly angel rather than a human princess, who is truly of such goodness that we who serve her deserve to be envied, loving her as we do not just as a courteous mistress but as a loving mother. And I, especially, am far better treated by her than I deserve. And since I know that your Lordship is most desirous that I should maintain the skills that I learned while I was at home, I must tell you that not only does my mistress the Infanta give me the opportunity of practicing them but, indeed, commands me to do so, and I shall not fail to obey both her and your illustrious self in this, as in all other respects, in order to satisfy my superiors and to bring honor both to our house and to myself. And so I conclude by kissing your hand, praying that you will enjoy health and a long life.

Turin, 15 March, 1586
Your most obedient daughter, Lady Lavinia Guasca[2]

1. Roberto L. Bruni and D. Wyn Evans, in their work *Italian Seventeenth-Century Books* (Exeter, 1984), list some forty printing firms operating in Turin during that century, many of which would doubtless have already been in existence by the 1580s.
2. Note that Lavinia here uses the feminine form, Guasca, of her family name, a not uncommon

A D. Lavinia
SVA Figlivola
QUAL più tenera madre à più diletto,
Care di lei delitie unico figlio,
Diè con tanta pietate in gran periglio
Baci, e ricordi di materno affetto?
Quant'io pien di timor, e di sospetto
Ti porgo al tuo partir il mio configlio;
Che con geloso amor dal centro piglio
Del cor, trahendo alti sospir dal petto?
Deh segui figlia, per tuo padre almeno,
Se non per util tuo, le mie parole,
Tinte d'honor, e di paterno zelo.
Ond'io di te spogliato, e d'anni pieno
Mi consoli; e ringratij il sommo Sole,
Che voli il nome tuo famoso al cielo.

To Lady Lavinia, His Daughter
What tenderest of mothers ever gave to her most beloved only son,
Dearest of all her delights,
Kisses and reminders of her maternal affection
With so much solicitude at a time of great peril,
As I, full of doubts and fears,
Offer to you as you depart my advice
Which with anxious love I draw, sighing deeply,
From the depths of my heart?
I beg of you, my daughter, for your father's sake at least,
If not for your own benefit,
Follow my advice, imbued as it is with honor and fatherly zeal,

---

practice at this time. She has also prefixed her name with the title of Lady (Donna), which is something we find her father doing as well from the time of her court appointment onward whenever he refers to her in his letters. Since by birth she belonged to an untitled patrician family, it would appear that her title was conferred on her by her new status as lady-in-waiting to the infanta. Similarly, when Guasco addresses, or refers to, any of her fellow court attendants, he invariably gives them this same title.

So that, though deprived of your company and heavy in years,
I may find consolation, and be able to thank the Lord of the heavens,
That your name is soaring famous to the skies.[3]

---

3. This is Guasco's valedictory sonnet to Lavinia as she departs for Turin from her parental home
in Alessandria. In the initial octet, he rather touchingly likens the advice he has written for her
to the counsels of a mother, imparting final reminders of her love and solicitude to her beloved
only son as he leaves her to face great dangers. In the sestet, Guasco predicts a happy and successful outcome to Lavinia's venture provided she follows his precepts. Note the role reversals
here, with Guasco presenting himself as a mother figure and Lavinia as a son.

DISCOURSE OF
SIGNOR ANNIBAL GUASCO
TO LADY LAVINIA
HIS DAUGHTER

PART 1: LAVINIA'S EDUCATION

Great is your debt of gratitude to God, my daughter. Indeed, I know of no one who could have more obligations to Him than yourself.[4] Let us set on one side His gift to you of your life, which is certainly a great mercy and the basis of all His other gifts, but one which you hold in common not just with irrational beings but with the whole of creation. You have been brought up a Christian, truly an incomparable blessing and one that takes precedence over all the rest, but a blessing common to many other people. You were nobly born, assuredly a gift of outstanding worth but shared with many. You are of healthy and robust physique, and your looks are such that you can hold your own with other girls, but such advantages apply to many. However, I am now coming on to consider some other, more particular, favors for which you have need to be grateful to the Lord and for which you must thank him a thousand times every hour. Where could you ever find a father and mother as solicitous in bringing up their children as your mother and I were in caring both for your soul and for your body? And, speaking just of myself, you well know with how much love and diligence I began, right from the time when you could scarcely utter your first words, to teach you and have you taught the things that now do you honor. Moreover, having discovered that you were of a very ready understanding, and perchance more so than one would have believed possible at so young an age (and for this again it is your duty to render especial thanks to God), I started instructing you in so many different skills that I am at a loss to know how you could absorb them all. But little

---

4. It is unusual to find a didactic work of this period launching directly into its central message with no preamble. Guasco's dramatic opening to his *Discourse* is clearly intended to arouse Lavinia's attention and to make her reflect on all the benefits of her life to date and the obligations toward God and her parents that these benefits now entail for her.

would my solicitude and efforts, or your ease of comprehension, have availed you if you had not been in a place where your talents could be given full scope, and to this end Almighty God placed the idea in my heart of abandoning our native city and leaving our affairs in the hands of others, to be attended to as God willed, in order to move at great expense to Pavia, a city as well-equipped as our own city is ill-equipped for educating children well and for adorning them with all the attainments required in those of noble birth. Furthermore, I can see no other reason why my heart should have persuaded me to make such a move but for your honor and benefit alone, since your cousins and your brother, whose advantage was my chief concern in moving here, have made such poor use of their opportunities that, as far as they are concerned, our expenses and inconveniences have been to no avail.

What teachers of reputation did I not employ for your benefit? And do you not recall that at times I appointed three and four teachers in the same profession simultaneously, all well paid, to instruct you, who, in competition with one another, dedicated themselves to you so affectionately and conscientiously that what another girl would have taken months to learn, you achieved in a few days?[5] But this would not have sufficed, since the loving care and diligence of your teachers alone would not have enabled you to retain all the things they had taught you if, in their absence, you had not mulled them over on your own. And this you would not have done had I not been at your side at all hours, making continuous and fervent efforts to spur you on. But not even this would have been sufficient, since being urged on by me, and often when you were least anxious to be, would have been of little avail if I had not (and this was no easy task) recruited a domestic staff to keep you in mind of those things. Although among these some were to be found already possessing a certain grasp of the subjects you were learning, soon all of them became experts under our roof, thanks to the opportunity I gave them, due to my residing in Pavia and, as you know, bringing so many teachers versed in so many different professions into our house to enhance the education of you children. And since the acquisition of knowledge and reputation are wont to give rise to pride, it was unavoidable that these servants should have felt their own sense of conceit, which made the overseeing and ordering of them all the more difficult for me, so that I was less well served by this large staff than I would have been by a small one.[6] These

5. Guasco does not specify what these disciplines [*lettioni*] were, but later on we find him using the term *arti liberali* for Lavinia's general education, which would imply that she had been given a training in at least some of the subjects that comprised the standard curriculum for boys at this time of the trivium and quadrivium—perhaps grammar, rhetoric, dialectics, and certainly music. The first three subjects would probably have been taught to her in Latin.

6. A vein of wry and self-deprecating humor surfaces from time to time in the *Discourse*, lighten-

things were hard to bear, but for your sake I continued to endure them, concealing my troubles, in order not to lose their services, and those with skills were so well treated by me, and I was held to be so well placed to promote them, that all those who happened to be in the city applied to me, with the result that I always had a good supply of the best of these, with whom you could at all hours practice your skills. And whether this has been to your advantage or not, only you can say; an advantage that was all the greater in that in no other household of a private nobleman bar that of your father could so many experts have been found assembled. Moreover, the trouble I went to in order to help you in every way that lay in my power to make good use of your time and of the labors of others is so great that I can only express it like this, namely, that I can guarantee I was held to be the most importunate and perhaps the most tyrannical father that any daughter ever had, demanding from you at every moment an exact account of what you were doing and wanting to know precisely how you were doing it; being constantly present during your lessons, admonishing, shouting, threatening, and at times beating you, until you had perfected them; since I had so honed my mind with the whetstone of natural paternal love, that I knew how to tell where, how, and when you were committing errors even in things of which I had no true knowledge. Of all this you were made aware by me, nor did I desist until you had corrected your mistake.[7] And to mention just one of these things, do you not recall how you had not even attained your seventh birthday before I myself set to work to teach you to write, not just in the characters in which I myself write, oh no, but in those that I did not know how to form, and how, with the printed examples of Crescio, you began little by little, and with what assistance I could give you, to master the art of forming chancery script, although I myself did not know how to form a single one of those characters.[8] And,

---

ing the tone and conveying the humorous and playful side of Guasco's personality that is so evident in his letters.

7. It was normal practice at this time to beat one's children, and something for which they should be grateful; indeed, not to do so was regarded as showing a neglect of parental responsibility. A child should be brought up in a wholesome fear of his or her parents, who must on no account allow their affection for their offspring to hinder them from using the rod. The moralist, Lodovico Dolce, reflects the attitude of the age in his *Dialogo della Institution delle donne* (Venice, 1545) when he urges fathers to show severity toward their children and restrict their freedom, especially in the case of a daughter for, he claims, "it is a good thing for a young girl to cry often and to be made sad during her childhood" (10v). Guasco later reminds Lavinia of the servile fear in which she had held him in her early childhood and of the frequent tears she used to shed during her lessons with him.

8. For further information on Cresci and chancery cursive, see n. 22 in my introduction. For the development of chancery cursive from the second half of the fifteenth century onward and the various methods by which it was taught, see Paul F. Grendler, *Schooling in Renaissance Italy* (Baltimore and London, 1989), 323–29.

pray, did this labor last for two or three months or thereabouts? No, but rather for four or five years did I continue this difficult task every single day and, sometimes, for many hours at a stretch in a single day, with how much tribulation on both our parts we both know well. But finally, with God's help and my own tireless efforts and, I should say, importunity, and in spite of your vexation, often accompanied by tears, you finally reached such a degree of excellence that you could do honor and service to others with your pen. Indeed, it would probably be impossible to find another girl of your age with such a high standard of competence as yourself.

Oh my Lavinia, are they few in number, these blessings of which I have so far reminded you, which you owe to God? No indeed, they are copious, but not so copious that there are not many more for which you are held bounden to Him. How would you have been able to grasp so many different subjects, and gain the profit you have derived from them in so few years, if God had not kept you in good health? And so favored you that you never had so much as a headache? So that without ever pausing for a moment you made steady progress, gaining ground and conserving all you had gained, which would not have happened if your lessons had been interrupted at times due to some indisposition on your part. Moreover, it also pleased the Lord at the same time to keep your father in good health, which was no less essential to your education than was your own health, since without his care, as you know, you would not have been nearly as advanced in your attainments as you are. This was a favor from God all the greater in that it was tremendously difficult, indeed almost impossible, for both of us to preserve our health, with all the worry and toil we had to undergo, summer and winter, day and night, over so long a period that everyone was filled with infinite amazement, and truly it was a miracle, and a special benefit on God's part.

But in order for you to realize fully the extent of God's favors toward you, just pretend that you now know nothing at all of the many things that you do know, and that it would be necessary for you to begin to learn them at this present time, as do many young girls of your age, and that you were starting out as from today, not to be taught to read, for by the age of four or little past it you had mastered that skill just as well as I myself who was teaching you, but rather to write, and imagine, in addition, that you had no one to teach you but me who, knowing neither how to do nor how to explain what I desired of you, was about as much use to you as a dumb man would be: what would you say, if I desired you to embark upon such an undertaking without a teacher? Would you not lose hope of ever being able to bring this work to its conclusion? And yet with God's help and with great efforts and sufferings on your part and with a contained impatience and long penance on mine, I guided you to your goal and, as you know, you have now fully acquired that proficiency.

But, if not content with the aforementioned burden, I had wished to lay yet a further, no less weighty, load on you at the same time, what would you say of my common sense? And what hope would you ever have of singing your part confidently at sight from every score if you had only now begun to learn the principles of singing? All the more so in these times in which the number of musical compositions has proliferated so greatly and reached such a peak of difficulty, and when modern composers compete among themselves to make their compositions as demanding as possible, and particularly since you were at the same time so absorbed in acquiring the art of writing that you scarcely had an hour to spare in which to regain your breath, let alone to take respite; and yet, thanks to God, you have mastered this skill also and can take the most complicated songs in your stride.[9]

And what would you say then if not only did I make you apply yourself to these two such lengthy and exhausting trainings simultaneously, but if at the same time I had a viola da gamba placed in your hand and began to have you taught how to play up and down the scales of its six keys? And it seems to me that you would say, "My noble father, how do you expect me to be capable of grasping so many things all at the same time? I shall gain some skill in them but not master them." And yet you did both; and you have gained such proficiency with your viola and bow that you can accompany any song creditably and effortlessly, and not only the soprano part but all the others too, tuned to the fourth and fifth.

But let us continue and suppose that, in addition to so many and diverse things, you were simultaneously burdened by me with yet another most weighty and difficult skill, and that together with the aforementioned labors you were set down in front of the clavichord, and that you were expected to learn at this present time how to adapt your fingers to it and to grasp with great effort those principles of how to play it that today you would scorn. And recall how, in the end, not contenting myself with one teacher alone, I employed four to instruct you on this instrument every day who, in rivalry with one another, taught you a variety of difficult harmonies, nor did it satisfy me that you should just learn your lessons at the hands of these teachers, but I insisted that you should make entablatures of them and should learn to score the music yourself,[10] to last as long as it might please you, so as to be

9. The art of counterpoint reached its apex at the end of this century. For a discussion of sixteenth-century court music, see Walter H. Kemp, "Some Notes on Music in Castiglione's *Il libro del cortegiano*" in *Cultural Aspects of the Italian Renaissance*, ed. Cecil H. Clough (Manchester and New York, 1976), 345–69.

10. Early Italian keyboard music was generally written or printed like present-day piano music on a two-staved score, though the staves often contained more than five lines each. This method was called *intavolatura* (entablature).

able to play the said instrument for two whole hours at least, with continual variations, not only dances and *canzonette* but also learned madrigals and good *ricercate*[11] and to be as much master of the notations as your teachers themselves? I am sure you never dreamed of progressing so far and that you would have held me to be the most unreasonable and perhaps cruel of fathers to ask so many almost impossible things of you in this art at the same time as your other studies, and yet you succeeded, and well know that none of your accomplishments adorns you more than this one does.[12]

But let us say still more and suppose that, while you were busy mastering all these skills, I had decided to have you taught counterpoint. How harsh and vexatious such an undertaking would seem to you, and how shocked you would be that I should want to drive you into so vast a labyrinth. And yet enter it you did, and emerged from it with honor.

And how would it seem to you if, in addition to these exhausting undertakings, I made you apply yourself to the abacus, what would you expect to gain from it? And when would you imagine you could master all the rules and apply them promptly? And this skill too I had you taught.[13]

Let us add still one more thing, that instead of allowing you to seek relaxation from all your toils in some childish game, I insisted that even before you had reached the age of nine, your games should be chess, backgammon, *toccadillo*, and such similar testing board games, would you not rather be frightened off by the difficulty of such games than expect ever to derive honor and

---

11. The *ricercata*, from the Italian, meaning to search out or to seek out, was similar to the *canzonetta*, but generally more serious in character.

12. At no point in the *Discourse* does Guasco state that he had devised Lavinia's musical education with the specific aim in view of obtaining a post at court for her, but this seems a likely supposition, in view of the intensity and urgency with which her lessons were imparted, Guasco's conviction of the great promise he saw in her from her earliest infancy, and his realization that musical ability could pave the way to success at court. In bk. 1 of Baldassarre Castiglione's *The Book of The Courtier* (ed. George Bull [Baltimore, 1967]), Count Lodovico had remarked, "Gentlemen, I must tell you that I am not satisfied with our courtier unless he is also a musician and unless as well as understanding and being able to read music he can also play several instruments" (94). (Subsequent references to Castiglione's book are to the edition cited here.)

13. Here Lavinia would doubtless have been given one of the practical arithmetics common in Renaissance Italy, usually written by *maestri d'abaco* or mathematics teachers. More than a hundred of these were published between 1478 and 1600. The main topics they dealt with were: reading and writing Hindu-Arabic numbers, four fundamental operations with integers, fractions, the rule of three, roots, geometrical progression, mensuration, the rules of algebra, and mercantile arithmetic (see S. A. Jayawardine, "The 'Trattato d'abaco' of Piero della Francesca" in *Cultural Aspects of the Italian Renaissance*, ed. Clough, 229–43).

In *Schooling in Renaissance Italy*, Grendler explains that "abbaco treatises did not assume the use of an abacus; instead, *abbaco* meant solving practical mathematical problems on paper" (308). These problems were usually business-related.

delight from them?[14] And yet here too you acquit yourself estimably, having very frequently beaten me who was teaching you.

Of all these things I have desired to remind you in this very diffuse manner, in order to be able to marshal them before your eyes as if they were happening here and now, even though I have not conveyed one thousandth part of the sufferings undergone by both of us in the process of arriving at the point where you now find yourself. I have done this so that I should be the better able to remind you of the obligation you must feel toward God and of how greatly you should prize the benefits He has conferred on you, like the man who, having climbed a stony mountain road in order to ascend to a delightful flowery plain, turns back to gaze at the steepness of the mighty peaks and crags he has scaled, amazed to find that, sweating and panting, he has conquered them, while rendering a thousand thanks to his Creator for having done so.[15] And let us inquire of any intelligent person how long it would take him to learn with ease all the things you find you have now learned, and if I am not much mistaken, he will say a full twelve years, which is an age you have not yet even attained and for a part of this time you were a suckling babe in your cradle. And you well recall what a wise matron asked you two years ago, which was whether you had learned all these things before, or after, you were born, and let us add what last summer you heard another such matron say: that she was more astonished to see you so robust in your person than she was amazed by the things that you knew, since it seemed almost a miracle to her that, after being always burdened in your childhood with so many toils, you still had a single breath left in your body. And truly you would not have been left with either spirit or life if the Author of life had not preserved you, nor would you in so short a time and by so long a course have arrived at so glorious a journey's end if He had not given you the necessary breath and strength and if I myself, inspired and aided by Him, had not so weighed out your time as on a balance, in such a way that I never permitted you to fritter away even one ounce of it fruitlessly.

Tremendous in truth are these favors bestowed on you by God, but the

---

14. Chess is mentioned by Castiglione as a necessary skill for the ideal courtier, though not one in which he should employ great effort, a mediocre ability being sufficient here (*The Courtier*, 140).

As for *toccadillo*, I have been unable to identify this board game; possibly it is a sixteenth-century term for tric-trak, an old variety of backgammon.

15. "You will be affected no differently by this grim beginning than walkers confronted by a steep and rugged hill, beyond which there lies a beautiful and delectable plain. The degree of pleasure they derive from the latter will correspond directly to the difficulty of the climb and the descent" (Giovanni Boccaccio, *The Decameron*, trans. G. H. McWilliam [Harmondsworth, 1972], 49; all subsequent references to this work will be to this edition).

sum of them is not yet complete. What reward did He have in store for all your efforts? And to what end did He ordain such efficacious means? The attainment is a fully sufficient reward in itself for all the toils endured in acquiring it, in addition to the praise that follows after it as the shadow follows the body. I will not mention the enjoyment that it is wont to bring to those who possess it or the way it renders a person more agreeable to others, a pleasure known only to those who feel themselves loved for their merits. But God had wished to direct your efforts to a more specific end, and for a more particular reward, although it was already a great thing to have enriched you with so many talents capable of earning you glory in the world, and which fortune would not be able to steal from you, so that you might be able to enjoy them at all hours in your own room and, through diverting yourself with them, dispel idleness, the root of all vices and evil thoughts.

But it was the general opinion, and rightly so, that you would gain small advantage from remaining in your father's house with all your attainments, acquired with such care, in comparison with that which you would derive from them in the household of some princess, and so I let myself be persuaded by those who loved you to try and place you in such a situation. But I was restrained by paternal tenderness and by not knowing which court to choose, as I considered one by one the qualities of the various Catholic courts. And for my part I would readily have given you to one of their most Serene Infantas of Spain but not only was that hard to arrange but, even supposing I had obtained a place for you there, I could not imagine how I would meet the costs or how I would be able to send you so far away from me, with the fear of never seeing you again. And consequently I resolved that when the moment came to deprive myself of you, I would willingly entrust you to one of their Serene Highnesses of Savoy, both for their illustrious rank and for the proximity of their court. But while I was giving thought to this, it had not yet been made known that the Lord Duke of Savoy was on the point of taking a wife, and still less was it known whom he had in mind to be his consort. I myself was burning with desire that it should be one of the aforementioned Infantas, as was generally desired by Catholics, but the outcome was nevertheless uncertain. But all of a sudden the plan was realized, and that great Prince was espoused to no less high and glorious a companion than the Infanta, Lady Caterina,[16] daughter of our noble King,[17] and a lady who in addition to her exalted rank is of a goodness and sanctity of life unsurpassed

16. The marriage contract was signed on August 23, 1584, some nine months after the union had been arranged.

17. Charles V had acquired the Duchy of Milan, still technically a part of the Holy Roman Empire, by escheat in 1535 and had bestowed it on his son, Philip II of Spain, in 1546.

in any other great lady of any age. And thus it was that through your own great good fortune, the very mistress in whose service I would have wished to place you came into our vicinity, when otherwise the distance and the difficulty of obtaining the post for you would have deterred me from so doing.

But the opportunity in itself would not have sufficed if I had not had some diligent and stalwart intermediary who could put your name forward to the Infanta and give her such an account of your achievements that she would be prepared to welcome you among her ladies-in-waiting, a boon that was procured by many very eminent people by means of great influence. And yet it was God's will that this too should be obtained for you, and what more diplomatic and well-disposed friend could I have found for this purpose than Baron Sfondrato, held as he was by their most Serene Highnesses in the high esteem that his merits deserved, who with his tact, skill and integrity so convinced the Infanta of your attainments and qualities that she felt disposed to receive you into her service?[18] The Baron reported this to me just when I was fearing the matter would not go ahead, not having heard any news at all of the plan for a long time, indeed having already put the thought of it out of my mind, due to the high costs that I had heard were borne by the other ladies entering that service, which were beyond your means.[19] Nor would I have been able to avail myself of the placement obtained for us by the Baron if those costs had not been, to some extent, reduced for me, and in this, too, God found a remedy, so that the undertaking might succeed despite all, for He so ordained that through the agencies of the aforementioned Baron and of Lady Sanchia di Guzman, the Infanta was willing to grant me a special favor and waive a part of the expense, with the result that I was able to place you in this most honorable service, even though, in spite of your privileged terms, the expenses were still too heavy for me, due both to your numerous sisters and brothers and to the financial burdens of our situation and the insufficiency of my fortune. Nevertheless, taking courage and fresh heart under

18. The Sfondrati were a noble Milanese family, originally from Cremona, who had risen to eminence in the fifteenth century. The baron here alluded to is Paolo Sfondrato, count of the Riviera and of the Holy Roman Empire and baron of Valassina, who was made a member of the Milanese Senate and a Secret Counselor by Philip II of Spain and was later sent as his emissary to the court of Duke Carlo Emanuele. He died in 1587, so his presence in Turin would have coincided with Lavinia's residence there by less than a couple of years. Later in the *Discourse* Guasco says that a family tie exists between him and the baron.

19. The practice to which Guasco here alludes of exacting a high fee from the parents of a girl who was coming to serve at court as a lady-in-waiting has never, to my knowledge, been researched thus far. It would be extremely interesting to know whether the level of fees varied substantially from court to court and whether other rulers, like the infanta in Lavinia's case, sometimes offered a reduced-fees place to an especially talented girl.

divine inspiration, I boldly embarked upon this course, although in truth I did not think I would be able to meet all the costs; and yet I have done more than I either expected to do or thought I was capable of.[20] As a result, you will be able to hold your own among the other ladies to an extent I would never perhaps have imagined, and did I not believe this to have been the express intention of the Lord, it would weigh heavily on my conscience that I had done so much for you to the detriment of my other children. But I know they will be content, seeing you going to a situation where, provided you for your part do what is required of you and what we are hoping for, you will be able to bring profit and honor both to yourself and to them.

Well now, your mother and I have brought you up until this day with every care and good example. We have adorned you with every possible accomplishment. We have placed you with one of the leading princesses of the world, where you will be honorably treated and piously directed. We have expended more on your behalf than our resources really permitted. We have provided you with a good domestic staff and with all the things you could possibly need. We are prepared to continue to assist you in every way that we can in the future. We have both of us been doing all that we could to prepare you for what will be expected of you. Nothing more remains for us to do, all our duties toward you are now fulfilled. Just one precious jewel I have yet in my bosom to give you, which is all that I have left for you, having already given you all that I had. But this will be so rich a gift that nothing you have received from me up to now will be worthy to rank beside it.[21] You must wear

20. On the costs involved, see below, the section titled "Concerning Her Person" for a list of the main items Guasco had needed to purchase to equip Lavinia for her court post.

21. From this point on, the *Discourse* contains numerous borrowings from a work written some forty years earlier by the eminent writer Sperone Speroni, namely, his *Dialogo della cura della famiglia* (Dialogue concerning the care of the family) (in *Opere Tratte da' MSS. originali*, ed. Mario Pozzi. Vol. 1. [Venice: 1740; Rome: 1989]), first published in Venice in 1542. In both cases, the work is addressed to a young girl who is on the point of leaving home and is to be the writer's parting present to her. Here, however, the similarities end, since Speroni is writing for a girl who is about to be married, his goddaughter, Cornelia Cornaro, and is offering her as a wedding gift his advice on how to become a good wife and housewife, a purely domestic role very different from Lavinia's situation. Nevertheless, Guasco succeeds in adapting many of the comments and precepts contained in his source to his own purposes. (The translations from the original are mine.) Compare Speroni: "But what rare and lovely jewel shall I give you with which, as a bride, you can adorn your nuptials? . . . I am sending you this one therefore, at the present time, wrapped up in a few brief words of vernacular speech, since I have no power to mount it in finer metal, nor with greater artifice" (76). Like Speroni, Guasco is vividly conveying to Lavinia here, by means of a verbal guessing game, the message that the guidance he is offering her on her future conduct through his prescriptive work is a more precious gift than the most priceless of jewels. (Speroni [1500–1588] was a Paduan writer, who spent much of his career in Rome and achieved literary renown for his polemical tragedy *Canace* [1542] and for his many orations, letters, dialogues, and commentaries on Virgil and Dante.)

it always upon your bosom like a precious necklace, cherishing it day and night in memory of your father, and through this gift bringing your father, who bestows it on you with so much love and tenderness, constantly before your eyes. True, this gift is no rare gem, set in gold, for I have spent so much on you that I have no money left to buy you such an object, and so you must needs accept it in this paper. You look at my hands and wait expectantly for this jewel I am promising you. Ah, but it is no diamond or ruby or sapphire, but something infinitely more valuable, nor does it come from the bowels of the earth but, rather, from the depths of your father's heart, and it will serve as a rule book to govern your conduct when I am not there; and since your mother and I will no longer be constantly available to remind you of what is best for you in this, your unwary childhood, you will be able to refer to it, imagining that your father is with you and speaking to you, and that you are sitting listening to him with that respect and attention that are appropriate in a girl born to so high a station in life and so deeply loved by her father.[22]

PART 2: PROPER COURT CONDUCT FOR LAVINIA

So, having given you my gift, nothing remains for me to do but to pray Almighty God and your Guardian Angel that they will supply what your mother and I will no longer be able to provide for you, now that we are consigning you to the care of another. But so that you might be able to make the best use of my handbook, I decided to divide it up for you under various headings, which will offer you certain guidelines on how to regulate your life and actions in the place to which you are going. It is not that I intend to tell you all you will need to do, for that I could not teach you, human affairs being so infinitely varied that one cannot prescribe precise rules for every single occasion But I have decided to provide a few general precepts for you, like an artist drawing upon a primed canvas, which must later be painted in a variety of ways.[23] And likewise you will be able to paint in all your activities under the headings of my rule book. These precepts will be grouped under eight captions: "Concerning Your Soul," "Concerning Your Honor," "Concerning Your Duties toward Your Mistress," "Concerning the Preservation and Improvement of Your Skills," "Concerning Your Person," "Concerning

22. Guasco here uses the tool of emotional blackmail against his daughter, as he does on several other occasions in the *Discourse*.

23. Compare Speroni: "It is not therefore my task to inform you fully on every matter; . . . my office is to dispose you by means of my plain advice, without digressing from general principles, to learn well from the ways of others, just as a good painter is wont to do, who first oils his canvas, where later it will be colored and painted in" (*Dialogo*, 88).

Your Possessions," "Concerning Your Social Relations," and "Concerning the
Treatment of Your Domestic Staff."

1. Concerning Your Soul

Where the first is concerned, which is the most important, and from which
the benefits of all the rest will derive, keep always uppermost in your mind
the fear of God, which is the beginning of all human wisdom. Be devout in
every way you can, modeling yourself on your mother, knowing as you do
how diligent and punctilious she has always been in these matters, so much
so that in my opinion it is her prayers that have been the main cause whereby
God has up to now prospered you and all our family. Consequently you must
insure that you never allow any day to pass without performing the holy office of prayer, and if you cannot find another time for this, you must steal an
hour from your slumbers and from your very eating rather than fail to perform it; for prayers are like the fodder a traveler gives his horse along the way,
which ultimately speeds up rather than slows down his journey time, even
though it may cause a short delay.[24] But your prayers must not come from
your mouth alone but from the depth of your heart, and they must be accompanied by appropriate reverence: you must kneel down, therefore, before your crucifix for at least half an hour, and more if you can. This crucifix
was the first item I gave you with which to adorn your bedchamber when I returned from Milan, where I had gone to provide you with what you would
need when you set off to enter the service of your mistress. And to this glorious symbol you will humbly appeal each day, with your missal and your
rosary in your hand, or at times just with your mind, thanking your Lord for
all the gifts you have received from Him and praying Him to give you the
strength to serve Him and to direct your steps to a good end. For He must be
the light that will guide your way in everything you do and, especially, in the
vocation upon which you are embarking in the service of Her Serene Highness. He will be as a father and mother to you in counseling you, as a teacher
in instructing you, as a doctor in preserving you, and as a shield and defense
against the envy and persecution that are wont to be found in courts. He will
bestow on you at this early age the wisdom of a woman, making you prudent
in many things where lack of prudence could trip you up, and He will accompany you at every step, teaching you and moving your heart to observe
the precepts with which I am adorning this jewel that I am bestowing on you.

---

24. A homely image typical of Guasco's style in conveying his fatherly admonitions to Lavinia
in an easily remembered form.

He will be the best possible painter to color in for you the drawing that I am making for you here. Indeed, He will make a far better painting of it than I can make a drawing. And yet He also makes the drawing, using me as His means, and speaking to you through my mouth.[25] And so you will have Him as your father and mother, as your teacher, and as your defense to be invoked in every eventuality, knowing that your prayers will always be heard and answered. And I shall live secure and happy, where before I was anxious and sad, due to the fear that once you had left this house and were far away from all my continual, loving, fatherly reminders and from the care you have always received up to now, you might fail to keep your promises to me regarding these matters and also fail yourself, through losing the attainments you had acquired and, with these, perhaps the favor of your mistress.

To sum up, what will God not do for you, if you do this small thing for Him? Do it, my child, I entreat you. By the authority that I must have over you as your father, I command it of you, and if my command is not enough, do it because you are commanded to do so by God who, if you fail to obey Him, will take His revenge upon both of us for your disobedience. But I know that you will do it and that instead of His revenge, you will receive God's reward for so doing.

In addition to praying, you must observe God's precepts and keep a pure and chaste conscience, as is required in any well-born and well brought-up Christian girl. Here the reading of spiritual books, in which I would exhort you to spend all the time you can possibly spare from your duties, will greatly avail you and produce admirable fruits. Nor should I forget to tell you that just as a good courtier is wont not only to win the favor of his prince through his own merits but also to obtain it by approaching another, more highly placed with his master than he is himself, so you should firstly address yourself to the blessed Virgin, to whom you should have recourse at all times as if to a most compassionate advocate, and then select for your special devotion some saint, such as Saint Anthony, on whose Feast-Day you were born, in the year of grace 1574, who will be your intercessor with Almighty God for your requests and will pray to the Lord continually on your behalf.[26]

25. Guasco's solemn, almost sermon-like, tones here earnestly convey his message to Lavinia that his precepts are being written under divine guidance and that God is speaking to her through the medium of her father. Once again he likens his *Discourse* to a painting, which will be completed by God, the supreme artist. There are faint resonances here from the *Courtier,* where in his dedication Castiglione describes his portrayal of the court of Urbino as the work of "a worthless painter who knows only how to draw the outlines" (*The Courtier,* 32).

26. Here, in an image appropriate to Lavinia's situation, Guasco likens the intercessions of the saints to the patronage system of sixteenth-century courts. As Guy Fitch Lytle comments in his chapter "Friendship and Patronage in Renaissance Europe" (in *Patronage, Art, and Society in Renais-*

2. Concerning Your Honor

Let us now move on to the heading of your honor, which I have placed second to that of your soul, since after the latter, there is nothing else that can be more highly prized, and indeed to lose one's honor means to lose one's soul. The honor of which I have to speak to you in this section is of course that conferred by your chastity. Remember, daughter, that no adornment bestows greater honor on a woman than this; its worth is such that through possessing it the poorest and plainest woman can call herself rich and comely, while without it, as has been remarked, she is neither truly alive nor truly a woman,[27] let alone comely and rich; and if the jewel with which I promised to adorn you were to contain nothing else but this, it would still be a treasure beyond price and a thing to be cherished more than your life's blood. This is that snow white and stately gown in which a woman may appear in all honorable places, but a gown that the smallest spot will stain in such a way that the wearer will be unable to retain her own self-esteem, let alone that of others, so hideous and hateful is such a stain. Nor is there any means of removing it, for it will persist even after the dress has been torn up and burned to ashes, since the stain of dishonor remains with a woman not only in her lifetime but also after her death. That is why honorable women, even those who were not guided by the light of faith, laid so much store by their honor that, in order not to taint it, they were happy to suffer the cruelest of deaths, like the ermine that allows itself to die of hunger and deprivation rather than stain the whiteness of its coat.[28] And if ever this were the duty of any woman, it must surely be yours, knowing from what lineage you come and from what a mother. Her chastity should serve you always as a mirror, alongside that of

---

sance Italy, ed. F. W. Kent and Patricia Simons with J. C. Eade [Oxford, 1987], 47–61), "The saints had long been known as the 'friends of God', and one's various patron saints were perhaps the most powerful friends one could hope to rely on" (53).

Saint Anthony's Feast-Day, on which Lavinia was born, takes place on June 13. This means that Lavinia would have been aged just eleven-and-a-half when she first arrived in Turin, since her journey is clearly taking place in midwinter, and in any case it is obvious from the way she speaks that she had already been in the palace for some time when she wrote her foreword to the *Discourse* on March 15, 1586.

27. Compare Speroni: "That chastity without which, as has truly been said by others, no woman can be called a woman nor truly alive" (*Dialogo*, 92). See also Juan Luis Vives's *The Education of a Christian Woman: A Sixteenth-Century Manual*, ed. and trans. Charles Fantazzi [Chicago and London: University of Chicago Press, 2000]): "A woman's only care is chastity, therefore when this has been thoroughly elucidated, she may be considered to have received sufficient instruction" (para. 3, p. 47).

28. The ermine, with its coat of purest white, was frequently cited and depicted during the Renaissance as a symbol of chastity, as, e.g., in Leonardo's famous portrait of Cecilia Gallerani.

so many other matrons both of her family and of ours, both past and present, who do honor to their houses with their names. And all the more must this care be your concern, in that you are descended from a line so ardent in the pursuit of honor that, in addition to the chastity of our women, a great number of the men of our family have risked their lives to win honor in tournaments and battles. Thus you for your part will have to conduct yourself in such a manner that you can legitimately be included in our lineage and not be the one to lose that which so many others in our family have preserved.[29] And among all the other things, take care not to stoop for a moment to consider which to give preference to, honesty and honor or self-advantage and favor, but always regard as the vilest of dirt any great favor and gain in comparison with the smallest loss of honesty and honor. And be assured, my child, that honor is so fragile a thing that the smallest breath can ruin it,[30] and therefore it will behove you to safeguard it not only in yourself but also in the opinions others hold of you, always conducting yourself in all your actions with the modesty befitting a young girl of your rank, employed in so honorable a situation. And above all take care to nurture chaste thoughts in your breast, for they will be reflected in your face and your eyes in such a way that the goodness of your soul and the chastity of your heart will be read there. And this will make you pleasing and lovable to others, and especially to your mistress, and more full of grace and beauty than could any artificial device; and how dear this honesty is to your mistress will be demonstrated by the regime that you will find in her house, which is something that brings great consolation to your mother and myself as we send you away from our care. And thus you must value this precious token all the more highly in that this great and honored Princess lays so much store by it.

3. *Concerning Your Duties toward Your Mistress*

I now come to the third heading, which concerns your duties toward your mistress, on which there are a great many things I could say to you, but I will gather together just a few of them. You must first of all consider that in leaving your father's house to go to the palace of so great a lady, you will find the same degree of difference in the way of life between the one and the other as there is between the house of your father and that of so great a mistress. And so it will be necessary for you to alter your mode of life as such a move re-

29. The emulation of one's illustrious forebears is a motif that runs throughout Italian Renaissance literature.

30. Compare Speroni: "The honor of the woman . . . is a flower that any breath of ill wind despoils and destroys" (*Dialogo*, 80).

quires and to consider how different a daughter's situation with her parents is from that of a lady-in waiting with her mistress. But this transformation will not be very troublesome for you, since you are going to this employment at an age that is not so mature that you cannot graft new habits onto it, nor equally so immature that you cannot adapt yourself to it judiciously.[31] Consequently, you will have to resolve in your mind that if, up to now, you were often indulged in your wishes by your mother and father, from henceforth you will have to deny your own will and aspire only to what is pleasing to your mistress, in such a way that, like a chameleon, all your wishes take on the hues of her mind, not only in what you know for a certainty she requires of you but in all you will be able to conjecture. And this you must do not only in your exterior actions but also with inner devotion and love, for from this two benefits will ensue: one, that through loving your mistress you will transform yourself wholly into her and feel that the things you are doing for her you do for yourself, so deriving the greatest delight from them, in such a way that serving her will be sweeter to you than commanding others;[32] and the other, that when she sees herself loved and served by you with affection, her love for you will increase day by day, for love by its nature has this particular power to arouse reciprocal love in all who feel they are loved by another. And because one can only know the intimacy of another's heart by means of external acts, you must always appear before her with a modest cheerfulness that will denote on your face your loving compliance with her wishes, nor must you ever present yourself before her with a countenance that is perturbed or full of melancholy, for seeing this she might start to suspect that it was due to a distaste for service on your part, or to a lack of love toward her, whence instead of her love and favor you might arouse her hatred and scorn.

For the same reason, you must take great heed never, either due to lack of thought, or maybe to not finding there all the comforts to which you have been accustomed in your father's house, or due to some other chance circumstance, to allow any expression of regret concerning your employment or of a reluctance to remain in it to escape from your mouth, in any company whatsoever, for such words could reach the ears of your mistress and lead her to form the view that you lacked love and respect toward her, causing you to fall from her favor, perhaps never to regain it. And, again, supposing she

31. Compare Speroni: "I am invited to do so by your youthfulness, which is not so immature that I lack hope that my counsels will produce good fruit, nor so ripe and full of years that new customs cannot be grafted onto it" (ibid., 88–89).

32. Compare Castiglione's *The Courtier*: "Well then, I want the courtier . . . to devote all his thought and strength to loving and almost adoring the prince he serves above all else, devoting all his ambitions, actions and behavior to pleasing him." (125).

should show you some slight disapproval or dislike, either because she had received a bad impression of you or perhaps because she wanted to test you out in this way, you must, notwithstanding, never react by displaying any vexation or dismay but persevere in serving and loving her with even more diligence than before, so that finally, when she sees your efforts to serve her being refined in such adverse circumstances as gold is by fire, she will come to hold you in higher regard than ever. To this I must add that should you see anyone receiving more favors than yourself, you must not show any displeasure or envy in consequence but rather cherish that person more than the other ladies, for not only will such a one, when she sees herself honored and loved by you, endeavor to speak favorably of you with her mistress to the very best of her ability, but moreover the sight of someone not only loving us, but also loving those whom we love ourselves, has the greatest possible power to inflame our souls with love for that person. In such a situation, you should think to yourself that your mistress, being a wise and just judge of the merits of her ladies, gives preference to the other lady because she is of superior worth to you,[33] and therefore you must strive not just to equal but to outdo her, if you can, in excellence, so that you can finally win your due reward. Hence it will be very profitable for you to study your mistress's humor and to note what is most wont to please her in her women, and in you in particular, and to put every effort into gratifying her in this respect, learning from those older than yourself and who entered her service before you.

And because our presence and modes of behavior are the first things that create an impression of us in the mind of an onlooker and possess the power at first sight to gain that person's goodwill toward us or to alienate him from us, you will have to use special diligence here and insure that your mode of behavior in your mistress's presence is always the most charming and attractive possible, overcoming your deficiencies by noting what the other ladies do, for this is an essential prerequisite to making oneself agreeable to others, being as I told you what first and most frequently speaks to the heart via the eyes. Bearing this in mind, you must endeavor to carry out all the duties that are required of you, either out of respect for your mistress or in her service, with such charm and grace that they seem to be part and parcel of a naturally

---

33. Through obtaining her post at court, Lavinia had placed herself within the orbit of the greatest patron of all in contemporary society, the absolute prince, whose power to confer benefits, when disposed to do so, was almost limitless; however, no service a courtier performed for his prince could guarantee a reward, since, as Biagioli points out in his *Galileo Courtier: The Practice of Science in the Culture of Absolutism* (Chicago, 1993), the absolute prince resembles a god, "one who is infinitely powerful and great so that his terrestrial clients cannot expect him to react to what they are doing to please him" (51). Likewise, Lavinia had to learn to accept that dedicated service to her mistress is no iron-clad guarantee of the latter's favor and approbation.

charming disposition rather than due to effort and art.[34] In this context I must not omit to warn you that whenever you are in her presence, whether in her bedchamber, or serving her at table, or on any other occasion and in any other place, you should behave sedately and, if you happen to be standing, not fidget about nor crane your neck now to one side and now to another nor maybe at times start yawning but remain as still as a statue, planted firmly on your two feet, for nothing is more aggravating than to be served in the former manner, since it gives the impression that it springs from a regret at being employed in that service and from a lack of reverence and love toward it; and in addition such behavior denotes a flighty mind and is something in a servant that arouses his employer's scorn and perhaps his hatred, as well as discrediting him; indeed, such gestures are wont to irritate not only one's employer but one's companions as well. Moreover, you must take care, if you should find yourself in the presence of your mistress when she is accompanied by the Lord Duke, or his courtiers, or anyone else, to keep your head and eyes bent over your canvas and needle, or your clavichord and songbook, or such-like things, if you are engaged in such exercises at the time or, if you are unoccupied, to keep your eyes modestly fixed upon your mistress, without letting your gaze dart all around, for that would be interpreted not just as lack of self-restraint but as wantonness, and God alone knows what damage such negligence could cause you. This is something you must avoid at all costs, not just in the presence of your mistress but no matter where you are or with whom.[35]

In addition to these considerations, you must have as your principal aim solicitous and diligent service for, to sum up, serving with consistent atten-

---

34. Guasco has in mind here Castiglione's concept of nonchalance [*sprezzatura*] that underpins the grace and charm of his ideal courtier, concealing whatever effort has gone into them and making all that he says and does appear natural and spontaneous. See Count Lodovico's comments in bk. 1 of *The Courtier*: "To labor at what one is doing and, as we say, to make bones over it, shows an extreme lack of grace and causes everything, whatever its worth, to be discounted. So we can truthfully say that true art is what does not seem to be art; and the most important thing is to conceal it" (*The Courtier*, 67).

35. Guasco's prescriptions here to Lavinia to behave sedately, to control her bodily movements, and to keep her gaze modestly lowered echo the advice of the majority of moralists of this period concerned with seemly female behavior. Compare the great Spanish educationalist, Juan Luis Vives: "She will keep her eyes cast down, and will raise them but rarely and with modesty and decorum. She will not stare at anyone intently or in an unbecoming manner" (*Education*, 128). Vives's educational manual, *The Education of a Christian Woman*, was written in Latin in 1523 under the title *De institutione feminae Christianae* while he was lecturing at Cardinal College, Oxford; it was dedicated to Queen Catherine of Aragon and was intended to offer guidance on educating her daughter, Princess Mary. It was thus written in an English context, and despite its conservative approach to the education of women it enjoyed enormous popularity throughout the sixteenth century. An Italian version was published in Venice in 1546.

tiveness is what earns one the favor and recompense of one's employer. For this reason you must not only consider the comfort and convenience of your mistress before your own but endure any trouble and inconvenience to insure her smallest comfort.[36] You must make sure that not only are you not one of the last to appear when attending to her needs but always one among the first and, if possible, the very first. You should also be present even when a particular duty is carried out in turns by you ladies, provided it is not contrary to the orders of the household to be in attendance then. And because you will have a few little things you will need to do for yourself, especially when you are dressing in the morning before going to attend your mistress, you will have to be somewhat vigilant and make sure you allow plenty of time, so that as soon as the moment arrives to make your appearance you will be ready to present yourself punctually without lagging behind the other ladies or having to make yourself tidy in a rush and emerging from your room all rumpled, for this would be contrary to what I reminded you of earlier and also give you a reputation of being negligent, sluggish, unhelpful, and, I might also add, badly brought up.

There is one other thing I need to say to you under this heading, and that is that you should pay great heed only to speak of your mistress, whether to a servant or to a lady companion, whether in earnest or in jest, in short in whatsoever way and with whatsoever person, with the respect and honor befitting such a lady and your own obligations to her, but I cannot in my heart believe that you would fall into so shameful an error as to do any differently, in view both of the vileness of such an act and of the danger inherent in it. Indeed, I would say that if ever you hear someone speaking of her less honorably than is befitting, not only should you not lend an ear to them and just remain silent but you should stand up to them and rebuke them sharply, protesting that if ever again they allow themselves to be so carried away in your presence, not only will they be rebuked by you but also accused, something which you should do, indeed, if the matter be serious enough to merit it, even on the first occasion. And if perchance someone were to come and tempt you, either due to their evil nature or out of envy from seeing you in your mistress's favor, hoping to seize some opportunity to make you fall from grace, think immediately that this is the work of the devil and rebuff this man or woman as such.

But setting this aside, two matters still remain for me to discuss, one on

36. As Ruth Kelso puts it in her discussion of the *Discourse*, "The central fact of life at court is the will of the rulers. Lavinia is advised in terms reminiscent of advice to the girl about to marry, to learn to subdue her will and her every wish to her lady's until she has no other" (*Doctrine for the Lady of the Renaissance* [Urbana, Ill., 1956], 222).

how to conduct yourself if you are receiving favors from your mistress and the other on knowing how to request some favor from her. In the matter of favors you must do in this wise: if your mistress, either in public or in private but especially in public, should display at any time more than her usual familiarity toward you, do not become too brazen and start acting as if you were her sister but receive this honor modestly and so as to indicate that you realize it derives rather from her goodness than from your own merits, but at the same time not with so homely a demeanor that you seem not to appreciate the favor. And if she does grant you one, not just with her countenance but also in deed, accept it with equal amounts of humility and respect, without appearing to get swollen-headed about it, for this would result in your losing other favors later on, in that, just as God is wont to exalt the meek and cast down the proud, so princes, demigods on earth, are wont to humble those who set themselves up and elevate those who humble themselves. Nor should humility toward your mistress be your only concern in this regard, but you must also take care, where the ladies-in-waiting are concerned, not to make a great clamor in their presence about the favors you have received, as if you wanted to arouse their envy, for the harm that this deadly poison of envy is wont to cause is sufficient, alas, on its own, without your setting out to arouse it in the hearts of others; for if the other ladies see you not only more favored than they are but also puffed up with pride, not just their envy but also their hatred will be kindled against you, and you will be in danger of being angrily dropped from your mistress's favor.[37] The remedy against being poisoned by this toxin of envy is, therefore, to display ever greater humility toward everyone as the favors toward you increase, showing always that you recognize them as flowing from the generosity and courtesy of your mistress and not from your own merits; indeed, if you need to refer to them, you should avow that no lady-in-waiting ever deserved them less than you and that the other ladies, on the basis of their merits, should hope for far greater things from their mistress than you, and in this manner, instead of hatred and envy, you will receive their love and congratulations.

---

37. The problem of dealing with envy at court is a recurrent theme in the Renaissance. Compare Giraldi Cinzio's *Discorso intorno a quello che si conviene a giovane nobile e ben creato nel servire un gran principe* (Discourse concerning what is appropriate to a well-mannered and well-born youth when serving a great prince [1569]), in which the writer warns the newcomer at court on how fellow courtiers of lesser ability than himself will disparage his efforts and try to discredit him in the prince's eyes. (See Philip Horne's discussion of this treatise in the preface to his edition of Giraldi's *Selene* [*Selene: An Italian Renaissance Tragedy*, ed. Horne (Lewiston, N.Y., 1996)] in the section titled "The Gentleman at Court," xiii–xxii). For this darker side of Renaissance court life, see also Sydney Anglo's chapter, "The Courtier, the Renaissance and Changing Ideals," in *The Courts of Europe, Politics, Patronage and Royalty 1400–1800*, ed. A. G. Dickens (London, 1977), 33–53.

When requesting a favor, you should copy the person who, playing at ball or any other game in which he possesses some advantage, always reserves it [that advantage] for his moment of greatest need, striving to win without it but exploiting it if in the end he is unable to achieve victory in any other way. Similarly, you must hold back from asking a favor of your mistress, always reserving such an advantage for your greatest need and considering carefully for whom, why, how, and when you are requesting it, making sure that the person for whom you are asking it deserves it and very rarely, if ever, asking a favor for yourself, since it could come about, were you to do so, that your mistress, either because of your importunity or for some other reasons of politeness, might indulge your request but perchance with reluctance; whence the favor her boon conferred might diminish the favor she bore you in her mind, in which case the loss would outweigh the gain. And were she to refuse you such a favor, the ensuing damage to you would be shame and confusion, leaving you fervently wishing you had never asked it and, in addition, it would block the way for you ever again to dare request favors from her, either for yourself or for anyone else. What is more, your mistress herself might suspect she had left you poorly satisfied and so never more hold you in such high regard as before, believing that due to your lack of satisfaction, your love toward her had cooled. And so you must consider most earnestly not only for whom but of what nature is the favor you are requesting, asking always something honest and such that she can easily grant it you; and in your manner of asking it, proceed so diplomatically that, if she does not grant it, she will not think she has left you poorly satisfied and, at the same time, choosing the most opportune moment to put your request, for this is a most important consideration.[38] And may what I have said on this topic suffice.

---

38. Federico had issued the same warnings to his ideal courtier in bk. 2 of Castiglione's great work:

> Very rarely, or hardly ever, will he ask his master anything for himself, lest his prince, being reluctant to refuse, concedes it grudgingly, which is far worse. And when he asks for something on behalf of others he will take careful note of the time and place, and will only request what is right and reasonable; and he will present the request in such a way, leaving out the items he knows could be displeasing and cleverly smoothing over the difficulties, that his lord will always grant it or, if he wishes not to, will be able to refuse without worrying about giving offense to the petitioner. For very often when lords have refused to grant a favor to someone who has been seeking it importunately, they imagine that the person who has been so insistent must be very anxious to get what he wants and therefore, when he is baulked, must be ill-disposed towards the one who has denied him; and this belief breeds in them a hatred of the person concerned, whom subsequently they can never see without distaste.
>
> (*The Courtier*, 126–27)

4. *Concerning the Preservation of Your Skills*

So now I come to my fourth theme, that is to say, to the care you must take in preserving and augmenting the liberal arts you acquired in your father's house. My child, this is a matter so close to my heart that if I had a thousand tongues, I would not be able to express all my feelings about it to you, nor do I know what words to use to inflame your heart as much as I would desire.[39] And it is only right that I should feel so fervently about it, in view of the intolerable, yet still endured, efforts that you and I invested in this endeavor, and rightly this passionate desire should touch your heart as well as mine, and more so, knowing as you do the suffering and torture you underwent in order to arrive finally at the point where you now stand in these aforementioned skills. If the things that are acquired with effort and hardship are wont to be highly esteemed and preserved more carefully than most, whoever had such cause as you to hold anything in such high esteem as this of which I am speaking to you? And when no other consideration could persuade you to gratify me and to benefit yourself, this consideration should be overwhelmingly compelling. But if this consideration will not persuade you to do it, there are an infinite number of others that should do so. Do it then for the sake of the achievement itself, if you will not do it for the sake of the efforts we have both invested in it, for the difficulty of acquiring it is a demonstration of how precious it is, having been set by God as something of outstanding value in a sublime and lofty place, which can only be attained with toil and sweat, and this is demonstrated by the honor and delight it is wont to bring to the person who achieves it. This is something I have already discussed, showing you in this discourse how it is a reward in itself, without taking into account all the other rewards it is wont to bring people with it, to which I will now add that it is so noble and excellent that it has been seen by some as the source of all human happiness. And although we Christians have to place our happiness in God and to look for it not in this life but in the next, nevertheless it is very true that no greater happiness is attainable in this world

---

39. Guasco now brings all his eloquence and his keen psychological insight to bear to convince Lavinia of the vital importance of keeping her various skills in good working order while employed at the court of Turin. Much is at stake here: the credibility both of Guasco himself and of those in high places who had vouched for Lavinia to the duke and duchess (see my introduction, n. 20), Lavinia's own future reputation during her time in the palace, and her father's understandable desire to see a good return on the huge expenditure he has made for her education. He argues his case powerfully and convincingly, point by point, at times in sermon-like mode, invoking the wrath of God Himself on her, should Lavinia fail in her duty here. To bring home to her the cost of what she has achieved, he describes their joint efforts in terms that denote great effort and suffering.

than through intellectual achievement. It is for this reason that we all have a natural inclination toward this blessing, and many endeavor to acquire it, although due to the difficulty of doing so the majority abandon the undertaking. But since, thanks be to God, you have made great progress here, it would be great cowardice, indeed impiety, not to esteem it as it deserves and as I so ardently desire you to do.

But if you will not esteem intellectual achievement for its substance, value it at least for its shadow, that is to say for the renown that (as I told you) is wont to accompany this great lady. Well you know what praise and honor it has earned you even now in your childhood, and what great hopes people hold for you in the future, after so exalted a beginning.[40] And if you are not prepared to do it either in the pursuit of glory or in fulfillment of the expectations of others, do it for fear of the blame you will incur if you do not maintain and augment, with pleasure and delight, in your adolescence what you acquired with effort and anguish in your childhood. And do it because of the scandal it would arouse if you failed to meet the expectations people hold of you. And if none of these things move you to do it, I entreat you to let the thought of the blame you will incur in the future motivate you, if both I myself and others can see that you have not improved in your adolescence upon your childhood and that you are abjectly depriving yourself at this stage of what you acquired then with the courage of a man. And if this does not suffice, do it so that, if the time ever comes that you are put to the test by people who know you only by lofty repute, you do not give the lie to those who did you honor in their words, and so that I myself, whether dead or alive by that time, am not held to be one of those liars, since I have so often praised you to people who did not know you. Recall how, more than three years ago, I filed away a sample of your writing, destined to remain there to your honor as a perpetual record, in proof of your excellence in such writing before you were even nine years old, and consider on the other hand that it would be to your shame and confusion were you to lose so great a skill with the passage of time, and the same would apply to many other things that have been witnessed in you in the past.

But if these incentives do not suffice to induce you to comply with so worthy a desire on my part, at least be persuaded by the knowledge that it was the fame of your skills that paved the way for you to enter the service of so great a lady, and it is upon these same skills that all our hopes of your suc-

40. Guasco's ambitions for his young daughter's successful court career stand in marked contrast to the narrowly domestic view Speroni expresses in his dialogue regarding female achievements: "It is no mediocre commendation of a wise woman that while she is still living, her praises, like her works, should be enclosed and contained within her own four walls" (*Dialogo*, 96).

cessful career rested when we placed you in such a situation and that it was in view of them that I have spared no expense, convinced that you deserved to be rewarded for your abilities, even though it imposed a great burden on our family.

Most powerful are all the arguments I have adduced up to now, and in view of each and all of them you yourself should take to heart what I am speaking of. But if they do not suffice to persuade you to pursue your own best interests, do so for many other more important reasons than those already mentioned. Do it for my sake, remembering the obligation you as a daughter have toward your father, and no ordinary father at that, but one who is more loving toward you than any father that ever a daughter had. Remember that it is your duty to undergo for my sake any kind of ill, but I do not desire you to suffer ill, indeed I desire no benefit at all for myself but only your own profit and honor, in those things that you can do with pleasure and delight.[41] And if your love for me and your duty toward yourself do not avail, then do it at least out of fear of me, not any longer the childish, indeed even servile, fear you so often showed me in my house due to the effort of the task and your very young age; but do it from a loving, daughterly fear, imagining your father is with you in your chamber and at an appropriate moment exhorting and commanding you to do it and that you are doing it more willingly out of reverence for him than you would do it for yourself. This fear must motivate you not only when you are away from me and subject to a rule other than mine but even when I am in my grave and nothing remains of me but a memory.

But if you will not do it out of either love or fear of me, do it in order not to slight me, placing your hand on your heart and asking yourself whether or not you yourself would feel slighted, had you given someone a present, no matter how small, with great affection, and they had then cast it into a corner, to be consumed by dust and moths. And how would you feel, if such a gift were not just a small one but something of great value, and all the more if you had acquired it with enormous effort? By thinking in this manner, you will be able to judge rightly whether I would have just cause to consider myself held in contempt if, upon entering your chamber, I saw you treating with little regard every small gift I had lovingly offered you, and how much greater would I have to consider the slight if not just a small present but something of much value, gained through huge effort on my part, were to be

---

41. Guasco's remark that "it is your duty to undergo for my sake any kind of ill" says much about contemporary attitudes toward children: they were regarded as the property of their parents, with few, if any, rights of their own, while the will of a father was paramount and buttressed by law.

neglected by you in such a manner: but what greater gift, acquired with what greater labor on my part, could I bestow on you, than the skills which I am now commending to you, and which, as you know, I helped you gain by playing so great a part in the effort they involved.

And if, as you were taught in the Ten Commandments of our Christian doctrine, you are bound, under pain of mortal sin, to honor your father and mother, what tremendous sin, and worthy of what chastisement, would be yours, if you not only failed to honor them but slighted them in what could most offend them and in what, moreover, could cause you most harm?[42] But if you are so obdurate that you refuse to do it for so many and such powerful reasons, do it for some others even greater than the aforementioned. Do it for the love of God, for Whom you will be doing a most pleasing thing, both to show how you value your skills, which He holds in high esteem, and in order to obey your father in so honorable a matter. Do it from fear of Him, and so as not to be punished by Him for such ingratitude. Do it, that He should not feel slighted by you if you were to fail to do so, for if I myself could feel myself slighted if you failed to value the dowry of skills with which I had gone to such lengths to enrich you, how much more might God do so, He having been their principal author and I the mere instrument? And if you need to be shown how jealous He is of the talents He is wont to bestow, He Himself reveals it in the parable of the man who, before going on a journey, consigned a certain number of talents to his servants and on his return asked them to account for them and who, when he found that the servant who had been given a single talent had buried it in the ground and that the servant who had been given five had made as many again, held the first servant in low esteem but promised the second to set him in charge of great matters, since he had shown himself faithful in small ones.[43] So will God do for you if, in a little while, when He asks you to account for your management of the talents you received from Him, He finds that you have accumulated more in addition to the initial ones, just as on the contrary He will hold you in poor esteem if He finds you have merely buried them. And not only will He rightly hold you in low consideration but He will show you His wrath if you have not only failed to increase your talents but have even lost them, which you will find much easier to do than it was for you to acquire them. And the maintaining of a talent is no less commendable than the acquiring of it.

Maybe you will say to me, "I shall no longer have the same leisure and

---

42. The fifth of the Ten Commandments is "Honor thy father and thy mother, that thy days may be long in the land which the Lord thy God giveth thee."

43. The parable of the talents is found in Matthew 25:14–30.

opportunity I had at home, without the care of my teachers and our servants, and now that I am being kept busy with other matters than I was then," to which I would reply that the care you received at home was directed only at making you apply yourself to the enterprise; and since, thanks to God, you have now reached the point where you can manage on your own and need only preserve them, (something that depends on your own will-power), this argument of yours is invalid.[44] It is true, I admit, that you will be kept busier at court than you were at home, but your merit will be all the greater if you do manage to steal the time to insure you do not lose what you have already acquired by practicing one thing on one day and another on another, like the painter who, albeit outstanding and of consummate skill, would never let a day pass by without drawing at least one line; and just as steel, when put to even a little use every day, never becomes rusty but, when left in disuse, rusts up in a short space of time, in the same way acquired skills that are not used are very soon lost but equally can be conserved by just a small amount of daily practice.

It is very true that the little you will have time to do, you must do well, for the excellence of the operation derives not from its quantity but from its quality, and in this you will have to invest much effort, all the more so because you will have no one to make you repeat anything you do negligently by reminding you that, just as children tend to resemble their parents and produce offspring similar to them, so our habits come to reflect the deeds from which they derive and to produce other similar habits. Thus it is that, when you practice your skills carelessly instead of diligently, they will deteriorate from good to bad, and in no time you will have lost them. So you must do what you can, and do it well, and if you can do no more, insure that every week, at least once, you practice all your skills, for it may be months, rather than days, before your mistress desires you to demonstrate one of them, and so you will have to remain prepared, or you could be caught unawares one day, and instead of earning her favor and making her wish to enjoy your skills frequently, to your own honor and repute, you will end up a laughing-stock, and she will finish by holding you in contempt and never again wish to honor your performances with her presence; indeed, she might even feel she had been misled by those who had brought your name to her notice, and become so disaffected toward you that never again would she hold you in good esteem. It behoves you, consequently, to follow the example of those who, having to appear on stage or in some other public capacity, sometimes re-

44. Clearly Guasco has thought through and anticipated every possible excuse that Lavinia might raise regarding the difficulties of maintaining her skills in her post at court and is systematically countering them all here, one after another.

hearse for this throughout a whole year in order to do themselves honor in that one short hour. Moreover, as your judgment matures in the future together with your years, you will see yourself refining your skills and will derive day by day ever greater honor and delight from them, which would not be the case if you were such a good-for-nothing as to let them fall from your grasp, to the point where, when you reached the years of discretion, you could no longer avail yourself of them. And if you should reply that some of these skills require to be exercised in company, such as singing, for example (something you will not be able to do every day as you were wont to do in my house), this is perfectly true, but if you practice on your own, with all the care you can muster, you will manage in that way at least to maintain your skill, even if not as well as you would in company, and when the occasion arises, you will be able to acquit yourself creditably, which will be all the more praiseworthy since both your mistress and the others will know that you have not been able to practice in company. And if singing when you are alone serves no other purpose, it will certainly avail you in this one respect, that it will keep your voice in good shape, provided you make every effort to hold a note, to go even higher than seems possible, to intone accurately, to go gracefully from one pitch to another, to extemporize a little, to sing a few scales, just as you know how to do with your pen on paper, things which, as I told you, you will do much better than you now know how to do, as your judgment, and also the power of your lungs, increase with your years, provided always that you maintain your skill in good shape, for this is the whole thrust of my argument. And in your chamber you will have to hand a great number of songbooks from which you will be able to select now one song and now another, and in this way keep yourself in practice, so as to be able to sing them with greater confidence when the occasion arises.

But I want to show you one companion you should always keep ready at your service in your chamber, that is to say, a well-tuned viola da gamba, with which you will be able to practice both your playing and your singing at the same time, and such an instrument will assist you greatly in your singing, as it did up to now. And in addition to the viola, your clavichord will be the best of companions to you, a much more accomplished instrument than the viola, with which you will be able to assist yourself when you are singing on your own. And I feel sure that in that honored company of ladies, you will find others trained in similar skills, with whom you will be able to practice both your singing and your other accomplishments in praiseworthy competition. As for your other attainments, you will be able to improve upon them, not just maintain them, all on your own, and who knows but that your mistress may not allocate you a teacher in whichever of your skills is most to her liking, with whom you will be able to make more progress in the future than you have up till now.

It really grieves me that just as I was helping you make headway in composing a reasonably good letter and writing correctly, I shall not be able to continue my instruction. However, I shall provide you with some manuals relevant to this profession, which, if you read them and note what is said in them, will, together with the grounding I have given you, little by little enable you to master this expertise, which will be a very great adornment and a necessary accompaniment to the beauty of your handwriting.[45] This last is something of which you must take the greatest care of all, both for the nobility of the art and because one day your mistress might desire to capitalize on it. Should this ever come about, I will give you this one piece of advice while I have the chance, namely, that the duty of serving employers, especially those of high rank, with the pen, involves mastering not only your writing but also your tongue. This is why such officials are called secretaries, since silence is their duty.[46]

So there now, my child, you can see how many incentives there are to spur you on to do as I have argued in this section: virtue, praise, the hopes we have formed of you, the fear of blame, the fear of scandalizing others, of not showing any improvement during your adolescence upon your childhood, of giving the lie to those who praised you, the renown that led you to be accepted into your mistress's service, your love for me, your fear of me and of showing disrespect toward me, your love and fear of God, and your desire not to show disrespect toward God Himself, to which reasons you may add the avoidance of idleness, the source of all evil, and in order to have at all moments of your life a means of entertainment to hand, which will enable you to

45. During the late sixteenth century, numerous manuals on the art of letter writing were being published in Italy, many of which specifically targeted aspiring court secretaries requiring models from which they might learn their profession, and contained examples for them to copy of the different types of letters they might be required to write. See the comprehensive bibliography given at the back of Amedeo Quondam's *Le carte messaggiere* (Rome, 1981), 279–331. Typical of such manuals is Francesco Sansovino's *Del secretario libri quattro*, published in Venice in 1564, subtitled, *Nel quale si mostra et insegna il modo di scriver lettere acconciamente e con arte, in qualsivoglia soggetto* (In which is demonstrated and taught the way to write letters appropriately and with due art on any subject whatsoever). Sansovino states that to be worthy of so honorable an office, the court secretary must be well-lettered, loyal, of fine and pleasing wit, hard-working, prudent, and well-versed both in the main areas of learning and in the languages in which letters are most commonly written, i.e., Latin and the vernacular, for he is the heart and mind of the court he serves.

46. Guasco is here alluding to the etymology of the term "secretary" [*secretario*], which derives from the Medieval Latin term *secretarius* meaning a confidential officer or someone privy to a secret [*secretum*].

pass your time happily, whatever the circumstances and place.[47] And so, since I, together with all your friends and relatives, have based our hopes of your future success on this alone, which we all commend to you but which only you can maintain, take, I beg of you, more care of it than of my very life and of your own person, the care of which I am now going to address under the fifth heading.

5. *Concerning Your Person*

My main aim here is to remind you to endeavor to maintain your health, for in addition to the advantages of being healthy, it is very necessary to someone entering another's employment, and especially to you, with so many undertakings on your hands which you can only maintain if you are in good health. Although this blessing, like all others, is bestowed by the hand of God alone, He nevertheless placed it so much under our own control that we for our part can do much in this regard, especially someone like yourself who is endowed with a healthy disposition, as you are and who, despite all the toils you have undergone in the past, have never required any medicine. To preserve your health for the future, then, and not to spoil your robust disposition, the best remedy will be a sound mode of life, for you must think that although, thanks be to God, you lacked for no kind of sustenance in your father's house, you nevertheless did not enjoy there either such varied or such sumptuous dishes as are to be found in the households of princes, and especially in that of so great a lady as your mistress, and so you must restrain yourself somewhat and not be carried away into excesses by your appetite and the variety of dishes but, instead, leave the table still hungry rather than sated, for since you have to remain for most of the time in your chamber, the abundance of food and the lack of exercise might easily end up causing you some sickness. In addition, you will have to avoid the types of food that used to be

47. The danger of idleness, or *otium,* is a Renaissance topos, something against which preachers and moralists regularly issue warnings, especially to women. The Church subsumed it under *accidia* (sloth), one of the Seven Deadly Sins, and recommended that to avoid its perils a woman should be kept constantly occupied in domestic tasks. Leon Battista Alberti stresses in his *Della famiglia,* written in 1434-41 (*The Family in Renaissance Florence,* trans. Renée Neu Watkins [Columbia, S.C, 1989]), that the young wife should busy herself in her household all day long and never sit idle, and Ariosto offers his readers an allegory of the soul-destroying effects of abandoning oneself to *otium* in the well-known story of Alcina and Ruggiero in canto 7 of the *Orlando furioso.* Anne de France cautions her daughter to avoid it at all cost, for it is the child of the devil, leading women to perdition (*Les Enseignements d'Anne de France duchesse de Bourbonnais et d'Auvergne a sa fille Susanne de Bourbon* (Lyon, n.d.).

forbidden you in our household, due to being harmful to children. And apart from lunch and dinner, avoid overrich foods, for so as to restrain your nature while you are growing up, a bread roll and an apple should suffice as nourishment at breakfast and at teatime, just as they were wont to do at home.[48] And even if some of your female companions should do differently, you must not follow their example, remembering that not being accustomed to them as they are, such foods could do you great harm in a short space of time, since it is unwise to try and alter the habits of your stomach.

And as well as in what you eat, remember to be sparing in your wine drinking, and here you will have before you the example of those Spanish court-ladies who, as Spanish custom dictates, are wont to drink water; not that you must follow suit, since this is not normally the practice of us Italians, and hence what is natural and beneficial to those ladies would be not only harmful but even deadly to you. But you can certainly imitate them by drinking your wine moderately and by watering it down whenever possible and, instead of drinking water, which is wont to arouse great hunger and to be less nutritious than wine, you can be more restrained than them in what you eat, and in this way, as our proverb says, cut even with them, for large quantities of food would be far more harmful to you than to them.[49] This advice will not only help to keep you healthy in body but will also be of the greatest assistance to your mind, which will remain more alert when you are exercising your skills, and at the same time help you to maintain your voice, which as you well know is of the greatest importance to those seeking to do themselves honor through song. And it will also be useful to you in promoting vigilance in your duties, not just an important but an essential part of the office of serving at court, and chastity and sobriety were always portrayed as friends and intimates. And if (God forbid), you should succumb to some indisposition, be sure to restrict your food intake immediately and remedy the ill through your diet from the start, for in this way many illnesses can be avoided. And may this suffice where your physical well-being is concerned, the care of which is the basis not only of your health but also of your social graces, which are of such importance in that they are what distinguish men from beasts. And if they are something that needs to be held generally in high esteem by all of us, how much more should they be so by a well-born gentlewoman and lady-in-waiting in such a palace as that of the Infanta, your

48. Juan Luis Vives had recommended that the diet of a young girl should be "light, plain, and not highly seasoned" (*Education*, 87). Like Vives, moralists frequently urge that, in addition, she should drink only water. Guasco's attitude is a more practical and realistic one.

49. "Cut even with them"—i.e., by eating less than her Spanish counterparts but by drinking wine to make up.

mistress, and these social graces appertain both to one's person and to its adornments.

Where your person is concerned, it seems to me that there are three things to which you need to pay special attention, and these are your hair, your hands, and your teeth for, provided she takes cares of them, a woman's beauty radiates especially from these three bodily parts. And hence it is that the ladies of Spain rightly attach great importance to the last two, as you will see instanced at the court of your mistress. But with what arts they cultivate these features it is not my job to teach you, nor would I know how to do so, but you will not lack for instructresses here. However, let me say that I do not mean that you should dye your hair blond, since this is extremely dangerous to the head and contrary to the preservation of your health that I have so urgently commended to you.[50] And you will be able to learn from those who know about such matters, as I do not, how to care for your hair without doing yourself harm. As far as your face goes, there is nothing I want to say, since it seems to me that it requires nothing but clear fresh water to cleanse it, especially in your case who, through God's grace, have nothing to complain about to Nature in this regard, and who never saw any cosmetics in your father's house. Whatever others may do, you must be sure to avoid them in the future, for they are an offense against God and ruin the teeth and the face itself.[51]

50. Since Guasco exhorts Lavinia not to dye her hair blond we can assume that she was a brunet. Blond hair constituted the contemporary ideal, however. Renaissance theorists on female beauty specify that a woman's hair should be golden, lustrous, long, and wavy, as Petrarch describes Laura's to be in his *Canzoniere;* in addition, her hands should be small, white, and graceful and her teeth like gleaming pearls within her ruby lips. (The most famous exponent of the Renaissance ideal of feminine beauty was Agnolo Firenzuola in his dialogue *Delle bellezze delle donne,* in *Prose,* ed. Bernardo di Giunta (Florence, 1548); *On the Beauty of Women,* trans. Konrad Eisenbichler and Jacqueline Murray [Philadelphia, 1992], 44–68.) It is interesting that, like Guasco, Castiglione makes particular mention in his *Courtier* of a woman's teeth and hands as helping to create an impression of uncontrived elegance:

> In a woman, lovely teeth are always very pleasing, for since they are hidden from view most of the time, unlike the rest of the face, it can be believed that less effort has been spent on making them look beautiful. . . . The same is true of the hands which, if they are delicate and fine, and are uncovered at the right time, when there is need to use and not just to display their beauty, leave one with a great desire to see more of them, especially after they have been covered again with gloves. For it appears that the person who covers them hardly cares or worries whether they are seen or not, and has beautiful hands more by Nature than through any effort or design.
>
> (87)

51. Almost all moral and preceptive works written for women at this time inveigh in the strongest possible tones against the use of cosmetics, which was considered a deplorable practice and a sign of licentiousness. On health grounds, the noxious substances they contained were likely to age a woman prematurely and even to lead to premature death, while on moral

Not only must you insure your bodily cleanliness, but also that of your clothes and adornments, endeavoring to wear your clothes with all possible gracefulness, keeping them carefully mended and, above all, protecting them from grease and stains, and here you will have to take special care, since your mistress is in the habit of making her ladies serve her at table, in the process of which one runs the risk of spilling the dishes over oneself, to one's own shame and to the scorn of the onlookers, as well as incurring the unsightliness of having to wear greasy clothes and to look like a kitchen maid instead of a court lady. Where the adornment of your head is concerned, this is something that in my view requires the greatest attention, since I believe that there is no means through which a lady can do herself more honor, and even if I cannot speak specifically here, since it is not within my competence, I will still not refrain from telling you that in my opinion the care you apply should not be such that your hair is ruined by art, for it is so fragile that it can easily be damaged. Nor would I recommend the arranging of your hair to be such that it takes up a great deal of time, for this is troublesome both for the person being adorned and for the adorner and especially so for those who, like yourself, are employed in another's service. Nor would I wish you to cover your head all over with embellishments, as some women are wont to do, for you do not want to look like an ox at a feast, but maintain a middle way and give the impression of having taken no special care in adorning your hair, rather than of having applied great effort to it, for the revealing of so much

---

grounds they demonstrated a perverse desire in a woman to alter her God-given appearance and to falsify Nature in the interests of vanity and of arousing male lust. Alberti's main protagonist in his *Della famiglia* censures his young wife on the single occasion when she applied cosmetics to her face before receiving guests to the house one Easter, and Castiglione ridicules the mask-like and grotesque appearance of a heavily made-up woman that, through revealing an excessive desire on her part to look beautiful, makes her appear so unlike the seemingly uncontrived ideal of beauty he sought:

> Surely you realize how much more graceful a woman is who, if indeed she wishes to do so, paints herself so sparingly and so little that whoever looks at her is unsure whether she is made up or not, in comparison with one whose face is so encrusted that she seems to be wearing a mask and who dare not laugh for fear of causing it to crack, and who changes color only when she dresses in the morning, after which she stays stock-still all the rest of the day, like a wooden statue, letting herself be seen only by torchlight, in the way a wily merchant shows his cloth in a dark corner.

> (*The Courtier*, 86)

Speroni (*Dialogo*), too, admonishes his young bride not to fall into the sin of trying to beautify herself by falsifying her complexion with a vile coating of white lead. The idea that the use of cosmetics amounted to a deception on the woman's part derived originally from Xenophon's *Oeconomicus*, in which Ischomachus takes his young wife to task for using white lead to whiten her complexion and alkanet juice to heighten the rosiness of her cheeks (*Xenophon: Memorabilia and Oeconomicus*, trans. E. C. Marchant, Loeb Classical Studies [London, 1923], 447–51).

art eliminates that grace which on the other hand is conferred by a sem-
blance of negligence. And you must apply this same consideration to all your
actions in order to avoid affectation, the very antithesis of grace.[52]

6. Concerning Your Possessions

And so, since it seems to me that I have said enough on this topic, I will pass
on to the sixth heading, concerning the care you must take of your possessions, which will consist not of rents nor of farms, although for the price of
them one could have bought a sizable farm or rentable property. But instead
they consist of a four-poster bed, draperies, bedcoverings, curtains, ornaments
suited to a bedchamber, all made of silk and extremely sumptuous, jewels,
gold and silver items, many dresses of gold and silk, an abundance of linen of
high value, musical instruments, books, and a great many other items for your
use that I will not stop to list here, with which I have provided you by means
of a heavy expenditure, on the same level as the other things, in such a way
that I do not know how anything could be lacking, either in your personal effects or in the furnishings of your chamber.[53] Just as it has been my responsibility, with great inconvenience to myself, to provide these things, so it will
be your responsibility, with the greatest of ease, to preserve them, reflecting
that since I have done more in this regard than my means permitted, in addition to all the many traveling expenses and other financial commitments that
this event has incurred, so you will need to take such care of these aforementioned possessions that they may do you great honor, recalling the proverb
you have heard so many times that he who honors his possessions is honored
by them in his turn. And so you will have to treat them in such a way that

52. Guasco clearly has Castiglione's advice to his ideal courtier in mind here, where Count Lu-
dovico says in bk. 1: "However, having already thought a great deal about how this grace is acquired . . . , I have discovered a universal rule which seems to apply more than any other in all
human actions or words: namely, to steer away from affectation at all costs, as if it were a rough
and dangerous reef, and (to use perhaps a novel word for it) to practice in all things a certain
nonchalance which conceals all artistry and makes whatever one says or does seem uncontrived
and effortless" (*The Courtier*, 67). To offer her a specific example of nonchalance relating to her
own person, Guasco is here advocating that Lavinia should adopt a hairstyle that will appear
natural and uncontrived, even though it may have involved a considerable degree of effort,
rather than one that will destroy any impression of grace due to being overelaborate. In this way
she will be observing the Golden Mean and avoiding Castiglione's "dangerous reef" of affectation.

53. This inventory of the items a lady-in-waiting needed to take with her to court is almost certainly unique in Italian Renaissance literature. It is clear from Guasco's list that the chamber allocated to Lavinia in the palace would be empty of any furnishings, all of which she would have to
transport with her, specially since she was far too young to go out and buy such items for herself
on arriving in Turin.

these expenses do not have to be repeated every other day, for it would be
beyond your father's means to do so. To discuss your responsibilities here in
rather more detail, let me tell you that there are four ways in which your belongings can be damaged: through tearing them, through staining them as
you use them, through not taking care of them when not in use, and through
allowing some of them to be stolen. You can guard against the first of these,
especially where your clothes are concerned, by taking care how you come
and go, how you act, and in short by paying heed to all situations in which
you might crease your clothes, for just as they get worn out little by little by
such lack of care before you are even aware of it, so by giving thought to
them on all occasions, they can be made to last twice as long as they otherwise would. For instance, if perchance one of your dresses or some such garment were to begin to tear in one place, someone who has the skill can mend
it with a few stitches, possibly thus avoiding a really large rent, and in this
way your clothes can be made to last for a good length of time still without
your having to run to the shops every other day, purse in hand. You must
guard against staining your garments by watching your step in muddy places
and taking care how you handle items that could stain, remembering that it is
far more dishonorable to have clothes that are greasy and stained than ones
that are worn and ragged, for while the latter is to be ascribed to time and
poverty, the former is due to the ineptitude of the wearer.[54]

Where the second heading is concerned, that of neglecting items that
are not in current use and so of causing them also to be ruined, you will be
able to guard against this by keeping them tidily in their proper place and
knowing exactly where to put your hand to find them when you do need to
use them, rather than turning a hundred things upside down to find one particular item so that they all suffer damage, and at the same time guarding
them from moths, dust, and mice, the natural enemies of the contents of a
house.

To guard against the theft of your possessions, you must watch over
them diligently, trusting no one, but without showing you mistrust anyone,
realizing that it is far better to look after your possessions well than to run
around seeking them after they have been stolen, very often imputing the
blame to the wrong person and so losing your friend along with your belongings. What I would advise you to do in order to minimize your efforts
and perhaps to maximize your security is to give your maid an inventory of

54. Respectable women are constantly reminded by prescriptive writers of the importance of
keeping their garments clean. Stained and greasy clothes were often associated with lewdness.
Vives comments regarding the clothes of the unmarried girl that they "should not be luxurious
or too expensive, but neat and spotless" (*Education*, 91).

all you own, which she must keep carefully, from time to time letting you see it, both so that you can check that nothing is missing and so that you can see how she is looking after your things. Where money is concerned, you need to be especially vigilant, for it is all too easily embezzled, both due to the need we all have of money and due to the ease of concealing it, and so, even when you are consigning a sum of money to your own maid, you must do so with great caution, writing down the exact sum in a little notebook on one side of the page, and on the other entering all the monies you receive, so that you cannot be tricked. In this context it behoves me to remind you to be as economical as possible in your outgoings, since you do not have so wealthy a father that his children may spend lavishly; and as he has already expended so much for your benefit, so you must endeavor with all the means in your power to save him expense in the future and restrain yourself from lavishing money on vanities and from spending more than you need do. In this way you will have sufficient for your needs and for situations where you cannot get by with less, remembering that parsimony is a woman's natural virtue.

But just as I mentioned cleanliness as well as usefulness in connection with the care of your person, so it seems to me that the care of your belongings also comes down to these, not using the term cleanliness here in the sense of preserving your clothes from stains but in that of a desire for beauty and order, leading you to keep the things in your chamber so well arranged that they seem to have been put there not as an encumbrance but as an adornment, so that anyone coming into it will be compelled to praise you for them, rather than censuring you due to finding them in disorder. This you should endeavor to do not only if you have a whole chamber of your own, no matter how numerous your possessions but even if you have to share one, supposing that due to a scarcity of accommodation in the palace only this amount of space is allocated to you, for it is a great advantage to know how to make a virtue out of necessity.[55] In this connection I feel compelled to relate to you the very words I once saw written by a man worthy to be believed:

I once saw in Venice (he writes) *a new and diligent manner of adeptly organizing many ordinary objects in a small space, when I was taken by my German friends to their warehouse on the Rialto to see the room of a merchant from Augusta in which, in addition to a vast multitude of lengths of cloth of many different colors from his country, in addition to his bed and the desk on which he did his bookkeeping, in addition to a hundred different instruments for making music, keyboard, wind, and string, in addition to the handbasin and the*

55. Since there was no ducal palace in Turin when the dukes of Savoy returned there, they commandeered the former bishop's palace. It was, however, insufficiently large for their ever-increasing needs, and sleeping quarters would certainly still have been cramped in the 1580s.

stove, in addition to a number of tubs of beautiful lemon and orange trees, which gave the impression of a garden, there was no type of domestic implement or utensil necessary to domestic life such as any noble and wealthy inhabitant of Bologna would possess, which was not to be found in abundance in that room. But he was far more to be commended in that, although the room was filled on all sides with every commodity and type of possession, yet at a first glance the observer saw there nothing that could not be ascribed to the simple adornment of its floor and walls.

This account in the actual words of the man who wrote it, which I read over and over again so many times that they always stuck in my memory, I wanted to repeat to you, so that you could comprehend what industry can do.[56] And if that merchant, hard at work in his dealings, living in a small rented room, could keep so many things so well arranged, how much more will you be able to do so, not having so many haversacks and being much less busy than he was? And all the more so in that you are a woman, the which sex is far more inclined to such thoughts than ours is;[57] and in addition, having a maid whom you will be able to direct in all this, something that that worthy man could not do, having no help but his own. But I do not want to tell you only to make use of your tongue in this regard, by giving orders to your maid but, rather, that you should very often do the tidying up with your own hands, both to avoid idleness, which is something that can never be sufficiently blamed, and for the sake of exercise and physical health, in addition to which, if your maid sees you are doing with your own hands what you could have ordered her to do, she will hurry to do it without being ordered to do so. In this way, accustoming yourself in these early years of your life to look after your possessions in the manner I have explained to you, you will come to be prudent and skilled in domestic management if at some future date it should befall you to have a house to run,[58] and although the running of a family and a whole house is a very different matter from looking after just one room, with the small number of things you will have in it, nevertheless

---

56. This description of the merchant's room on the Rialto is taken verbatim from Speroni (*Dialogo*). Both writers cite it as a commendable example of how order and beauty can be imposed on a small space even though filled with a great many objects. It is in fact more applicable to Lavinia's situation than to that of Cornelia, who will have a whole palace of her own in which to arrange and display her belongings. The account derived originally from Xenophon's *Oeconomicus*, in which Ischomachus describes to his very young bride the hold of a merchant ship he had visited as an exemplum of how to order many things in a small space (433–37). (Orderliness was a prime requirement in the female sex in the Renaissance, a disorderly woman being regarded as a threat to the very stability of society.)

57. Compare Speroni: "To you, who are a woman, that is to say naturally inclined to such thoughts" (*Dialogo*, 90). The view that women are more disposed by nature than men to order and care for the household goods is to be found in both Xenophon and Aristotle.

58. This is one of only two references Guasco makes in the *Discourse* to Lavinia's eventual future role as a wife and housewife.

the quality of a person's character makes itself known in small matters just as well as in great; for however large this city of ours is, it could still be drawn on a small piece of paper with its towers, its churches, its bridges, and all the structures it contains, and not just our own city, but Europe, and the rest of the world, are wont to be represented to us on a small drawing board.[59]

7. *Concerning Your Social Relations*

I think I have now said enough to you under this sixth heading, and so I shall move on to the seventh, concerning your social relations with others, on which topic, if I wanted to speak to you in detail, I would need to write a complete book as others have already done, in that it relates to civilized living, which involves innumerable considerations concerning customs that it is not my intention to deal with in this little discourse of mine, so, instead of discussing them point by point, I shall give you some books in which you will find them expounded without my laboring to sum them all up for you here. And these books will be Castiglione's *Courtier*, newly republished, with right and due authority, truly a most noble work and absolutely essential to anyone who has to live at court, and in addition to *The Courtier*, Monsignor della Casa's *Galateo*, a most invaluable book, not less for the excellence of its style than for the way it carefully details all the different sorts of topics that can be discussed, not just at court, but in any social intercourse; and then there is Guazzo's *Conversation*, so useful a book that there is no one professing a knowledge of letters and social customs who does not keep a copy of it in his study, and a work all the more to be valued by you in that it is written by an honorable neighbor of ours and a dear friend of mine.[60] All these books I earnestly beseech you to read with close attention, in that you can learn from

59. An interesting allusion to the new and highly fashionable science of cartography, which during the sixteenth century became an important means to all rulers of centralizing their power, of propaganda, and for use as an instrument of government. Both Machiavelli and Castiglione allude in their writings to the importance of mapmaking. (See Peter Barber's "Maps and Monarchs in Europe, 1500–1800," in *Royal and Republican Sovereignty in Early Modern Europe*, ed. Robert Oresko, G. C. Gibbs, and H. M. Scott, eds. [Cambridge, 1997], 75–124).

60. A new edition of *The Courtier* had been published as recently as 1584 in Venice: *Il Cortegiano del Conte Baldassare Castiglione, riveduto e corretto da Antonio Ciccarelli*. This was the first of a series of expurgated editions of *The Courtier*, necessitated by the decision of the Roman censors in 1576 that the book was heretical and immoral. Not long afterward, it was placed on the Index where it remained until 1996, Ciccarelli's edition being the only one during all those centuries that the faithful were permitted to read. Between its first appearance in 1528 and 1584, *The Courtier* had gone through fifty-seven Italian editions, as well as being translated into all the major European languages. It was first translated into English by Sir Thomas Hoby in 1561.

The *Galateo* was first published in 1558, and the *Civil Conversation* in 1574. For English versions of these last two works, see Giovanni della Casa, *Galateo*, trans. Konrad Eisenbichler and Kenneth R. Bartlett, Centre for Reformation and Renaissance Studies (Toronto, 1986); and M.

them in a short space of time what you could not learn from the experience of many years, in addition to which you could commit a great many errors through not having read them, while gradually acquiring through practical experience the art of conversing with others.

Leaving you, therefore, to rely on these writers and on the example of the many well-mannered lady companions that you will find in that court, as far as most of the matters relating to correct social manners are concerned, I shall deal briefly with those that happen to come to mind while I am writing to you in general terms. The first point about which I wish to warn you is that you should learn well how to control your tongue, considering that Nature enclosed it mysteriously within the lips and teeth, as if behind two doors, so that we could use them to conceal our thoughts and hold them back with our teeth, even if they had got as far as the tip of our tongue, and then restrain them with our lips, if they had escaped the confines of our teeth. It is for this reason that verbosity was always censured, and rightly so, for it is inevitable that he who talks a lot, no matter how intelligent he is, should sometimes blunder, while on the other hand, an honest taciturnity has always been commended. There was once a great teacher who, for this reason, refused to allow his pupils to speak in his school until the age of five, desiring to show that one needs to learn before one speaks, else one says stupid things, to the derision of him who hears them and to the dishonor of him who says them. So you must learn from this example to restrain your speech, listening much and speaking little, above all during this apprenticeship of yours, in which as well as your extreme youth and lack of experience, and your never having associated with any company outside your father's house, there is the additional factor that you are going to find a great diversity of temperaments and nationalities there and be in a place where the manner of life is very different indeed from what you saw at home. Little by little you will begin to understand court affairs and the personalities of the people living there, and as you grow older, so will you gain in wisdom and acquire greater confidence in talking.

When you do need to speak, take care never to do so randomly but only when you have thought in advance what you are going to say, for just as you can tell from the ring of a piece of metal when you strike it what its value is, so from what someone says you can value their worth and how to appraise them. Consequently, if you make a favorable impression on your hearer, you will be commended as a person of discretion and intelligence, which will make you well-liked and highly regarded; just as on the other hand you

Steeven Guazzo, *The Civile Conversation,* trans. George Pettie and Bartholomew Young (1586; London and New York, 1925).

would lose this credit and be poorly esteemed if you were to utter inepti-
tudes. You will be able to avoid this provided you think before you speak,
which is something you will easily manage since, thank God, you are neither
silly nor a fool, and so you could not go wrong here unless from lack either of
reflection or of experience.[61] When you are speaking with someone, it behoves you to consider their rank very carefully, in order to preserve the decorum due to them, for one converses in one way with a superior, in another
with an equal, and in another again with an inferior, and in one way with men
and in another with women; in one way with servants and in another with
other people, adapting your topics to the condition of the aforementioned
people and never speaking about matters that do not appertain to them and
that you do not understand.[62] And above all you must reflect well on your
mode of conversing with those men with whom, in conformity with the us-
age of that court, it will be permissible for you to speak, both because far
more caution and modesty are required when a gentlewoman is conversing
with a man than with another woman, and also because, generally speaking,
men have greater knowledge and so you need to give a better account of
yourself with them than with the ladies, emulating with all your might that
pleasing gravity and dignified charm of the ladies of Spain who, in my view,
surpass in this respect all other ladies in the world.[63] It will be very easy for
you to acquire these qualities at that court, with the example before you of so

61. The advice Guasco here gives his young daughter is highly progressive and enlightened
compared with the endless exhortations of earlier moralists to women to remain silent in all situations except domestic ones. Francesco Barbaro, e.g., had warned that to utter in public endangers a woman's chastity, "for the speech of a noble woman can be no less dangerous than the
nakedness of her limbs" (*On Wifely Duties*, trans. Benjamin Kohl, in *The Earthly Republic*, ed. Benjamin Kohl and R. G. Witt [Philadelphia, 1976], 205), while Juan Luis Vives, although writing
for Princess Mary, a likely future queen of England, had declared, "If she is a good woman, it is
best that she stay at home and be unknown to others. In company, it is befitting that she be re-
tiring and silent, with her eyes cast down so that some perhaps may see her, but none will hear
her" (*Education*, 72).

62. Compare *The Courtier*: "And then, since words are idle and childish unless they are concerned
with some subject of importance, the lady at Court, as well as being able to recognize the rank
of the person with whom she is talking, should possess a knowledge of many subjects; and when
she is speaking she should know how to choose topics suitable for the kind of person she is addressing, . . . she should not be inept in pretending to know what she does not know, but should
seek modestly to win credit for knowing what she does" (213–14). Ian Maclean comments that
the court lady as described by Castiglione, unlike her far more restricted domestic counterpart,
"must have all the accomplishments required to sustain conversation in civilized company; her
very position in such society runs counter to the structure applied to her as a moral, domestic
and intellectual being. The *taciturnitas* for which domestic woman is praised is abandoned" (*The
Renaissance Notion of Woman* [Cambridge, 1980], 64).

63. Castiglione, too, had referred to the "calm dignity characteristic of the Spaniards" (*The
Courtier*, 146).

many such gracious ladies, whose Spanish dignity and charm are manifested not only in their speech but in everything ladies of their race do. Indeed, so natural and proper are these qualities to the ladies that they confer charm and distinction on them, in addition to that keenness and readiness of wit with which the Spanish are wont to spice their conversation, which is something you will have to copy with all your might.[64] It is very true that just as jesting is a delightful and noble thing and proof of a ready wit, so too it is a rare ability, since it requires promptness of mind and originality, and must not appear premeditated or insipid or borrowed from another. It is something that requires nature rather than art, even though here, as in all things, art can assist nature. But who can say that you may not prove a success here? I have often heard you make extremely witty remarks, which I have from time to time related to my friends, arousing their amazement.[65]

But what matters still more, and that has no need of either nature or art but only of modesty, which is in our own hands, is to avoid offending anyone, whether present or absent, in your jesting, whence derives the commonplace saying that one should not make fun of those who grieve or utter witticisms at the expense of the truth. So, in addition to the aforementioned conditions, your sayings must be polite quips rather than biting comments, and you must use them in such a way that they scarcely graze the skin, let alone the heart, of him with whom you are conversing. And here a fine example comes to my aid, highly relevant: let your quips be like those playful nips that your little dog is wont to give you with its teeth, which, although applied to your flesh, nevertheless never do you any real hurt but, rather, afford you pleasure through feeling yourself harmlessly gripped by the teeth of that dear little creature.[66] And while I am on the subject of not causing distress to anyone through your jesting, I must remind you in addition to avoid at all costs giving offense to people by word of mouth in any other way whatsoever, either directly or behind their backs, whether in jest or in earnest. And above all, take care not to let yourself be so carried away as to come to insults and quarrels with your female companions, for this would be shame-

64. Compare *The Courtier:* "It also seems that the Spaniards are instinctively witty" (152).

65. In his *La donna di corte* (The court lady), printed in 1546, Lodovico Domenichi had identified urbanity, or the ability to be witty, as central to courtiership (see my introduction, xxx–xxx), but had pronounced women to be incapable of this property. Guasco clearly would not agree with this and is offering his daughter every encouragement to exercise the ready wit that he says he knows her to possess.

66. Compare Lauretta's comment at the start of the third story of Day 6 of the *Decameron:* "Lovesome ladies . . . I should like to remind you that . . . the nature of wit is such that its bite must be like that of a sheep rather than of a dog, for if it were to bite the listener like a dog, it would no longer be wit but abuse" (488–89).

worthy, and were it to become known in court, maybe even reaching the ears of your mistress, it would place you in her disfavor and in disrepute with the others, and you would find yourself shunned by one and all, like a troublesome horse that is wont to be kept separate from the rest with every sort of barrier, even becoming hateful to its very owners. The remedy against entering into these squabbles is to know your companions' personalities and to learn to accommodate yourself to them and also to avoid situations that could have such a result. Since these can easily occur, one way is to refrain from unpleasant topics of conversation, and if such a one should happen to arise between you and some other lady, you must immediately change the subject; and above all take care not to start drawing comparisons between either yourself or your possessions and those of other people, for this is a most odious topic and one that leads not only to the cooling of friendships but also to the arousing of enmity. So, even given that someone were to tempt you into this, you must still avoid talking on such a topic, nor must you give any indication that you care about being at an advantage either in worldly goods or in personal endowments, but at the same time you must endeavor with commendable emulation not to allow the other ladies to outdo you in their moral qualities or habits.

But if it is bad to offend someone verbally in front of them, to do so behind their backs is far worse, just as it is to wound someone who is off their guard rather than someone who is defending themselves; for he who acts like that is regarded as infamous and, in addition, commits the grave sin of defaming another, which is more to be avoided than death itself, even if one knew for sure that this person would never get to hear of it. For even if it never did leak out, the conscience alone of the guilty party would be sufficient accusation and punishment, in addition to the chastisement prepared for him by God, who rarely permits this sin to remain concealed, so that others should take greater care not to commit it. Make sure, therefore, that you guard against this, for not only would it be unworthy of your noble rank, but the very earth itself would repeat it if men remained silent, and in order that this piece of advice should stick in your memory, I am going to include a fable here:

There was once a king called Midas, whose ears Phoebus had, due to some grudge or other, changed into ass's ears.[67] This fact was known to no

---

67. King Midas had voted in favor of Pan against Phoebus Apollo when judging a musical contest between the two, and in consequence the angry Apollo had ass's ears bestowed on him. Ovid tells the tale of Midas's barber and the reeds in *Metamorphoses* 2.153 ff. This well-known fable is cited by Speroni (*Dialogo*, 81), as a general warning that wrongdoing will always become known eventually. Guasco, however, cites it in the more correct context of speaking ill of some-

one except a barber, by whom the king was washed and shaved. This barber, bursting to spread abroad so great a piece of news but fearful of the risk of doing so, went one day into some secret and hidden valleys where, after gazing carefully all around to make sure no one could either see or hear him, dug a hole in the ground and gave vent to his secret with these words: "Midas has ass's ears." And then he filled in the hole and left, confident that no one would ever get to hear of it. But the patch of earth, filled with the voice of that barber, then produced some reeds through which resounded those same words: "Midas has ass's ears." Although this fable is only a poetic fiction, it nevertheless contains beneath its surface this mystery, that there is no crime, no matter how secret and well concealed, that will not ultimately be disclosed. This admonition should not only be of use to you in all you do but will avail you especially in the matter I am currently discussing. Not only must you refrain from offending people in what you yourself say, but you must also not allow anyone else to do so in your presence: not that I mean that you should come to blows with someone who is speaking ill of another, but that at least you should demonstrate through remaining silent that you take no pleasure in hearing it and that you could never possibly entertain any bad opinion of the other ladies, especially of your fellow ladies-in-waiting or any other well-born gentlewomen. Similarly, it would give you a bad reputation if you appeared ready to believe evil of the other ladies, for people might conclude that you held a similar view of them. And should you hear one of your companions being blamed in her absence for some trifling fault, you should discreetly set about finding excuses for her rather than joining in the accusations with the other girls.

There is one other thing I want to remind you about in this context, more important, in my view, than the others already mentioned, though I cannot believe you would ever fall into such an error, since you never acted so foolishly at home, and since it is something that is quite unthinkable in a noble and well brought up person like yourself. Nevertheless, in order not to omit any of the points that it seems most important to recall in this discussion, I will still mention it to you, and it is this: that as well as taking care not to offend anyone through what you say, either to their face or behind their back, beware of going from one to another of those ladies telling tales about something you have seen or heard, especially things that could give rise to squabbles and discord, for that would be an abomination and would make everyone hate you down to the very stones of the house, and you would be

---

one behind his back under the delusion that your words will never leak out. Christine de Pizan devotes a section of her advice to court ladies to considering the evils of their maligning one another in her *Book of the Three Virtues.*

pointed out as a little troublemaker, unworthy of the name of gentlewoman; it would turn everyone against you, nor would anyone have a good word for you, and your misconduct would be all the worse if you reported what was false. I mention all this not because I consider it possible that you would ever commit so vile a sin but to satisfy myself that I have not omitted so important a reminder, for well you know that there is no worse insult than to call someone a liar, and truly with good reason; for since Nature has granted us speech to express what is in our minds, liars do a great wrong to Nature and to God when they tell untruths, that is to say, express the opposite to what is in our minds, for not only are they abusing this gift of Nature but also acting against civilized society, which cannot be preserved unless people speak truthfully. And for this reason it is right and proper that this vice of telling lies should be so abominated by the world, all the more so when told with the intention of harming one's neighbor and discrediting him, for such an action renders you accountable to God and under an obligation to restore the reputation you have damaged. I am quite sure you would not commit a sin of such magnitude, but I would exhort you still further to make sure you never tell any lie whatsoever, even if it does no one any harm, because of the aforementioned wrong that one commits in so doing against Nature and God. Moreover, even if not all lies are mortal sins, they are certainly venial ones, which predispose a person to commit sins that are mortal. I will leave aside the fact that lies are wont to be discovered, whence the liar reaps this punishment for his sin: that even when speaking the truth no one will believe him, even though he should swear to it with oaths.

There are many more precepts in addition to those already mentioned that can be cited regarding this matter of how to control your tongue, for there is, in short, nothing connected with social intercourse that could not be included here, and so I will proceed by reminding you of any others that spring to mind as my pen runs on. Take care you continue to deserve the praise I have so often bestowed on you for the fact that up to now you have never been heard boasting or praising yourself for any of your accomplishments, for as you increase in years and perhaps acquire a modicum of ambition, you could end up lapsing from the prudence you used to show in your childhood, which would be all the more blameworthy inasmuch as it would be less excusable in your adolescence than it would have been in your childhood. And not only would you be rebuked for blowing your own trumpet but you would arouse hatred against yourself in the hearts of others, for it would give the impression that you were pushing yourself forward and considering yourself superior to them, which is something our human nature cannot endure, since no one likes to be outdone by another.

But just as it is unseemly to praise yourself, so equally is it improper to speak ill of yourself, partly because this is a sin, and against charity to oneself, and partly because, unless he who does so is not just a fool but a madman, no one will believe that he does it in order to find fault with himself but so that his listener should be prompted to praise him, and this aim is all the more reprehensible in that it is highly affected and indiscreetly importuning, for it gives an opportunity to people either to flatter this foolish self-denigrator or else to praise him sneeringly, if not derisively.

You must take care, moreover, to avoid quibbling and, as people say, splitting hairs, for this is a very serious vice that makes a person's conversation truly odious, due to the irritation of having to deal with someone so determined to oppose one's opinions and maybe also the very truth, through love of their own views and through an arrogant desire to get the better of others both in this and in all other matters. Nothing loses you the sympathy and goodwill of other people faster than this. And should you ever happen to find yourself in a group prone to such quibbling, do not give them any cause or chance to argue with you but agree with them immediately, in order neither to receive annoyance nor to cause it.

You must learn not to overreact when your companions play a joke on you, as is wont to happen among young people and especially at court, and not to treat it as an outrage but learn both to give and to take a joke with good humor, for if you lose your temper at being teased, you will appear rude and inexperienced in such matters. This would give your companions cause to tease you all the more, seeing you becoming upset, while on the other hand, if you show no irritation, you will be rid of them all the sooner. I would certainly advise you not to be too persistent in teasing the other girls, for it could perchance happen that one or two might take it amiss, and that instead of a joke, a quarrel could result. But your teasing should be done with that tact with which one should chaff a friend, which we call playfulness. For a while it arouses laughter in its victim, but if it persists too long, it gives rise to pain and grief, thus becoming no longer a jest but an offense. And so you must do the same and not persist in teasing so near the quick or so persistently that the jest becomes an annoyance. And take all the more care to observe this rule with those girls that you know are little inclined to take a joke, such as those that are more wont than the rest to fear becoming a butt of jests and so less able to put up with it. And let the other girls do as they will, for your aim is simply to make yourself loved in every way possible and to cause displeasure to no one.

Avoid being the bearer of sad news to anyone, for just as we acquire favor and even sometimes a reward from those to whom we bring good news, so we earn resentment and animosity from those to whom we carry ill-tidings, since they feel that we neither love them nor hold them in regard if causing them pain and grief is of no consequence to us, and all the more must you take care not to display happiness for another's ill or vexation when good befalls them.[68] Rather, you should always share in every misfortune that befalls your companions and friends and rejoice in their good fortune, in response to the law of true love that we should show ourselves to be as concerned for what affects our friends as we are for what affects ourselves.

In addition, you must be on your guard against ever criticizing anything at all in which someone takes delight, and in which they claim expertise, nor still less criticize any defect which is found in them, for these are the paths that lead not only to being disliked but also to being hated. Instead, you should praise the good qualities in the person to whom you happen to be speaking, for this has the virtue of making us loved, just as the opposite has of making us hated. Remember, moreover, never to rebuke anyone for any fault they may have committed, nor remind them of any kindness you may have done them, for that has the power of violently offending those with whom we are conversing.

There is another thing I have just thought of on the subject of ruling your tongue, in addition to those points already mentioned, and one that is most important and that warrants my reminding you about it, and that is that you should be very discreet in confiding your secrets, for once told they can no longer be called secrets, and if they are things you do not wish people to know, take care not to confide them. And you must hold your tongue regarding not only your own secrets but also those of any friend who may have confided in you, always providing the interests of your employers are not at stake. And in this connection I must not omit to mention that those who live at court cannot help knowing about the things that take place in the palace, some to a greater and some to a lesser extent, but nevertheless it would not be permissible for those things to become known outside, nor would it please your employers themselves that they should be reported, so make sure that you never allude to them under any circumstances.

I have reserved one reminder in this connection to the end, since it seems so necessary to me that nothing matters more, and that is that at all times and in all places you should preserve an honest decorum in your speech, for as a person's words are, so their character is judged to be, and so you must keep this thought constantly in mind, knowing that without it you would fail to earn praise for any other virtues you may possess, and it would

68. Castiglione, too, warns against being the bearer of ill-tidings (*The Courtier*, 126).

be the greatest disgrace to you to fall into such an error. There are many other things that one could maybe say on this subject, but if I am not mistaken, all of them are comprised in those already mentioned.

Next, I need to explain to you that an offense depends on the intention of the offender, whence it comes about that if someone feels even a single hair of his head being pulled on purpose to slight him, he will take offense and seek revenge, which is something he would not do for a heavy blow received in jest or accidentally. From this you must understand that one can do injury to a person not only by word of mouth but also through gestures and physical movements, since our intentions are made clear not just through words alone but with bodily signs, as we see the dumb doing, even though we have no more sure or more natural way to reveal our feelings than through speech. And so you will need to guard against any of those acts and gestures that could be taken as an indication of ill-will and a desire to offend those with whom you will have to associate, such as certain jeering and grinning expressions and a twisting up of your mouth at the words and deeds of others, for these are indications that you hold this person in scorn and are tacitly criticizing them. Indeed, such offensive manners are wont to be more hurtful than if someone were to deal us an injury openly, inasmuch as in that way we would know what someone was saying about us and how to refute his remarks, giving vent as we do so to our anger; but when someone says nothing, we do not know what sort of grudge he may have against us, even though we are aware in a general way of being slighted by him, and we sometimes imagine he bears us more animosity than he really does; moreover, we do not know how to show our resentment toward him, and hence our vexation and anger weigh all the heavier on us, due to not being able to unburden ourselves of them.

Indeed, it is not only by means of outward signs that one can do someone an injury but at times even through remaining silent. For example, if someone were to relate to us some good fortune that had befallen him, or else some evil that greatly concerned him, and we failed to lend an ear to him and repaid him with silence, that person would have good cause to think that we cared nothing for his good or ill and that we held him of small account, which he would regard as a great insult. The same would occur if we were in the company of a person who was praising the excellence of someone of whom he thought much and who was a relation or friend of his, and we failed to confirm that praise, or even to utter a single word, for that would lead that same person to conclude that we were prevented by envy and malice from appreciating someone else's good qualities, in consequence of which he would consider himself wronged not only on the part of his friend but also of himself, since true friends hold the wrongs done to their friends as wrongs done to themselves. And the same view would be taken of us by the person that was being spoken of, if he should get to discover how we had behaved in that situation, and indeed with good reason, if his friend should report it to him, as a result of which we would make two enemies with one blow. So be sure to think most carefully about this advice of mine and avoid falling into this error, placing your hand on your heart and considering how you would regard anyone who treated you like that and what impression you would form of their friendship.[69]

In conclusion then, I feel I should say to you that alongside all the others, you must observe the general rule that even children grasp as soon as they gain the use of their reason, which rule Nature has so imprinted on our souls that men of every race, no matter how savage, recognize it and know they must observe it, that is to say, that in all your actions, you should do to others as you would they should do to you, and consequently, if you wish to be loved, honored, respected, considered, and cared for in your needs in the place to which you are going, then love, honor, respect, consider, and care for others in your turn. Respect, cherish, visit, praise, excuse, defend, never insult, blame, deride, wound, scorn, envy, or hate anyone, share in other people's troubles and rejoice in their happiness, if you want them to respect you, to cherish you, to visit you, to praise you, to excuse and defend you, and not to malign you, to censure you, to sneer at you, to goad you, to scoff at you, to bear you envy or hatred and if you wish them to sympathize with you in your troubles and to rejoice in your happiness. There is no lack of cases where I could apply the aforementioned rule, and you must observe it both because these are virtuous acts, agreeable to God, and also because they will all redound to your honor and favor, since as you do to others, so you will receive from them. And you will have to apply this thoughtfulness not only to the most important people in the palace but right down to the humblest little woman in it,[70] both because there are times and places when she too could be of use to you, and so that you earn a good reputation with all the ladies.

69. These shrewd comments, for which there are no obvious sources in Italian Renaissance literature, show that Guasco had thought deeply about the fragility of human relationships and how easily they can be impaired.

70. Compare Anne de France: "And further, be humble to the lowly as to the great, gentle courteous and amiable" (*Les Enseignements*, 22). Young, inexperienced, and far from the support of her family and compatriots as Lavinia will be, Guasco is very aware that his daughter can afford to make an enemy of no one in the palace. Moreover, from an opportunistic point of view, she should remember that no one is too humble to be of possible service to her. In his chapter, "Taking Patronage Seriously" (in *Patronage, Art, and Society in Renaissance Italy*, ed. Kent and Simons, 29–65), Ronald Weissman makes the apposite comment: "In this world . . . one sought to deal whenever possible with patrons, clients, family, and friends, or, failing this, to convert all neutral relations, all necessary contacts with strangers, into ties of obligation, gratitude, and reciprocity" (44).

And all the more will you have to honor and cherish each one according to her rank in that you will not have the company of any of your own compatriots, and so it will be necessary for you to seek to win the love of all of them, in order to know that you can turn to them when need arises with the confidence that you would use toward ladies of your own region and as they might use toward one another. For he who loves and knows how to make himself loved can create compatriots, brothers, and sisters for himself wherever he goes, so potent is the power of love, indeed often the tie of friendship binds people together more tightly than ties of fatherland or blood.

In addition to the ladies-in-waiting and all the other ladies of the palace, it will behove you to be civil, courteous, and full of cordiality and affection toward the gentlewomen who will be visiting the court from time to time, either to pay their respects to your mistress or to call on some of you ladies in attendance and converse with you. This is in order that a good report should be spread of you not just in the palace but also outside it, and that wherever such ladies happen to be, they should have cause to commend your courtesy and good manners, and all the more so in that those Piedmontese ladies are of such good lineage that they put everyone under an obligation to do them honor; and in addition to their praise, you might reap some benefit from them on some future occasion, for someone who is away from home needs to acquire friends on all sides.[71] But just as no day is so beautiful and so calm that some little cloud cannot obscure the sun and disturb the atmosphere somewhat, although a mere puff of wind could blow it away and make the day brighter than ever, yet if the cloud should grow bigger, it cannot be dispelled so easily and often turns to rain and hail, in the same way no friendship is so calm and serene that some small cloud of vexation may not disturb the sun of its love, but this can be removed by the smallest waft of an affectionate little word, making the friendship brighter and calmer than ever, which is why people say that a quarrel between friends reinvigorates their love. But if on the other hand that cloud of animosity is allowed to grow not only does it disturb and darken the friendship but at times it leads to a torrent of hatred and a hailstorm of enmity. And so for this situation too I must needs prescribe you a suitable remedy, which is this: do not allow any cloud of anger or vexation that may arise between you and any of your female friends to last, for the longer it stays upon your chest, the more it swells in size, and so you must show straight away that you have forgotten all that has passed between your-

71. Guasco here extends a nice compliment to the ladies of Piedmont who would be coming to court to pay their respects to the infanta and her entourage, while at the same time reminding Lavinia that she needs to win their good opinion as well, since they, too, could be of use to her and to her reputation.

self and that companion and be the first to greet her, showing yourself more affectionate toward her than ever and, if the blame was yours, sorry for having been the cause of past unpleasantness, while if on the other hand she were the cause of the quarrel, showing that you harbor no ill feelings toward her. In this way, all the rancor she had been entertaining against you will at once vanish from your friend's heart, and she will come to love you more in the future than she did before, seeing that nothing can diminish the affection you bear her.[72]

There is one thing that has just come to my mind, which I very nearly forgot to mention but which I would not want to omit under any circumstances since it is of great importance, and it is this: that the law of friendship requires outspokenness and that friends should feel enough confidence to be able to express their opinions freely to one another, and here there are two things I need to warn you about: one is that if your companion has some matter to attend to or is not in the mood for a conversation, you should not pester her or take it amiss that she does not desire your company at that time; and the other is that you should allow your friend, just as she should allow you, to speak her mind on any matter in which she might deem you had behaved unbecomingly, and you must not take this as an insult but be grateful to her, not only if she should point out to you some misdemeanor of yours but should actually rebuke you for it, and you should thank her over and over again and encourage her to perform the same friendly office in the future, rather than allowing yourself to fall into error for want of it, to your great detriment and shame.[73] This is something you should accept not only from those older than yourself but also from younger girls as well and not take exception if someone younger than yourself should chide and rebuke you for some error, for no matter how young, that girl can see another's faults more clearly than the person committing them can, especially in matters in which she may have more experience than the other person, which she may well have, even though considerably junior to you, if she has been for some time in the service to which you are going at the present moment. And if you should pay this deference to your juniors, how much more should you pay it

72. This vivid extended image depicting friendship in terms of sunshine, and squabbles and enmity in terms of clouds and storms, is intended to impress on Lavinia's mind the importance of maintaining her friendships and making up a quarrel before it is too late. As Guy Fitch Lytle remarks in his essay, "Friendship and Patronage in Renaissance Europe," "Friendship was both a fundamental value and an essential social relationship during the Renaissance. It recurred constantly in essays, plays, poems, sermons, works of art, wills, and private letters" (47). Like Guasco, Castiglione offers his courtier much advice on how to succeed as a friend.

73. Castiglione's courtier, too, is exhorted to correct his defects in the light of his friends' advice (*The Courtier*, 139).

to your seniors and, especially, to those elderly matrons to whom belongs not only the care of the young women but also the authority not just to reprove them but also to give them orders; and while I am speaking of such matrons, let me tell you that since your mistress has given them authority over you and the other girls, it is your duty to respect and obey them as representatives of your mistress herself and to consider that whatever they command you to do is based on her orders. So not only must you do it because you cannot do otherwise, but you must do it with genuine cheerfulness, so that your readiness to obey can be seen on your face, rather than doing it with a melancholy look suggesting that you are obeying out of compulsion and not from love.

And among the ladies you will need to respect and obey will be Lady Sanchia, chief lady-in-waiting to the Infanta and in charge of all the other ladies, and with the said Lady Sanchia, both because of her authority and because of her goodness and also for the kind office she performed on your behalf with her mistress and, again, for the goodwill she displays toward us, you must endeavor to conduct yourself so humbly and respectfully, and to make her so satisfied with you, that she may know she performed her good office for someone who deserved it, and so that she may come to love you more day by day. Do not just wait for her to order you to do what you regard as your duty but do it without being asked and with every readiness, so that she may know that you revere and obey her not only for the authority she holds over you but also for her merits. When she sees this, she will hold you in far more affection than she would do for any other reason, since it is natural to all of us to take pleasure in the honors people pay us, which are as it were symbols of our virtue and merits and which delight us far more than being obeyed just due to the authority we hold over them. For this reason you must serve and revere that lady on every possible occasion, conducting yourself in her presence with the same modesty you would display if she were your absolute mistress and not dependent on another lady, and wherever you may need to speak of her, always do so with the greatest respect you can, and if she should rebuke you for some fault, show a humble and modest remorse for it, admitting rather than denying your error and then endeavoring not to commit a similar fault again in the future. In these ways you will come little by little to win over that lady's affections so that, day by day, she will try to acquire ever greater goodwill for you with your mistress, giving such testimony of your activities when she speaks of you that your mistress will grant you every favor and reward. The aforementioned other matrons will do the same, and not just they, but all the ladies-in-waiting, when the occasion arises to speak of you, and so will your mistress's court officers, who in the course of conversation will hear you spoken of and learn of the good name you have in the palace. As they are your mistress's most trusted officers, it will be your duty to revere them as their function demands but, most especially, Baron Sfondrato, whom you must fear and love as an overlord and as a father, both for his rank and for the authority he holds in the palace and also for his merits and because he is my most revered lord and the person responsible for your having been given your present appointment. And he, for the duty I pay him, and because you are at court as his protégée, and also because there is a certain family tie between us, will give you on all occasions that most efficacious and prudent help and advice he is able to give by dint of his authority and wisdom. Due to the special regard you will have for him, you will have to make every effort you can to succeed at court, conducting yourself according to all the advice I am setting out for you here and to that which will be given you by that Baron and by your other friends, so that as a reward for the efforts he has made on your and on my behalf in obtaining this court position for you, he may receive the pleasure and comfort of seeing that you are as he portrayed you to be to their most Serene Highnesses and as they are expecting you to be. And should any circumstance arise in which you need advice and help, have recourse freely to him, for in either eventuality you could not fasten your boat to any more secure anchorage than that.[74]

And in saying this, I am reminded of another point, which is that in matters in which you feel you are ignorant, do not be ashamed to seek advice from others, especially from your superiors, for it is far better to seek advice from others in order not to err than to err through not asking for advice. And this applies not only to you, who are still so very young, but to the wisest and most prudent of persons; indeed, their wisdom and prudence are made evi-

---

74. Guasco is here reminding Lavinia that in Baron Sfondrato he and she have a patronage relationship with one of the most distinguished figures at the court of Turin, placed there by Philip of Spain himself as that monarch's representative. Lavinia is the baron's *creatura*, she is there under his protection, bound to him by the huge favor he had done her in commending her to the duke and duchess, and she must seek to repay him as best she can, both by succeeding at court and by demonstrating the esteem in which she holds him by going to him for advice. See Mario Biagioli's discussion of the central importance of the patronage system in Renaissance society, in his *Galileo Courtier.* Biagioli stresses that social mobility and a successful career were impossible without utilizing the system, pointing out that it had "specific structural features and a logic that bound patrons, brokers, and clients through their need to circulate power in order to obtain or maintain it" (28). But for Guasco's family tie with the Sfondrati, it is doubtful whether a mere patrician like himself could have approached so eminent a powerbroker as the baron. Given, however, that this relationship existed, Guasco would have been encouraged in his initiative by his daughter's outstanding attainments since, as Biagioli points out, Renaissance patrons were like talent-spotters, "looking for potentially upwardly mobile clients in which to invest their connections" (24).

dent through their not relying just on their own opinions in important matters, for many eyes see better than one eye alone, and our passions are wont to deceive us in our own affairs and to make us see evil as good and good as evil, and hence good lawyers are wont to seek advice from others concerning their own personal disputes, and worthy doctors call in other doctors to cure their infirmities. Similarly families, cities, republics, and kingdoms are all guided by advice, to which we can add that he who bases his actions on the counsel of another, even if some ill should befall him as a result, can console himself that he has acted prudently and in accordance with the views of wise people. So take this recommendation from me and conduct yourself always according to sound advice, remembering that although I am myself offering you guidance here, I am only speaking in general terms, as I already told you, without being able to foresee the countless eventualities that may arise in which you will need to seek advice. And so you must have recourse freely in such matters to those who know more than you. For in addition to the benefit you will derive from conducting your actions with prudence, you will be considered discreet and unassuming, and so in this way also you will win over the hearts of the people from whom you have sought advice, since they will realize that you hold them in high esteem and will be gratified that you consider them qualified to advise you. And so you will put them under an obligation of love toward you, for we all have the desire in our hearts to be of such worth that another may rely upon us, and for this reason it gives us pleasure to be sought after by others and to be of use to them, for it seems to us that this results from our innate worth, which we love in ourselves more than any other thing. And if we like to feel we are being admired for what Fortune has bestowed upon us, how much more does it delight us to be admired for our moral qualities, as for example being held to possess so much counsel and wisdom that not only do we have sufficient for ourselves but enough to spare for other people.[75]

Moreover, this humility of yours in showing you wish to be guided by others will protect you against persecution and the fierce and furious envy of the court, for not even wild bears will attack a prostrate prey. And so (as I know I have already told you in another section of this discourse) you must counter the frenzy and poison of envy[76] with this sole antidote of humility, no less pleasing to God than to men, and with this holy virtue seek to make yourself loved by all, never pushing yourself forward nor laying claim to the best amenities and the first place,[77] but always giving way in both to the

75. Another of Guasco's perceptive comments on human psychology.

76. On the subject of envy at court, see above, n. 37.

77. Compare *The Courtier:* "He will succeed by never pushing in front of others to secure the first and most honored place" (139).

other girls, and outdoing them, if possible, in courtesy, for this is the greatest victory one can achieve in society. Remember that he who wants to leap the highest must retreat backward a few paces, and in the same way you will find that by recoiling from the prime honors, you will be the first to whom they will be granted, just as on the other hand, in trying to seize them, you will be one of the last to gain them.

But because up to now we have only discussed how you should avoid offending anyone by deeds or words but, rather, how you should use both to make yourself pleasing to all, it still remains for me to tell you that there are some things with which we do people neither honor nor injury, and yet they have the power to earn us both love and hatred, according to how we do them. These things are our habits, demeanor, and manners, and consequently you will have to devote much thought to them. If these are engaging and attractive, we can so win over the hearts of those with whom we are associating that, without doing anything actually to serve and honor them, we put them under an obligation to do whatsoever lies in their power for us, and by the reverse type of behavior we can acquire people's hatred even though we have done nothing at all to offend them. For this reason you will need to cultivate politeness and charm of manner as a gateway to people's favor,[78] and to note in the other ladies whatever seems to become them, endeavoring to copy it, and if there is anything in which they seem to be wanting, since it is impossible for anyone to achieve perfection in all respects, then you must avoid in yourself what you judge to be unbecoming in the others.[79]

To these pieces of advice it is not inappropriate that one more should be added before I leave this topic, and that is that you should endeavor to learn the Spanish language as quickly as you can, in that not only does a knowledge of different languages confer benefit and praise on him who possesses it but a proficiency in this language will be not just useful and praiseworthy but essential for you, since you are going to where the majority of people with whom you will have to associate are Spanish, and the longer you take to learn the language of that nation, the longer you will remain deprived of the delightful conversation of those Spanish ladies, which will be a source not only

---

78. Guasco clearly has in mind here the comments Castiglione makes in bk. 1 of *The Courtier* on the vital importance of grace in achieving social success: "So in addition to noble birth, I would have the courtier favored in this respect, too, and receive from Nature . . . that certain air and grace that makes him immediately pleasing and attractive to all who meet him" (55).

79. Compare the well-known passage in *The Courtier*: "It is very profitable for him to observe different kinds of courtiers and, ruled by the good judgement that must always be his guide, take various qualities now from one man and now from another. Just as in the summer fields the bees wing their way among the plants from one flower to the next, so the courtier must acquire this grace from those who appear to possess it and take from each one the quality that seems most commendable" (66–67).

of pleasure but also of profit for you, since you will learn a great deal from those shrewd ladies. And until you have mastered this said language, you will be under the disadvantage of not being able to form such close bonds of friendship with the aforementioned ladies-in-waiting as you would if you knew their language, since there is no more opportune means of binding our souls together than through verbal communication. Moreover, in addition to the pleasures of conversation that the knowledge of language brings, situations often arise when it is not sufficient just to be able to make oneself understood as best one can but when a really good command of a language is needed, as when, for instance, you are making a request or petitioning, persuading, or dissuading someone, excusing or defending yourself or another, reporting events or bearing messages, and employed in a hundred other similar necessities, and hence you will need to gain a really good competence in the aforementioned language, and all the more so in that your mistress is accustomed to use no other tongue, nor do I know how well she understands ours.[80] So while you are still in the process of learning that language, you will be deprived of the opportunity to converse with your mistress, a loss that cannot fail to be harmful to you, both for the comfort that staff are wont to receive when they converse with their employers and because an employer sometimes becomes attached to an employee through hearing them talking, and all the more so if they discourse with discretion and wit. I will set on one side the possibility that if you master the Spanish language, it would perhaps come about that, in view of the excellence of your handwriting, your mistress, as I told you, might decide to employ you as her secretary, which would redound greatly to your honor and reputation.[81] But I would like you, when you are learning it, to endeavor to master the elegant Castilian form of the language, in doing which you will be assisted by reading good Spanish books, especially the ones I have given you, in which the rules and idioms of Castilian speech are set out, and from these books you will gain this further advantage, which you would not be able to gain from just listening to other

80. The duke had apparently set to work to learn Spanish as soon as his marriage was arranged, but it seems from Guasco's comment that, initially at least, the infanta continued to converse in her native tongue in Turin, surrounded as she was by a large Spanish entourage. In consequence, little Lavinia had yet another challenge to meet upon her arrival at court, i.e., to acquire an almost instant fluency in a totally unfamiliar foreign language.

81. Here, with appropriate nonchalance, Guasco alludes to what is probably his most cherished hope for his daughter's court career, the objective that would doubtless have spurred him on through the many years of tedious labor spent helping her to acquire her calligraphic skills. In the handbook that Panfilo Persico wrote especially for the secretaries of princes, *Del Segretario Libri quattro* (Venice, 1620), the writer says that such court secretaries are greatly esteemed, due to the very special relationship they have with their prince who, in return for their love and loyalty, will confide his most secret thoughts and concerns to them, which will bind their two souls ever more closely together in a bond of friendship.

people speaking, which is that you will learn how to write, and write correctly, in that language, just as through listening to it, you will gain what your books could not teach you, namely, the pronunciation and intonation that this language requires, since each language has its own, which can only be learned orally. And to this you will need to apply much care and diligence, since without this proficiency no one can boast of having mastered the tongue in which he is speaking.

These then are the reminders that I feel I should give you for now under this heading, that is to say, regarding your manner of conversing with others, and for the rest I rely on those writers that I mentioned earlier to you who have written on this subject and on the expertise you will gradually obtain on your own and through being advised by others in the palace. And if you are content to observe these recommendations of mine, as indeed you must be, I can confidently guarantee you will acquire the favor of your mistress and the love of all her court.

8. *Concerning Your Treatment of Your Domestic Staff*

Since I consider that I have now fulfilled my intention and said all I need to say under this seventh heading, I shall now move on to the eighth and last, which concerns your relations with those whose duty it is to serve you, and here you must realize that it is one thing to serve out of love and another to serve for a wage. Hence it is that we see the husband being served by his wife, and the father and mother by their children, and in short any relation or friend by another, with a diligence and affection not displayed by hired servants toward their masters. And so one should do all one can to be served by the latter with love, which can be done by showing oneself (as far as the difference of rank allows), so amiable toward one's servants that their service is made sweet, even though by its nature it is bitter. Since everyone loves their freedom and only serves another out of necessity and need, the person who does not do as I have told you only receives from his servants that very minimum of service that they are obliged to give and is hated rather than loved by them, in such a way that this type of person is the living embodiment of the proverb that we have as many enemies as we have servants. In this respect princes have the advantage over us private citizens in that they are served by nobles, who vie with one another to gain honor through their service, each one seeking to serve better than another,[82] while we have to make do with

---

82. Compare Torquato Tasso: "The court, then, is a gathering for the sake of honor" ("Malpiglio; or, On the Court," in *Dialogues: A Selection, with the Discourse on the Art of the Dialogue.* trans. Carnes Lord and Dain A. Trafton [Berkeley and London, 1982], 165). (This dialogue was written the same year as the *Discourse.*)

being served by lowly people whose only motive for serving is the small wage they earn. It is for this reason that the old household servants always serve with greater love than do the newly-hired ones, since a long stay in your employers' house ends up by generating love and, hence, renders the services of such servants better than those of the others who are serving only for recompense. You must therefore treat your male and your female servants with such affection that they repay you with no less love than they do service, and here you will also apply the rule I spoke to you about earlier, which is to do to others as you would wish them to do to you. This is something that you will know very well how to do, in that since you yourself are going to serve, you must behave toward those who will be serving you in the same way as you would wish your mistress (taking into account the difference in rank) to show herself toward you. In addition, you must consider that the staff that your mother and I have given you will be serving you under the same terms as they served you at home, that is, in order that you should receive service and convenience from them but not so that you might adopt a high-handed manner toward them, for this is unacceptable in someone who does not know how to command, and he who does not know how to serve does not know how to command, and until one has served, as you have not yet done, one does not know about serving. Your manservant and your maid-servant will be serving you, therefore, as your father's employees or, rather, as those of your mistress, from whom they will receive their board and keep, and so you must give them their orders not as your very own personal servants but as dependent both on your mistress and on your mother and myself. Indeed, you should be aware that even if they were entirely dependent on you, it would be unseemly for you at such a very young age to adopt the sort of authoritative manner that is expected in those of more mature years, just as a matron's style of dress would not be fitting for you even though the dress itself is perfectly proper. And this consideration of one's age is of such importance that even those who become fathers at an early age seem not to have the same authority over their children when they grow up as do older fathers and as they ought to have as their natural right, and they must needs go to pains to insure by their conduct that they do not completely lose the respect their children owe them.

I wanted to cite you this example here so that you might understand that in order to preserve the reverence and respect of those serving you, it will be unseemly in you to assume the kind of authority and command that older people use toward their servants, for in addition to the respect that comes with age, it seems to those who are given orders by young people that the latter should be doing the serving rather than the commanding and that their orders are frequently presumptuous; this is partly due to their not knowing how to give orders and partly due to a vainglorious desire to show that they are the masters, as a result of which they are obeyed by their servants almost resentfully. So please give some thought to this reminder and insure that very often, instead of giving orders to your maid in your bedchamber, you carry out the tasks with your own hand, no less for the reasons I gave you above than to accustom yourself to every kind of situation in life and so as to be able to do things on your own, should you have no one on hand to serve you, and also to learn how to cope with a little inconvenience at certain times and in certain places. And in this connection it will do no harm for me to tell you that you should not insist on having every possible comfort that might be available and on being served in every smallest thing, but at times you should forgo the comforts you could have, in order not to find it irksome when you cannot have them, for this is something that will not only benefit you while you are in the household of another but also in your own household, when the time comes for you to run one, at which point it will be a great advantage if you have already learned how to deal in a proper manner with your ser-vants, who will serve you with greater respect and with greater love as a re-sult. Not only will this avail you at all times of your life, but it will be of the greatest benefit to you now, finding yourself as you do away from home while still so lacking in years and experience, a situation in which a loving and loyal domestic staff will be an enormous help to you. Moreover, not only would they not serve you in every eventuality with the same affection if you did not treat them well, but they could also do you harm, at least with their tongues, if in no other way. And one of the most important things to avoid in this con-text is insulting your staff, especially in front of other people; for in addition to the wrong you would be doing them and the ill-feeling that you would be generating in them against yourself, your staff, stung by the insult, might an-swer you back with words that could be far more damaging to you than your words to them, to your own great shame and to the scandal of anyone pre-sent, indeed to their anger, should they be of noble rank, at the lack of re-spect you showed them in insulting your servant in their presence. And not only must you avoid offending them, but also avoid getting involved in an ar-gument with them, especially with your maidservant, whom you will always have in your chamber, for this would be a contemptible action that would make you the laughingstock of the palace. And another thing you must avoid is acting too much like a sister toward your maidservant, for this too could lose you her respect and make others think you come of an inferior back-ground.[83]

83. Guasco's practical and perceptive comments in this section of the *Discourse* offer Lavinia some sound advice on how she should behave toward her domestic staff of two and on how best

VALEDICTION

It does not seem to me that there is anything else I need say to you in this connection, and so I have arrived at the end of the discourse I have been writing for you while your mother is getting your luggage ready for your departure, and while she, your uncle, and I are making our preparations to accompany you.[84] It only remains, my child, that you should be content to insure that these words of mine, which I have written down for you with tears of tenderness, should remain so fixed in your mind that you never ever forget them. And furthermore I must ask two favors of you, the first, that when you arrive in Turin, you should undertake to read this discourse of mine at least once a month, imagining that you have your father at your side intoning the words into your ears with all the vigor and energy generated by the love he bears you, and the second, that since I have no other copy of this manuscript I am giving you, you should be pleased to make me a copy of it in your own hand, as and when your time permits, thus impressing it on your mind all the better.[85] And I shall wait for you to send your copy to me here and shall hold it as a pledge on your part of your intention to act in accordance with all the instructions it contains, if not in the interests of your own duty and honor, then at least for the sake of the love you bear me and your desire to satisfy me, or at least to compensate me for the inconvenience to which your mother and I are putting ourselves, she pregnant and near to giving birth, and I in poor health, in accompanying you on this journey of yours, on such snowy

---

to maintain a mean between, on the one hand, being peremptory and overbearing with them and, on the other, being too familiar. By reminding his daughter that she, too, is in the service of another, Guasco is trying to help her to appreciate her servants' situation better, while also underlining the danger it could do her reputation at court if she offends her staff. There appears to be no antecedent in Italian Renaissance literature for Guasco's detailed discussion here on the management of servants.

84. Guasco makes an interesting allusion to this impending journey in his first volume of letters. The letter is addressed to the archbishop of Turin, and in it Guasco entreats this prelate's assistance in enabling him to find good accommodation in that city when he brings Lavinia to court. Guasco will be accompanied not only by the immediate family members mentioned here in the text but also by "a large company of attendants" [*una grossa brgate, che sarà con noi*]. And so far he has failed to accommodate them, due to Turin's severe lack of lodging places. He is greatly hoping that the archbishop can arrange for them to borrow his sister-in-law's large townhouse, situated as it is conveniently close to the palace, since she is at her country residence at present. Clearly Guasco was intending to stage something of a triumphal entry into the city with his large party to mark this auspicious family occasion. (Annibal Guasco, "A Monsig. della Rovere, Arcivescovo di Turino, che fù poi Cardinale," in *Lettere: Di nuovo aggiuntavi in questa nostra seconda impressione la seconda parte delle Lettere dell'istesso Auttore* [Treviso, 1603], p. 70).

85. As Lavinia's foreword shows, she neatly sidesteps this onerous task by getting her father's work published, instead of transcribing it laboriously by hand.

roads and in so dreadful a winter.[86] But the fact that you are undertaking this journey readily, freely abandoning your own region and this paternal household where you were born and brought up with such love and tenderness, seems to me like a good omen, and I believe that just as fire naturally leaves the spot here below where it was kindled and soars upward to where it will perhaps find its own perfection awaiting it,[87] so your desire to benefit yourself prompts you to go willingly to Her Highness in order to earn profit and honor from so doing. And I am assuredly convinced that you will do so, if you follow all the advice I have laid down for you in these pages and that your mother and I have so often recalled to your mind. Let us be on our way then, my daughter, and may God in His goodness preserve us on our journey and give you His blessing, just as your mother and I give you ours.

86. Guasco's anxiety regarding the journey they were about to undertake from Alessandria to Turin, although only a distance of some fifty miles, was understandable: by this time most of the old Roman roads in Italy had deteriorated, and new roads, where there were any, were not being maintained, since the peasants objected to undertaking this labor. Guasco and his family would clearly have been traveling by carriage, and the bad roads and narrow bridges made such transport extremely difficult. On horseback a traveler could cover twenty to twenty-five miles a day but by carriage considerably less.

87. This Neoplatonic image, with its Dantean overtones, is taken from Speroni (*Dialogo*, 77). Just as a flame soars naturally upward to seek its perfection in the sphere of transcendent realities, so Cornelia goes readily to her future husband, in whom she will find her happiness and perfection. Similarly, Lavinia's eagerness to exchange her home for the new and more exalted sphere of the court augurs well for the success of her stay there. Both girls are, as it were, impelled by their aspiring natures to leave the parental home in pursuit of their own advancement and benefit.

APPENDIX

GUASCO'S CORRESPONDENCE AS A REFLECTION
OF HIS FAMILY LIFE

Guasco wrote three volumes of letters, which he published in 1603, 1607, and 1618, respectively.[1] Rather than arranging his letters chronologically, Guasco in each case groups them, undated, into categories, under a series of headings such as "Of Congratulation," "Of Thanks," "Of Consolation," and "Of Exhortation." Many of these missives are addressed to distinguished nobles and prelates and are couched in purely formal and conventional terms, complimenting his correspondents on some honor received, commiserating with them on a family bereavement, requesting a favor, and so on, and reveal little more about the writer himself than his impressively wide circle of notable correspondents. However, interspersed with such letters as these are a number of others that are far more personal in character, recounting family events to his closest friends and relatives. In contrast with the exhortatory and anxious tone of the *Discourse*, we here see Guasco in more relaxed mode, enjoying relating and commenting on the happenings of his family life and especially on the achievements of his children and, at a later stage, on those of his grandchildren. As his favorite child, Lavinia's name recurs frequently in such letters, and Guasco delights in including her greetings alongside his own whenever he writes to a mutual acquaintance.

Although seventeen years had elapsed between Lavinia's departure for

1. Annibal Guasco, *Lettere: Di nuovo aggiuntavi in questa nostra seconda impressione la seconda parte delle Lettere dell'istesso Auttore* ([Treviso, 1603], the first, incomplete volume having been published in 1601 by Ponzio and Piccaglia [Milan]), *Il secondo volume delle lettere del signor Annibal Guasco Alessandrino* (Alessandria, 1607), and *Lettere del signor Annibal Guasco Alessandrino, con alcune sue Rime secondo le occasioni accompagnate alle lettere* (Pavia, 1618). These three volumes of letters have never been translated into English, and all excerpts quoted from them are my translations. It should be noted that, in his letters, Guasco variously—and inconsistently—uses the titles "Signor" or "Signora" and the abbreviations "Sig." or "Sign."; care has been taken to reproduce these exactly as they appear in the original.

the court of Turin and the publication of her father's first complete volume of letters, this fortunately contains copies of missives her father had written regarding his daughter at a much earlier date, which provide a valuable background commentary to the *Discourse.* In one such letter Guasco states that Lavinia is only seven years old, so consequently he must have written it in 1581, a year after the succession of the new young duke, Carlo Emanuele, to his duchy. The letter is of great interest in that it shows that Guasco was already, at this early stage in his daughter's childhood, seeking to bring her skills to the notice of the duke, presumably in order to pave the way to obtaining a court appointment for her once the latter had taken a wife: Guasco tells his correspondent that he had written a *canzone* for the duke to celebrate his recent recovery from the plague, which his small daughter had transcribed for him in her beautiful calligraphic hand, and that the duke had expressed "gracious pleasure and agreeable amazement when he learned the age and sex of the writer."[2]

Another four years were to elapse before the marriage of the duke to the Infanta Caterina took place, and the duke did not arrive back in his duchy from Spain with his bride until August 1585. However, Guasco must have received the eagerly desired offer of a court appointment well before that date, since in his reply to the news he states that Lavinia had not yet turned eleven, which means the letter must have been written prior to June 13, 1585. Baron Sfondrato—ambassador to Philip II of Spain at the court of Turin and a distant relative of Guasco's, due to whose good offices, we learn from the *Discourse,* Lavinia had been brought to the notice of the ducal pair as a young girl of exceptional talent—had written to convey the good tidings to Guasco and his wife, and Guasco's reply reflects the spontaneous delight with which they had all three received the news:

> I am greatly rejoiced by the account that your Excellency has sent me in your letter just received, that Her Most Serene Highness has accepted my daughter into her service as lady-in-waiting, and I am at a loss for words to convey the pleasure it gives her mother and me. I can only say that although this daughter is our life and soul, the thought of parting with her in order to give her to Her Highness caused us no pain. And I trust Your Excellency will understand that this is no small admission, since my love for her is an immoderate passion. But there is no controlling these paternal excesses. With regard to what you write of the testimony you have given Their Highnesses of the child's merits, be assured that they will not be disappointed in her, for here I know pa-

---

2. "Al Signor Giuliano Goselini" (*Lettere* [1603], 35).

ternal affection does not deceive me. I send you my warmest thanks for all your assistance and beg you to convey my respects to Their Serene Highnesses and to kiss their hands on my behalf to thank them for the position they are giving my daughter, and, God willing, I shall shortly come in person to do the same, and to express my obligation to Your Excellency for your kind offices. On that occasion I will be guided by your views and advice regarding how and when to bring my daughter to take up her post. For her part, not only does she show no reluctance at the thought of having to leave her mother and father, but her heart is so full of eagerness to get there that I predict that it will be greatly to her advantage, all the more so in view of the affection Your Excellency reports Their Highnesses have shown in accepting her, and in view of Her Majesty's special dispensation, in addition to her initial agreement, regarding her appointment. May it please the Lord in His goodness so to assist such hopeful portents with His grace that an even better outcome may result from so good a beginning."[3]

The baron had done his work well, as the letter states, and Lavinia is to be given a reduction in the heavy fees normally payable by the family of a girl taking up a place as a lady-in-waiting [*dama d'onore*] in the palace, which would have been beyond Guasco's means.

In another letter to the baron, which must have been dispatched soon after the previous one, Guasco writes that he is enclosing a *canzone* he has composed in celebration of the duke's nuptials, which he begs him to pass on to the duke and which he proudly states has once again been copied out in her very best italic hand by "my dear little secretary, Your Excellency's protégée and through your agency destined for that palace." He continues: "With me she asks the favor that you will inform the Lord Duke not only who composed it but also who copied it out, and may His Highness condescend to take into account the fact that she has still only reached the tender age of ten years and that during this short span of her life she has been kept occupied in acquiring many other skills that have earned her a measure of praise. May Your Excellency forgive this imposition and be so kind as to let me know, at your own convenience, how His Highness receives this composition."[4] The

3. "Al Sig. Barone Sfondrato, Ambasciatore del Rè Catolico, presso l'Altezza di Savoia" (*Lettere* [1603], 180).

4. Ibid., 57. These letters also shed light on the patronage system obtaining at this time. As a fairly lowly client, belonging to the patrician class, and not to the nobility, Guasco could not possibly have approached such mighty princes as the dukes of Savoy directly, or through a patron of only slightly superior standing to himself, regarding so important a matter as a post at court for his daughter; instead, his only hope was to utilize his ties with a powerbroker as out-

visit Guasco had stated in his previous letter to the ambassador that he would be making to Turin had now taken place, for Guasco speaks here of the duke's goodness and charm, which had left such an impression on him that, on returning home, he felt inspired to write these same verses "on so glorious a topic." Here again we see Guasco communicating with the duke in the correct manner via this powerful intermediary, whom he can also use to convey and to gain vital information.

Perhaps because it would have been considered disrespectful and inappropriate to do otherwise, only one of Guasco's published letters contains an allusion to Lavinia while she was actually employed in the palace. This is to be found in a missive addressed to Guasco's friend and distinguished fellow writer, Stefano Guazzo, thanking him for sending him a volume of his letters that had recently been published. In this letter of Guasco's we learn that he had been visiting the palace and had already spent a month there. He had taken Guazzo's volume with him to show to Lavinia, and she and her companions have been reading it with great pleasure. He adds that she is greatly obliged for the honor Guazzo did her by mentioning her in some of these letters.[5]

As a caring and responsible parent, it was incumbent on Guasco to find a suitable match for his daughter as she entered her late teens but, having done so successfully, it was also essential for him to obtain permission for the marriage from Lavinia's employers, to whom she was primarily answerable. Now that his daughter had been at court for several years, Guasco could dispense with intermediaries and approach the duke on the matter directly, which he does as follows:

> This letter comes to convey my respects to Your Highness and to inform you that a few months ago, God sent us an offer of a match for Lady Lavinia, my daughter, which I considered suitable for her in view of the rank of the said person and his worldly means. Count Guido Emanuel Langosco, a knight of Pavia, is the person in question who, if it should please Your Excellency to confirm the Infanta's consent and the wishes of the young pair, will not, I am sure, disappoint you nor displease you as a new retainer, and so both he, Lady Lavinia and myself all rely on Your Excellency's magnanimous goodness to favor and help us in this matter.[6]

---

standing as the ambassador, especially in view of the fact that Guasco was seeking a job offer with special terms attached. Having done so successfully, Guasco is able, as we see here and in subsequent letters, to embark tentatively on a highly deferential relationship with the duke himself.

5. "Al Sig. Stefano Guazzo" (*Lettere* [1603], 79). See my introduction (35) for Guazzo's reference to Lavinia.

6. "Al Sereniss. Sig. Duca di Savoia" (*Lettere* [1603], 84).

From subsequent letters we learn that Baron Sfondrato's brother, Nicolò Sfondrato, had by now been elected to the Holy See, succeeding Urban VII as Pope Gregory XIV, which dates Guasco's letters fairly precisely between December 5, 1590, and October 16, 1591, in which case the duke would have been away in the south of France on a prolonged military campaign. Nevertheless, the latter was apparently prepared to find time to dispatch his consent for Lavinia's marriage to the young knight, for in another letter we find Guasco writing to Cardinal Paolo Camillo Sfondrato, son of Guasco's patron the baron and nephew to the Pope, informing him that Lavinia's ducal employers have now approved the match but that the family still needs a dispensation for a link of consanguinity proscribed by the church that exists between the young pair. Guasco describes Lavinia as a protégée of the baron (who is now dead) and adds, "it befell your father to give her her dowry through placing her with Her Most Serene Highness, and now it falls to His Holiness your uncle to give her a husband."[7] Guasco describes his future son-in-law as being of the highest integrity and extremely wealthy. In a subsequent letter to the master of the bedchamber of Pope Gregory XIV, Guasco states that the cardinal himself had dispensed this link of consanguinity, so the marriage can now go ahead, and he adds, "I would ask Your Excellency this favor, to be so kind as to kiss His Holiness's foot on my behalf, and to mention this marriage to him, for I am quite sure that in his goodness he will derive pleasure from hearing of it, due to our mutual relationship and my desire to serve him, and to the affection he has always shown both to the daughter and to the father." He also says the young couple request a papal blessing on their marriage.[8]

Although officially affianced to Guido Langosco before the end of the year 1590, Lavinia was still dependent on her ducal employers to decide when her wedding could take place, and this was not to be until the very end of 1591, in order that both the duke and the duchess might be able to attend it. It says a great deal for the regard and affection in which Lavinia was held by the ducal pair that they both insisted on being present. However, the long engagement in which this resulted, combined with the infanta's rigorous moral regime, seems to have created tensions for Guido and Lavinia, for we find Guasco writing to a lady friend who is in touch with the duke's movements: "Count Guido writes to me with great vehemence that he has returned from Turin with the thirst that he took there to visit his fiancée and to speak with her still unassuaged, since the Infanta would not permit him to see

7. "Al Sig. Cardinale Sfondrato" (*Lettere* [1603], 84–85).
8. "Al Sig. Fabrizio Berzi, Maestro di Camera di Gregorio XIIII" (*Lettere* [1603], 85–86). Nicolò Sfondrato became Pope Gregory XIV in December 1590 and died in October 1591.

her. I would dearly like to know when we can hope that the Lord Duke will be back in Turin, at whose coming the count is hoping to satisfy this thirst of his."[9]

The wedding was in fact finally held in Nice, where the infanta went to be reunited with her husband after his return there from his unsuccessful campaign in Provence. Lavinia was apparently permitted to accompany her mistress there in preparation for her wedding, while it fell to Guasco to escort the bridegroom to join the royal entourage in Nice. We find Guasco writing in high spirits to inform an old friend and neighbor, Hercole Grimaldi, lord of Monaco, that the opportunity to pay him a long-awaited visit has finally arisen:

> And what opportunity is this? Do you still recall, Sir, little Lavinia my daughter, who was being brought up in her childhood with so much care by her father in Pavia, while you and I were living so close to one another in that city? It is now nearly seven years since I gave her as lady-in-waiting to the Infanta, Lady Caterina, in whose palace this young woman has been such a success that one could not have wished for better, to the great satisfaction of Their Highnesses and of all their household. Last year she was betrothed to Count Guido Langosco by her mistress the Infanta, with my consent, and the wedding has been postponed until now, while the return of the Lord Duke to his states was being awaited.[10]

The duchess arrived in Nice on December 27, 1591, and the wedding of Lavinia and Count Guido Langosco must have taken place there within the next four days, since Francesco Guasco states in his genealogical table of the Langosco family that the count married Lavinia in 1591.[11] Guasco goes on to inform Grimaldi in the same letter that the wedding has just been solemnized and that he and the newly wedded pair had left Nice three days ago "after receiving many kindnesses from that princely couple and many tokens of their gratitude for the service of this lady-in-waiting."[12] He adds that he and they are all now in Villafranca and will shortly be sailing past Grimaldi's castle, where they hope to visit him. We later learn that the wedding in Nice was in fact a double ceremony and that Lavinia's young companion and friend in the service of the infanta, Lady Orintia Langosca, had been married on the same

9. "Alla Signora Adriana Gromis" (*Lettere* [1603], 93).

10. "Al Sign. Hercole Grimaldi, Sig. di Monaco" (*Lettere* [1603], 96).

11. Francesco Guasco, *Tavole genealogiche di famiglie nobili Alessandrine e Monferrine dal Secolo XI al XX* (Monferrato, 1939), vol. 11, table 1, "Famiglia Langosco."

12. "Al Sign. Hercole Grimaldi, Sig. di Monaco" (96).

occasion to a certain Count Giacopo, for in a subsequent letter he writes to Orintia's father, Count Alfonso Langosco della Motta, Guasco states of the two girls that "just as they had been companions in the service of Her Most Serene Highness, so the wedding of that lady was conducted together with that of my daughter, in the same house of Their Highnesses, with the same ceremonies, and at the same time."[13]

The visit to Grimaldi duly took place, for in a subsequent letter to his old friend, Guasco thanks him for the lavish hospitality that Grimaldi had bestowed on them, a detailed report of which had been sent by them to their ducal patrons, and goes on to describe the terrible storm they had encountered after sailing from Monaco, which had caused unimaginable sufferings to Lavinia, who was a poor sailor. They had finally reached home safely four days after disembarking at Oneglia, to find that the whole city of Alessandria had turned out to meet them with great solemnity and joy. Guasco himself was thankful to be able to rest at last, since he tells his friend he had been in constant pain during his travels from "that agonizing affliction of mine" (evidently some malady he had already mentioned to Grimaldi).[14]

The next news we have of Lavinia is conveyed in a flurry of excited letters from Guasco to his friends announcing the arrival of his first grandchild. Lavinia has been safely delivered of a baby son, Carlo (clearly named for Duke Carlo Emanuele), and Guasco writes that not only is the baby too beautiful for words, but also "so considerate in his arrival that he did little harm to his mother, so as not to be ungrateful to her for bringing him into the light of day."[15] Guasco adds that he is experiencing "that happiness which my affection for this daughter and the gift God has bestowed on me through her call for."[16] From another letter we learn that Lavinia's mother had been very ill with a high fever just before Carlo was due, so much so that they had feared for her life. Lavinia had nursed her day and night despite the advanced stage of her pregnancy, and Guasco says he had been almost out of his mind with anxiety. Fortunately, the baby had discretely delayed his arrival, and Lavinia's mother, though still very weak, had been able to assist her daughter at the birth. Even now she had not fully recovered from the *catarro* which had prevented her from sleeping, and she would be purged in two days' time.[17] Guasco makes the interesting comment, when writing his news to one of the

---

13. "Al Sig. Conte Alfonso Langosco della Motta" (*Lettere* [1603], 105).

14. "Al Sign. Hercole Grimaldi, Sig. di Monaco" (97–98).

15. "Al Signor Filippo Pirovano" (*Lettere* [1603], 112).

16. Ibid.

17. "Alla Signora Donna Mariana de Tassis" (*Lettere* [1603], 110).

infanta's senior ladies-in-waiting, Lady Beatrice di Mendozza, that Lavinia had borne her labor pangs "with a great patience, learned from Her Most Serene mistress in similar situations."[18] Guasco writes to Grimaldi that the child is more beautiful than gold, that Lavinia has had a good delivery and is very well, and that the duke and duchess have become his godparents by means of two proxies who stood in for them at the christening.[19] To another friend he says that the ducal pair have expressed the greatest delight at the news of the birth.[20]

From various allusions to little Carlo in Guasco's letters, it would appear that he was being brought up mainly in his grandparents' house, with a resident wet nurse, where his parents spent frequent extended visits.[21] Certainly Guasco seems to be in touch with his day-to-day progress. He tells Countess Zanna Langosca, "My very own Carlo is developing extremely well, but he fights all day long to free his hands from the tyranny of these swaddling-bands, although the poor little wretch will not have his way for another two months."[22] In a touching letter to one of the infanta's Spanish ladies-in-waiting, Lady Marianna, Guasco responds to the question she had put to him via Lavinia, as to which is the greater love, that which one feels for one's children or that for one's grandchildren: he replies that the two loves are inseparable, and each intensifies the other: "My love for Lady Lavinia makes me love her child, and my love for the child makes me love her all the more, and my loving her the more makes me love her child the more."[23] He adds that no grandfather could possibly feel greater love for his grandchild than he does, stemming as it does from his unparalleled love for the mother.

Despite domestic cares and pregnancies, Lavinia had by no means severed her connections with the court of Turin, for we are told that she had written home during one of these visits to ask for Carlo's measurements. Was she perhaps planning to weave him some small garment? In a letter to Lady Beatrice di Mendozza, another of the infanta's entourage, Guasco states that he had been on the point of sending her these measurements when tragedy

---

18. "Alla Signora Donna Beatrice di Mendozza, Dama della Serenissima Infanta" (*Lettere* [1603], 113).

19. "Al Signor Hercole Grimaldi, Signor di Monaco" (123).

20. "Al Sig. Bonifacio Pozzi" (*Lettere* [1603], 114).

21. Despite the thunderous rebukes of preachers and moralists, the women of upper-class Italy seldom, if ever, breastfed their babies at this time. Instead, they either sent them out to be nursed in the countryside by peasant women or, if sufficiently wealthy, as in Lavinia's case, employed a wet-nurse in the household.

22. "Alla Sig. Contessa Zanna Langosca" (*Lettere* [1603], 128).

23. "Alla Signora Donna Marianna de Tassis" (120).

had struck the family, for he tells her that the little boy "has all of a sudden grown so much and beyond all our expectations that his height cannot be measured by human means, in that he has arrived in Heaven, to which he soared in a great flight yesterday morning, the Sunday before Lent, so as to refresh Paradise and make a happy carnival up there with his little angel companions."[24]

The playfulness of Guasco's tone does nothing to mask the violence of his grief, indeed he adds that he is too distressed to hold a pen and is having to dictate this letter from his bed, unable even to hold his head up: "This *festa* of his has left this household in the floods of tears that your Ladyship can well imagine. It is perhaps fortunate that Lady Lavinia is in Turin, where she will have the affection of the entire palace to sustain her."[25] She is due to give birth again in three months' time and Guasco begs Lady Beatrice to do all she can to comfort her. He also beseeches her to ask the infanta to stretch out a helping hand to Lavinia and use her authority with the bereaved young mother to bring her some comfort. In another letter, to Lady Marianna de Tassis, Guasco says he would have died of grief had it been possible to do so, and he movingly evokes the mischievous little boy, who still seems present to him in all his exuberance and vitality:

> There is not a corner in this house where I do not seem to see him, nor does a moment pass when he does not appear before me with one of his little pranks. Now I see him in my mind gazing at the pigeon, now at the little garden, now he is ringing the garden bell, now he is playing one game, now another, now he is coming toward me laughing, now he follows me with his eyes as I go away from him, and seems to be calling me back to him as he used to do when he was alive: and with these sweet and yet bitter little tricks of his he tears my heart apart. . . . Your Ladyship will say that I am mad and that it is unseemly in a man in my position so to give way to my feelings, and I confess it, but I do not know how to endure it.[26]

He adds that no matter how much he tries to enlist his reason to restrain his emotions, he finds that he is unable to do so. This letter is singular for the deep and spontaneous grief it conveys, taken against the background of a period when infant deaths were a common occurrence in most families and when men of social standing and education were expected to endure be-

24. "Alla Sig. Donna Beatrice di Mendozza" (160–61).
25. Ibid.
26. "Alla Sig. Donna Marianna de Tassis (162).

reavement with stoicism, but clearly Guasco was not a typical man of his time in this respect. He then writes to try to console Carlo's grieving mother, reminding her that her parents, too, had lost their first-born son as well as three other little angels [*angioletti*] but that God had consoled them with other offspring of both sexes, "and you know just how much pleasure we take in one of these female offspring."[27] In a letter to a male friend, Guasco touchingly says that he had loved Carlo more than himself, "being the most delightful, the sweetest and the most lovable creature that ever came down from heaven," yet to Lady Marianna de Tassis he writes that "Lavinia must now dispose herself to forget her first Carlo and devote herself to nurturing the second, unborn, Carlo whom she has been carrying for the last six months."[28] Meanwhile, Lavinia's mother, whose extreme piety at times causes Guasco some anxiety, has for once agreed not to fast during this Lent, presumably in order to recover better from this terrible shock.

It was now Lavinia's task to supply her husband with a son and heir to replace little Carlo, and this did not prove easy. One daughter, Margherita, (named, no doubt, after the infanta's eldest girl, born not long after Lavinia's arrival at court), had arrived since the birth of Lavinia's first son, and the child she was expecting when the news reached her of Carlo's death also proved to be a girl, as was a subsequent baby. Before long she was pregnant yet again, and the hopes of her husband and grandparents were focused upon the outcome of this pregnancy.

Of Lavinia's three daughters, the first, Margherita, seems to have been Guasco's favorite, and he frequently mentions her in his letters by name, unlike the other two girls whose names are barely mentioned. Guasco is clearly fond of them all but cannot entirely forgive the younger two for not having been males. He remarks in one letter that daughters are a lesser good [*minor bene*] than sons. However, he reports affectionately on their progress. Of one he writes to his mother-in-law, "Lady Lavinia's little girl is perfectly beautiful, she is already eating like a horse and up till now she has cut her teeth without too much discomfort."[29] It was during the course of her fifth pregnancy that

27. "Alla Contessa Donna Lavinia sua figliuola" (*Lettere* [1603], 166).

28. The first letter is "Al Sig. Gio. Giorgio Giuliani" (*Lettere* [1603], 164); the second is "Alla Signora Donna Marianna de Tassis" (163). Compare Margaret L. King's apposite comment in her chapter, "The Woman of the Renaissance," in *Renaissance Characters*, ed. Eugenio Garin; trans. Lydia C. Cochrane (Chicago and London: University of Chicago Press, 1991): "The apprehension of child death hovered over birth. The newborn child may have been looked upon by Renaissance mothers as a transitory being in whom only a tentative if powerful affection could be invested" (210). The common custom of giving a subsequent child of similar sex the same Christian name as a dead offspring, as indeed we find Lavinia herself doing, seems to support such a view.

29. "Alla Sig. Veronica Bellona" (*Lettere* [1603], 226).

news reached Lavinia of another tragedy, this time of far-reaching implications, namely, the death of her former mistress, the infanta, who died on November 7, 1597, aged barely thirty-one, giving birth to her tenth child. Initially the news was concealed from Lavinia, since she herself was sick and about to give birth, but Guasco tells a friend that Lavinia's mother had gone three or four days ago to assist her and will be forced to break the news to her. Her presence would help to soften its impact, but Guasco comments: "For all that, I cannot imagine how the poor girl will have been able to stand up to this blow, and I feel sure that all the circumstances I have already mentioned, the very special role she played toward her lost mistress, and the love she bore her will have deprived her of her reason."[30] Guasco then writes a letter of consolation to Lavinia herself, describing the infanta's death as an earthquake, bringing down many buildings, but he says pragmatically that Lavinia must take some comfort from the fact that she herself is no longer employed in the palace and that it is now some considerable time since she left there, with so high a reputation and, in addition, the favor of Their Highnesses,

> by whom you and your husband were so well rewarded for your service that if you do your reckonings properly, you can call yourself privileged over all the other ladies, thanks to the grace of God; and in particular you are more fortunate than those who have remained there like lost sheep, deprived of so benign a mistress and shepherdess. May God be praised then for the role that it fell to you to play in the life of Her Highness, which must be attributed to the prayers with which the undertaking was commended to God, though we did not then anticipate the favor that has been shown to you.[31]

Now imminently expecting her fifth child, Lavinia had fallen gravely ill and was so weak that her parents feared she would not survive the pangs of labor. No doubt the shock of learning of the infanta's death, also in childbed, had not improved her situation. Guasco's letters become ever more despair-

30. "Al Sig. Gio. Giorgio Giuliani" (313). In the letter Guasco writes to his friend Giovanni Giorgio Giuliani regarding this sad event, he describes the infanta as one of the greatest princesses of all time, whose virtues and abilities could well be emulated by great men. She was so well loved by her people, and had ruled her states with such care and wisdom, that her husband the duke was freed from all worries. Guasco also laments the fact that her sister and aged father will never now see her again.

31. "Alla Contessa Donna Lavinia sua figliuola" (*Lettere* [1603], 314–15). This highly significant letter, the veracity of which can hardly be doubted since Guasco allowed it to be published, testifies not only to the great success of Lavinia's court career but also to the fact that she was privileged over and above the other court ladies in the role she played vis-à-vis her mistress. It seems highly probable, therefore, taking into account various other such allusions that her father proudly makes in his letters, that she did indeed achieve the coveted position of secretary to the infanta that Guasco had held up to her in the *Discourse* as representing her ultimate goal.

ing in tone, and the reader expects to be informed from one page to the next that Lavinia has followed her mistress to heaven.[32] But, almost miraculously, she survives the birth, aided by her mother who had flown to her side, and this time the long-awaited boy child arrives. Guasco's delight knows no bounds. He writes to his son-in-law: "Upon my word, Count, you will be impossible to live with now that you have finally discovered how to produce males after so many female children. But if it were possible to measure happiness, I do not know who would be the winner, the father or the grandfather."[33] His jubilation then gives way to solicitude for his beloved daughter's well-being: "The mother needs to rest now, and so since she has restored to you the son that you lost, do not be in such a hurry to molest her as you usually are, but above all endeavor to preserve her health after the birth, and guard her from every disorder, so that with God's help her recovery will be as satisfactory as her labor was."[34]

Although Lavinia plays the starring role in her father's letters, Guasco does also make references to the activities of three of her siblings. We learn that the eldest son and heir, Francesco, who had graduated in jurisprudence at Pavia, acquitted himself well when being examined for his doctorate in Rome; we also hear of the second son, Cesare, when he is about to enter the church, and of Lavinia's younger sister, Caterina, when taking the veil to become Suor Laura Caterina in the convent in Alessandria where she had been educated. Guasco writes a long and detailed account of her *monacazione* in a letter to Francesco, in which he describes how Lavinia, married and pregnant with her third child, had assisted her sister to prepare for the solemn ceremony:

> The morning of the said day, Lady Lavinia acted as lady's maid to her sister, the bride of Christ, and using all the art of the palace where Lady Lavinia was brought up, she applied every possible skill to her adornment, elaborately curling those locks, as fair as gold, that were destined that day for the scissors, and weaving a beautiful garland of flowers and precious stones to place on her head. She dressed her in rich garments, bedecking her neck and bosom with many more jewels, and thus adorned with all these embellishments and with her own nat-

32. In a letter to his son Francesco, Guasco relates that Lavinia is in childbed and that he is awaiting the outcome in the remotest room in the house, "not, as you know, being able to endure a proximity to those I love when they are in these torments" ("A Francesco suo figliuolo" [*Lettere* (1603)], 263–64).

33. "Al Sig. Conte Guido Langosco suo Genero" (*Lettere* [1603], 317).

34. Ibid.

ural charms, she emerged from her chamber more beautiful and more dazzling than the sun, while each moment seemed a thousand years to her until she could appear before her Lord in that array and change it for love of Him.[35]

Her proud father adds: "And that day her beauty was so radiant that she eclipsed all the other women who were accompanying her, who must have numbered at least a hundred, between married ones and maidens."[36]

Although a mere patrician with no claim to a noble title, it is clear from Guasco's account of the pageantry connected with his daughter's taking of the veil, that the central events in the lives of his family were treated as public spectacles by their fellow citizens of Alessandria. After the ceremony the great door of the convent is flung open and the young novice is led out, her hair shorn and dressed in her nun's habit, "all happy and laughing and looking so beautiful in her altered garb that she even excelled her previous appearance."[37] In an emotional scene she asks her father for his blessing, which he tearfully bestows on her, and she then embraces Lavinia, who bursts into floods of tears. This is all too much for Laura Caterina, who herself begins to cry, and begs her sister to desist or people will think she is unhappy to be entering the cloister. Writing to his mother-in-law a short time after this event had taken place, Guasco tells her that the young novice is now living in her convent so lightheartedly and joyously that she feels as if she were in Paradise and that all the sisters adore her for her goodness.[38]

Guasco's second volume of letters, which was published four years after the first one, represents a period of relative calm and serenity both in his life and in Lavinia's. Although still only in her early thirties, Lavinia appears not to have fallen pregnant again after the first volume of letters was published, so there are no more reports of difficult labors, nor harrowing accounts of infant deaths. She is able to enjoy the company of her brood of five living small children and the companionship of her affectionate and supportive husband, both in Milan, where the main Langosco residence seems to have been, and at their country villa, where Guasco was a frequent visitor, leaving his care-ridden and stay-at-home wife to cope with the running of his own estates and business affairs. He speaks of the great joy he derived during such visits from the company of his beloved daughter, his son-in-law, and his young grandchildren, with whom he seems to have been a very great favorite, and tells of

35. "A Francesco suo figliuolo" (221).
36. "Alla Sig. Veronica Bellona sua Suocera" (*Lettere* [1603], 226).
37. "A Francesco suo figliuolo" (224).
38. "Alla Sig. Veronica Bellona sua Suocera" (226).

how every evening at sunset, when holidaying on their country property, the entire family would drive out in their carriage, taking with them a picnic supper already prepared, and dine al fresco "in some woodland glade, to the murmur of water, to the song of the birds, with pastoral views and cooling breezes, and attended by the laughter and jests of five little angels who serve as our parrots and tiny clowns at these country repasts of ours."[39] On another occasion he writes home to his wife to tell her of the good recovery he is making at Lavinia's villa from a recent long and serious illness, enumerating all the factors that are contributing to his convalescence, and urging his wife to come and join him there: "Peace of mind, physical exercise, rest from my studies, even if not a complete break, good air, agreeable countryside, de-lightful company, continuous love and affection, choice wines (in fact better in my view than ours are), every sort of recreation, but above all, hare cours-ing, in which not just the count and I engage but the countess and all her chil-dren, who always come in the carriage to enjoy playing their part in the spectacle."[40]

Guasco reports two happy pieces of news in this volume of letters, the first being the betrothal of his son and heir, Francesco, to Chiaraluce Sta-geno, the daughter of a wealthy and highly esteemed Genoese gentleman. Guasco tells the various friends to whom he writes this news that she is a good girl, sixteen years of age, attractive, "well brought up, from what I hear, and with a good dowry to be paid immediately in cash." The second good tidings concern Guasco's eldest and favorite granddaughter, Margherita Lan-gosca, now aged ten, for whom her parents had apparently requested a post at the court of Turin. Lavinia's loyal friend, Lady Marianna de Tassis, who had mothered her during her years at court, has written to tell Guasco that Margherita is to enter the service of the young princesses of Savoy, and Guasco is so excited by the news that he has ridden in person to convey it to the Langoscos, overjoyed at the thought that the family link with the Sabau-dian court is to be continued into the next generation. Writing to thank Lady Marianna for her kind offices, Guasco says, "I base my hopes on the quality of this child, in addition to her lineage, trusting that these princesses may be as satisfied with her as Her Most Serene Infanta was in her lifetime with her mother."[41] He has no fears for the child, in that she is succeeding her mother in her vocation and because he knows that Lady Marianna will be like a grandmother to Margherita, just as she was a second mother to Lavinia, and

---

39. "Al Signor Giovan Giacopo Lughi, Podestà d'Alessandria" (*Il secondo volume* [1607], 41).
40. "Alla Signora Laura sua Moglie" (*Il secondo volume* [1607], 181).
41. "Alla Signora Donna Marianna de Tassis" (*Il secondo volume* [1607], 138).

he begs her to kiss the duke's hands on his behalf and convey his thanks to him for permitting his family to continue to serve him. This letter is succeeded by one to the duke himself, in which Guasco touchingly states that he gives thanks to God that "while the sun is setting over my house, I shall see the service being maintained in my own flesh and blood toward your house, which I shall bear in my heart into the next life, just as it has always been engraved on my heart in this one."[42]

Like her mother, Margherita, still aged only ten, possesses outstanding skills, one of which is calligraphy, an expertise in which her mother had perhaps instructed her, and the other of which is dancing, something Guasco never mentioned in connection with Lavinia, perhaps because as a musician her role would have been to provide the music for courtly dances rather than to participate in them. In the letter Guasco writes his wife inviting her to come and join him at the Langosco country seat, he tells her by way of encouragement that their little granddaughter challenges her to dance with her, "since she is indeed the most beautiful and willing ballerina of her age and sex to be found in this state, believe me, for it is absolutely true; and if you cannot believe it, come and see it, and I too will dance with you at your coming, if it is not enough that Margherita should dance for you."[43] Guasco has written a sonnet for his wife to show her how much he is missing her, which Margherita has transcribed for him, writing in her accomplished hand, which Guasco tells his wife is truly astonishing in one so young. She has authenticated her transcription with the words "Margherita Langosca wrote this" [Margherita Langosca scrisse], and she sends her grandmother "one of her long and measured dance curtsies that almost touch the floor, performed with such finesse as she sinks and rises again that you would long to watch her."[44]

Back home again, Guasco writes to Margherita to praise her for a letter he has received from her, telling her that she is as good a writer as her mother and that not only he but many others to whom he had proudly shown her letter have been amazed that she should possess so outstanding [singolar] a skill at so young an age. He also reminds her that she is just as admirable "in your feet, as in your hand" and that he and all his neighbors are longing for a visit from her so as to be able to watch her dancing at some festa, adding that she will tire of dancing long before her grandfather tires of watching her.[45] Writ-

42. "Al Serenissimo Signor Duca di Savoia" (Il secondo volume [1607], 139).

43. "Alla Signora Laura sua Moglie" (182).

44. Ibid., 183.

45. "A Margherita Langosca sua Nepote" (Il secondo volume [1607], 206). Dancing was, of course, a central activity of court life for both men and women and is mentioned many times in Baldas-

ing at the same time to her mother, Guasco tells her that the letter in which he had praised Margherita is destined for publication, to serve as a testimony to her achievements and to act as a spur to her to build on the fame of her mother, "concerning whose talents I found myself more than once unable to remain silent on paper, offering to God the thanks due to Him that they merited, seeming as they did to me so convincing that I knew they could not be ascribed to paternal prejudice, for no matter how loving a father I always was to her, I never allowed my tenderness to obscure my judgment in that respect."[46] It is interesting to note that although, by the time this volume of letters was published, some fifteen years had elapsed since Lavinia had left her court post to get married, Guasco is still proudly bearing witness to her skills, which he trusts will serve as an inspiration to Margherita in her own court career. In the same missive, Guasco lavishes the highest praise on a letter Lavinia has just written him, telling her that he was so impressed by it that he has shown it to his friends, "finding it has a true epistolary style, with a good choice of terms, numerous clauses that are pleasing to the ear and well-linked together, and such in short that one could do no better with a long effort, let alone with such a rushed pen, and the messenger in such haste, that you were forced to seize the first rough sheet of paper that came to hand, with no time to look for anything better." Guasco concludes by sending Margherita two kisses, "one for herself and one for her skills" [*le sue virtù*].[47]

This volume also includes a long exhortation on all the pitfalls of student life to Guasco's second son, Cesare, who has just gone away to study at the Studio of Pavia. Guasco solemnly reminds him of his duty to obey and revere his parents, "as if they were earthly gods," and goes on to pay what is clearly a well-deserved tribute to Cesare's mother, saying that from the day she entered Guasco's house she had taken upon her own shoulders every care and worry both for their domestic affairs and for the running of their country estate and had attended to all these responsibilities with such prudence and discretion that Guasco had been able to devote himself entirely to his studies, leaving everything else to her. He also speaks of his wife's great piety, reminding Cesare that it was due to his mother's prayers that he had been saved from a terrible illness fifteen months earlier. Guasco states that he and his wife have now been married for more than forty years, and her reputation as

---

sarre Castiglione's *The Book of the Courtier* (ed. George Bull [Baltimore, 1967]) as demonstrating the vital courtly attributes of grace and nonchalance.

46. "Alla Contessa Donna Lavinia Langosca sua figliuola" (*Il secondo volume* [1607], 213).

47. Ibid., 214. It is pleasing to note that despite her many years of domestic life, serious illnesses, and innumerable pregnancies, Lavinia seems not to have lost the epistolary skills and elegant style that doubtless served her so well at the court of Savoy.

the most caring of wives and mothers is known far and wide, "so lucky you and lucky all of us, while such a lady is living in our midst."[48]

A final volume of Guasco's letters was published in Pavia in 1618, the year before he died, which takes us right up to this date.[49] By now a very old man indeed by contemporary standards, Guasco continues to write in the same vein, part formal, part playful, and always full of sympathy and understanding for the afflictions of others, as well as full of affection and gratitude for any kindnesses and attentions he had been shown. But much of his subject matter now is of the saddest possible kind, since a recurrent theme of these later letters is that of sickness and death in his immediate family.

There are a number of references in this volume to the progress of Guasco's son, the above-mentioned Cesare, who had studied first in Pavia and then in Salamanca and who had risen to become a "gentleman of the bedchamber" of Cardinal Maurizio, son to the duke of Savoy. Just as he was about to be appointed prior to an abbey, however, at the age of thirty-three, he fell ill and died, to his father's immense grief. In a whole series of letters to family friends and relatives Guasco gives a graphic account of Cesare's month-long fatal illness and the agonizing remedies he was obliged to undergo each day at the hands of the team of doctors called in by his parents, all to no avail.[50] Cesare's demise at the very peak of his career left only the eldest son, Francesco, and the latter's own small son, Annibalino, to continue the male line. In that family, too, death had struck, carrying off their second little boy, aged only fourteen months. Guasco had gone to comfort the grieving parents, Francesco and his wife Chiaraluce, for the loss of this little angel [*angioletto*], as Guasco fondly refers to him, and in a heartrending letter written to his wife, he relates how he had journeyed on to Milan from this sad visit to seek consolation with his beloved Lavinia and her family. Lavinia's one remaining son, named Carlo after the deceased first-born child, had been indisposed but was believed by Guasco and his wife to have fully recovered, and Guasco was entirely unprepared for the fresh tragedy that was awaiting him when he arrived at Lavinia's house in Milan. He had hoped to surprise her, but she had been watching for him and she herself came hurrying down the steps to greet him, drying her tears so as not to cause him immediate dis-

---

48. "A Cesare suo Figliuolo" (*Il secondo volume* [1607], 146).

49. We owe this last volume of Guasco's letters to the initiative of the editor, Agostino Bordoni, in personally visiting the writer in his family home to enquire whether Guasco had any copies of letters he had written since the 1607 edition that he would allow Bordoni to publish. Not only did Guasco meet his request, but he also promised Bordoni to let him have copies of any others he should write while the volume was in the process of being printed.

50. See Guasco, *Lettere del signor Annibal Guasco Alessandrino* (1618), 229–74.

tress, and in reply to her father's inquiries after Carlo, even mustered the self-control to answer, "I believe he is quite well." Guasco, realizing at once from her tone of voice that some terrible event must have occurred, exclaimed, "What, has something happened to him?" whereupon Lavinia burst immediately into a flood of sobs and tears. She then recounted the dire events that had led to this new tragedy: Carlo, a promising boy of fourteen, had suddenly been taken violently ill in the middle of the night with internal bleeding; scores of doctors, barbers (i.e., surgeons) and later, priests, had been called in despite the hour and the dense fog that was enveloping the city but to no effect. The remedies applied were so violent and agonizing that the patient had cried out that he be allowed to die in peace, but he was spared nothing, in hopes that these extreme antidotes might save his life; however they were all to no avail, and the boy died at dawn the next morning after making a touching confession of his sins in an audible voice. All the aspirations of his father had been focused on this teenage son who was doing so well at his studies, and the couple had no hopes of any further male progeny, since no more children had arrived in recent years. Lavinia had related to Guasco how the count his father had done all that lay in his power that dire night to support his wife and dying son and to spare them the sight of his grief and how he had assisted the doctors in every way he could, only giving way to his feelings when he could leave them for a moment and retreat to some corner of the house to weep in solitude. The whole of Milan was now mourning Carlo's loss, both because of the great promise he had shown at so early an age, and because of the affection and regard in which his parents were held by all.[51]

Guasco also tells of a severe illness his wife had suffered but from which she had miraculously recovered at the advanced age of seventy-two, although the doctors had given up all hope for her. Guasco touchingly describes to his correspondent how deeply he and his wife loved one another and how profound was his relief at her recovery against all the odds.[52]

On a lighter note, we find Guasco writing a letter to his daughter Laura Caterina in her convent to accompany the portrait she had asked her father to send her to hang in her cell and enclosing a sonnet addressed to the portrait, beginning "Go, my hoary painted likeness." Guasco requests her prayers and promises to visit her in the near future.[53] Guasco clearly took a considerable pride in his poetic compositions, and several of the 1607 and 1618 epistles are accompanied by short poems. On one occasion he writes to

51. "Alla Sign. Laura sua Moglie" (*Lettere* [1618], 57).
52. "Al Padre Fra Carlo d'Alessandria Cappuccino" (*Lettere* [1618], 204).
53. "A Suor Laura Caterina sua Figliuola" (*Lettere* [1618], 15–16).

tell Lavinia that a sonnet he had composed concerning the violent storms both at sea and on land from which northern Italy had suffered lately had been read with especial enjoyment by a convention of distinguished literary figures assembled in Genoa. Not only that, but in Asti the preacher in the cathedral had taken this same sonnet as the subject of one of his sermons. Guasco encloses an eight-line madrigal in this same letter to Lavinia, which, with his wonted gallantry, he has written to celebrate the escape of her close friend, the beautiful Spanish countess of Oelves, from one of these sea storms. On another occasion he sends effusive thanks via Lavinia to the wife of the governor of Milan for her gift of a large quantity of candied plums, with a sonnet further expressing his appreciation of her kindness to him. He also encloses a touching little sonnet for Lavinia herself on the recent death of her devoted and much loved young page, who had expired with his eyes fixed fast on his mistress. In his sonnet, Guasco imagines the lad promising to continue to serve her even in heaven.[54]

Meanwhile Lavinia's gifted elder daughter, Margherita Langosca, had succeeded her mother at the court of Turin and was lady-in-waiting to the young princesses, daughters of Caterina and Carlo Emanuele. Her grandfather writes to acknowledge receipt of some eagerly awaited letters from Margherita that she had written both in Italian and in Spanish. Guasco is enormously impressed by her mastery of Spanish and by the elegance both of her hand and of the concepts she expresses, so much so that he tells her he has had copies made of these letters to send on to her mother, as he wishes to keep the originals himself in order to show them off to his friends whenever the occasion should arise. All who have read them so far have been amazed [stupefatti] and full of praise for them, and they have brought infinite joy to him and his household. He has written to her mother attesting to the beauty of Margherita's penmanship, and he presages a shining career for her from so excellent a start.[55] So while the Langosco male line had died out, the female line was continuing to flourish at the very center of power.

To conclude this family saga on a peaceful and idyllic note, Guasco writes to Lavinia expressing his pleasure that she has decided to leave Milan at the height of summer, where she has been in poor health, to spend a short sojourn at a country villa called Buffalora, which she is to reach by boat. He contrasts the scorching heat inside the city walls with the fresher air of the countryside and imagines her enjoyment as she floats comfortably down the

---

54. "Alla Contessa Donna Lavinia sua figliuola" (*Lettere* [1618], 111).

55. "A Donna Margherita Langosca, Dama delle Serenissime Infante di Savoia sua Nepote" (*Lettere* [1618], 68–69).

canal, watching the passing boats and cooling herself in the fresh breezes playing on the surface of the gleaming water.[56]

Guasco's letters provide a vital added dimension to the *Discourse*. The 1603 volume corroborates and illuminates the central events of Lavinia's early life on which the former work pivots and casts light on many questions that would have been left unanswered by the *Discourse* alone. Taken together with the two later volumes, these letters open up for us a unique window onto the life of a northern Italian patrician family at a defining moment in their history, as they successfully establish a foothold for themselves in the major power base of the court of Turin through the talents of two of their female members. The letters convey a portrait of Guasco himself as an affectionate and deeply involved father and grandfather, immensely proud of his family's, and above all his beloved daughter Lavinia's, achievements, as a devoted husband, and as the loyal friend of a wide circle of correspondents; they also show him networking with many of the leading figures of his day in northern Italy—dukes, cardinals, archbishops, ambassadors, literary figures, and highly placed noblemen and at times commenting to them on major contemporary events. They offer many glimpses of the contemporary postal system effected via speedy but unreliable and impatient messengers. Some of Guasco's missives have great poignancy due to the fact that they were written to convey news of tragic events to other family members as yet unaware of them. Others form a series, providing an hour-by-hour bulletin, with cliff-hanging suspense, concerning an event such as the progress of a difficult and dangerous childbirth. They bring home with enormous immediacy the extreme fragility of human life at this period, the ineffectiveness of the medical profession when endeavoring to cure even quite minor diseases, and the ever-present threat at any age of sudden death. They also chronicle, even if somewhat disjointedly, Lavinia's life over a period of some thirty-seven years, from her very early childhood up to the time of her court career and on to the period of her marriage, the births and, at times, the deaths of her many children, her later social and domestic life, and her continued links with the court of Savoy. We seldom hear her voice, but through her father's eyes we witness her experiencing the many different joys, griefs, triumphs, and vicissitudes of her eventful life, always sustained by her parents' love, care, and pride.

Whatever our views may be of the educational methods employed by Guasco, as detailed in the *Discourse*, to equip his precocious small daughter for a high-flying court career, and however much they deprived Lavinia of a

---

56. "Alla Contessa Donna Lavinia sua figliuola" (*Lettere* [1618], 217).

normal childhood, it is evident from his letters that they achieved their objectives and that his ambitions for her were abundantly realized: Lavinia was a phenomenal success at the court of Turin and won the lasting esteem and affection of her ducal employers, as well as of many of the infanta's entourage. Indeed, her reputation must even have become known at the Spanish court in Madrid, for we are told by the twentieth-century chronicler of the Langosco family that on July 2, 1599, two years after the death of her sibling Caterina, Isabella Clara Eugenia, the elder infanta, was passing through Tortona on her way to join her husband Albert, archduke of Austria, where a great crowd of people turned out to see her, among them Lavinia; Princess Isabella greeted them all with great benevolence, but she singled out Lavinia "for her illustrious lineage, her learning, her beauty and her accomplishments."[57]

57. Isabella, who in 1599 was aged thirty-three, had remained in Spain assisting and caring for her father, King Philip II, up until the time of his death on September 13, 1598. Only then had she married her cousin the archduke of Austria. She and Philip were in constant communication by letter with Caterina in Turin. The quote is recorded in F. Guasco, *Tavole genealogiche*, vol. 1, table 12.

SERIES EDITORS'
BIBLIOGRAPHY

PRIMARY SOURCES

Alberti, Leon Battista (1404–72). *The Family in Renaissance Florence.* Translated by Renée Neu Watkins. Columbia, S.C.: University of South Carolina Press, 1969.

Arenal, Electa, and Stacey Schlau, eds. *Untold Sisters: Hispanic Nuns in Their Own Works.* Translated by Amanda Powell. Albuquerque: University of New Mexico Press, 1989.

Astell, Mary (1666–1731). *The First English Feminist: Reflections on Marriage and Other Writings.* Edited and with an introduction by Bridget Hill. New York: St. Martin's Press, 1986.

Atherton, Margaret, ed. *Women Philosophers of the Early Modern Period.* Indianapolis: Hackett Publishing, 1994.

Aughterson, Kate, ed. *Renaissance Woman: Constructions of Femininity in England: A Source Book.* London and New York: Routledge, 1995.

Barbaro, Francesco (1390–1454). *On Wifely Duties* (preface and bk. 2). Translated by Benjamin Kohl. In *The Earthly Republic: Italian Humanists on Government and Society,* edited by Benjamin Kohl and R. G. Witt, 179–228. Philadelphia: University of Pennsylvania Press, 1976..

Behn, Aphra. *The Works of Aphra Behn.* Edited by Janet Todd. 7 vols. Columbus: Ohio State University Press, 1992–96.

Boccaccio, Giovanni. *Corbaccio; or, The Labyrinth of Love.* Translated by Anthony K. Cassell. 2d rev. ed. Binghamton, N.Y.: Medieval and Renaissance Texts and Studies, 1993.

———. *The Decameron.* Translated by G. H. McWilliam. Harmondsworth: Penguin, 1967.

Bruni, Leonardo (1370–1444). "On the Study of Literature (1405) to Lady Battista Malatesta of Montefeltro." In *The Humanism of Leonardo Bruni: Selected Texts.* Translated by Gordon Griffiths, James Hankins, and David Thompson, 240–51. Binghamton, N.Y.: Medieval and Renaissance Studies and Texts, 1987.

Cerasano, S. P., and Marion Wynne-Davies, eds. *Readings in Renaissance Women's Drama: Criticism, History, and Performance, 1594–1998.* London and New York: Routledge, 1998.

Christine de Pizan (1365–1431). *The Book of the City of Ladies.* Translated by Earl Jeffrey Richards; foreword by Marina Warner. New York: Persea Books, 1982.

———. *The Treasure of the City of Ladies.* Translated by Sarah Lawson. New York: Viking Penguin, 1985.

———. *The Treasure of the City of Ladies.* Translated by Charity Cannon Willard; edited by Madeleine P. Cosman. New York: Persea Books, 1989.

Crawford, Patricia, and Laura Gowing, eds. *Women's Worlds in Seventeenth-Century England: A Source Book.* London and New York: Routledge, 2000.

Della Casa, Giovanni. *Galateo.* Translated by Konrad Eisenbichler and Kenneth R. Bartlett. Toronto: Centre for Reformation and Renaissance Studies, 1986.

Elizabeth I: Collected Works. Edited by Leah S. Marcus, Janel Mueller, and Mary Beth Rose. Chicago: University of Chicago Press, 2000.

Elyot, Thomas (1490–1546). *Defence of Good Women.* In *The Feminist Controversy of the Renaissance: Facsimile Reproductions,* edited by Diane Bornstein. Delmar, N.Y.: Scholars' Facsimiles & Reprints, 1980.

Erasmus, Desiderius (1467–1536). *The Praise of Folly.* Translated by Betty Radice. Introduction and notes by A. H. T. Levi. New York: Penguin Books, 1993.

———. *Erasmus on Women.* Edited by Erika Rummel. Toronto: University of Toronto Press, 1996.

Ferguson, Moira, ed. *First Feminists: British Women Writers, 1578–1799.* Bloomington: Indiana University Press, 1985.

Firenzuola, Agnolo. *On the Beauty of Women.* Translated by Konrad Eisenbichler and Jacqueline Murray. Philadelphia: University of Pennsylvania Press, 1992.

Folger Collective on Early Women Critics, eds. *Women Critics, 1660–1820: An Anthology.* Bloomington: Indiana University Press, 1995.

Glückel of Hameln (1646–1724). *The Memoirs of Glückel of Hameln.* Translated by Marvin Lowenthal. New introduction by Robert Rosen. New York: Schocken Books, 1977.

Henderson, Katherine Usher, and Barbara F. McManus, eds. *Half Humankind: Contexts and Texts of the Controversy about Women in England, 1540–1640.* Urbana: University of Illinois Press, 1985.

Joscelin, Elizabeth. *The Mothers Legacy to Her Unborn Childe.* Edited by Jean leDrew Metcalfe. Toronto: University of Toronto Press, 2000.

Kaminsky, Amy Katz, ed. *Water Lilies, Flores del agua: An Anthology of Spanish Women Writers from the Fifteenth through the Nineteenth Century.* Minneapolis: University of Minnesota Press, 1996.

Kempe, Margery (1373–1439). *The Book of Margery Kempe.* Translated by Barry Windeatt. New York: Viking Penguin, 1986.

King, Margaret L., and Albert Rabil, Jr., eds. *Her Immaculate Hand: Selected Works by and about the Women Humanists of Quattrocento Italy.* 2d rev. ed. Binghamton, N.Y.: Medieval and Renaissance Texts and Studies, , 1991.

Klein, Joan Larsen, ed. *Daughters, Wives, and Widows: Writings by Men about Women and Marriage in England, 1500–1640.* Urbana: University of Illinois Press, 1992.

Knox, John (1505–72). *The Political Writings of John Knox: The First Blast of the Trumpet against the Monstrous Regiment of Women and Other Selected Works.* Edited by Marvin A. Breslow. Washington, D.C.: Folger Shakespeare Library, 1985.

Kors, Alan C., and Edward Peters, eds. *Witchcraft in Europe, 1100–1700: A Documentary History.* Philadelphia: University of Pennsylvania Press, 1972.

Krämer, Heinrich, and Jacob Sprenger. *Malleus Maleficarum* (ca. 1487). Translated by

Montague Summers. London: Pushkin Press, 1928; reprinted, New York: Dover, 1971.

Larsen, Anne R., and Colette H. Winn, eds. *Writings by Pre-Revolutionary French Women: From Marie de France to Elizabeth Vigée-Le Brun.* New York and London: Garland Publishing Co., 2000.

Lorris, William de, and Jean de Meun. *The Romance of the Rose.* Translated by Charles Dahlbert. Princeton, N.J.: Princeton University Press, 1971; reprinted, Lebanon, N.H.: University Press of New England, 1983.

Marguerite d'Angoulême, Queen of Navarre (1492–1549). *The Heptameron.* Translated by P. A. Chilton. New York: Viking Penguin, 1984.

Persico, Panfilo. *Del Segretario libri quattro, Ne' quali si tratta dell'arte e facoltà del segretario.* Venice: D. Zenaro Heirs, 1620.

Russell, Rinaldina, ed. *Sister Maria Celeste's Letters to Her Father, Galileo.* San Jose, Calif., and New York: Writers Club Press, 2000.

Teresa of Avila, Saint (1515–82). *The Life of Saint Teresa of Avila by Herself.* Translated by J. M. Cohen. New York: Viking Penguin, 1957.

Weyer, Johann (1515–88). *Witches, Devils, and Doctors in the Renaissance: Johann Weyer, De praestigiis daemonum.* Edited by George Mora with Benjamin G. Kohl, Erik Midelfort, and Helen Bacon. Translated by John Shea. Binghamton, N.Y.: Medieval and Renaissance Texts and Studies, 1991.

Wilson, Katharina M., ed. *Medieval Women Writers.* Athens: University of Georgia Press, 1984.

———, ed. *Women Writers of the Renaissance and Reformation.* Athens: University of Georgia Press, 1987.

Wilson, Katharina M., and Frank J. Warnke, eds. *Women Writers of the Seventeenth Century.* Athens: University of Georgia Press, 1989.

Wollstonecraft, Mary. *A Vindication of the Rights of Men and a Vindication of the Rights of Women.* Edited by Sylvana Tomaselli. Cambridge: Cambridge University Press, 1995.

———. *The Vindications of the Rights of Men, the Rights of Women.* Edited by D. L. Macdonald and Kathleen Scherf. Peterborough, Ontario: Broadview Press, 1997.

Women Writers in English, 1350–1850: 15 vols. Oxford: Oxford University Press. (Projected 30-vol. series suspended.)

Wroth, Lady Mary. *The Countess of Montgomery's Urania.* 2 pts. Edited by Josephine A. Roberts. Tempe, Ariz.: Medieval and Renaissance Texts and Studies, 1995, 1999.

———. *The Poems of Lady Mary Wroth.* Edited by Josephine A. Roberts. Baton Rouge: Louisiana State University Press, 1983.

de Zayas, Maria. *The Disenchantments of Love.* Translated by H. Patsy Boyer. Albany: State University of New York Press, 1997.

———. *The Enchantments of Love: Amorous and Exemplary Novels.* Translated by H. Patsy Boyer. Berkeley: University of California Press, 1990.

SECONDARY SOURCES

Akkerman, Tjitske, and Siep Sturman, eds. *Feminist Thought in European History, 1400–2000.* London and New York: Routledge, 1997.

Backer, Anne Liot Backer. *Precious Women.* New York: Basic Books, 1974.

Barash, Carol. English Women's Poetry, 1649–1714: Politics, Community, and Linguistic Authority. New York and Oxford: Oxford University Press, 1996.

Battigelli, Anna. *Margaret Cavendish and the Exiles of the Mind.* Lexington: University Press of Kentucky, 1998.

Beasley, Faith. *Revising Memory.* New Brunswick, N.J.: Rutgers University Press, 1990.

Beilin, Elaine V. *Redeeming Eve: Women Writers of the English Renaissance.* Princeton, N.J.: Princeton University Press, 1987.

Benson, Pamela Joseph. *The Invention of Renaissance Woman: The Challenge of Female Independence in the Literature and Thought of Italy and England.* University Park: Pennsylvania State University Press, 1992.

Blain, Virginia, Isobel Grundy, and Patricia Clements, eds. *The Feminist Companion to Literature in English: Women Writers from the Middle Ages to the Present.* New Haven, Conn.: Yale University Press, 1990.

Bloch, R. Howard. *Medieval Misogyny and the Invention of Western Romantic Love.* Chicago: University of Chicago Press, 1991.

Bornstein, Daniel, and Roberto Rusconi, eds. *Women and Religion in Medieval and Renaissance Italy.* Translated by Margery J. Schneider. Chicago: University of Chicago Press, 1996.

Brant, Clare, and Diane Purkiss, eds. *Women, Texts and Histories, 1575–1760.* London and New York: Routledge, 1992.

Briggs, Robin. *Witches and Neighbors: The Social and Cultural Context of European Witchcraft.* New York: HarperCollins, 1995; Viking Penguin, 1996.

Brink, Jean R., ed. *Female Scholars: A Tradition of Learned Women before 1800.* Montreal: Eden Press Women's Publications, 1980.

Brown, Judith C. *Immodest Acts: The Life of a Lesbian Nun in Renaissance Italy.* New York: Oxford University Press, 1986.

Cervigni, Dino S., ed. *Women Mystic Writers.* Volume 13 of *Annali d'Italianistica* (1995).

Cervigni, Dino S., and Rebecca West, eds. *Women's Voices in Italian Literature.* Volume 7 of *Annali d'Italianistica* (1989).

Charlton, Kenneth. *Women, Religion and Education in Early Modern England.* London and New York: Routledge, 1999.

Chojnacka, Monica. *Working Women in Early Modern Venice.* Baltimore: Johns Hopkins University Press, 2001.

Chojnacki, Stanley. *Women and Men in Renaissance Venice: Twelve Essays on Patrician Society.* Baltimore: Johns Hopkins University Press, 2000.

Cholakian, Patricia Francis. *Rape and Writing in the "Heptameron" of Marguerite de Navarre.* Carbondale and Edwardsville: Southern Illinois University Press, 1991.

———. *Women and the Politics of Self-Representation in Seventeenth-Century France.* Newark: University of Delaware Press, 2000.

Davis, Natalie Zemon. *Society and Culture in Early Modern France.* Stanford, Calif.: Stanford University Press, 1975. See, esp. chaps. 3 and 5.

———. *Women on the Margins: Three Seventeenth-Century Lives.* Cambridge, Mass.: Harvard University Press, 1995.

DeJean, Joan. *Ancients against Moderns: Culture Wars and the Making of a Fin de Siècle.* Chicago: University of Chicago Press, 1997.

————. *Tender Geographies: Women and the Origins of the Novel in France.* New York: Columbia University Press, 1991.

Dixon, Laurinda S. *Perilous Chastity: Women and Illness in Pre-Enlightenment Art and Medicine.* Ithaca, N.Y.: Cornell University Press, 1995.

Dolan, Frances, E. *Whores of Babylon: Catholicism, Gender and Seventeenth-Century Print Culture.* Ithaca, N.Y.: Cornell University Press, 1999.

Donovan, Josephine. *Women and the Rise of the Novel, 1405–1726.* New York: St. Martin's Press, 1999.

De Erauso, Catalina. *Lieutenant Nun: Memoir of a Basque Transvestite in New York.* Translated by Michele Ttepto and Gabriel Stepto; foreword by Marjorie Garber. Boston: Beacon Press, 1995.

Duby, George, Michelle Perrot, and Pauline Schmitt Pantel, eds. *A History of Women in the West.* Vol. 1, *From Ancient Goddesses to Christian Saints,* edited by Pauline Schmitt Pantel. Vol. 2, *Silences of the Middle Ages,* edited by Christiane Klapisch-Zuber. Vol. 3, *Renaissance and Enlightenment Paradoxes,* edited by Natalie Zemon Davis and Arlette Farge. Cambridge, Mass.: Harvard University Press, 1992–93.

Erickson, Amy Louise. *Women and Property in Early Modern England.* London and New York: Routledge, 1993.

Ezell, Margaret J. M. *Writing Women's Literary History.* Baltimore: Johns Hopkins University Press, 1993.

Ferguson, Margaret W., Maureen Quilligan, and Nancy J. Vickers, eds. *Rewriting the Renaissance: The Discourses of Sexual Difference in Early Modern Europe.* Chicago: University of Chicago Press, 1987.

Frye, Susan, and Karen Robertson, eds. *Maids and Mistresses, Cousins and Queens: Women's Alliances in Early Modern England.* Oxford: Oxford University Press, 1999.

Gallagher, Catherine. *Nobody's Story: The Vanishing Acts of Women Writers in the Marketplace, 1670–1820.* Berkeley: University of California Press, 1994.

Gelbart, Nina Rattner. *The King's Midwife: A History and Mystery of Madame du Coudray.* Berkeley: University of California Press, 1998.

Goldberg, Jonathan. *Desiring Women Writing: English Renaissance Examples.* Stanford, Calif.: Stanford University Press, 1997.

Goldsmith, Elizabeth C., ed. *Writing the Female Voice.* Boston: Northeastern University Press, 1989.

Goldsmith, Elizabeth C., and Dena Goodman, eds. *Going Public: Women and Publishing in Early Modern France.* Ithaca, N.Y.: Cornell University Press, 1995.

Greer, Margaret Rich. *Maria de Zayas.* University Park: Pennsylvania State University Press, 2000.

Grendler, Paul F. *Schooling in Renaissance Italy Literacy and Learning, 1300–1600.* Baltimore and London: John Hopkins University Press, 1989.

Grierson, Edward. *King of Two Worlds: Philip II of Spain.* London: Collins, 1974.

Hall, Kim F. *Things of Darkness: Economies of Race and Gender in Early Modern England.* Ithaca, N.Y.: Cornell University Press, 1995.

Hampton, Timothy. *Literature and the Nation in the Sixteenth Century: Inventing Renaissance France.* Ithaca, N.Y.: Cornell University Press, 2001.

Hardwick, Julie. *The Practice of Patriarchy: Gender and the Politics of Household Authority in Early Modern France.* University Park: Pennsylvania State University Press, 1998.

Haselkorn, Anne M., and Betty Travitsky, eds. *The Renaissance Englishwoman in Print: Counterbalancing the Canon.* Amherst: University of Massachusetts Press, 1990.

Herlihy, David. "Did Women Have a Renaissance? A Reconsideration." *Medievalia et Humanistica,* n.s. 13 (1985): 1–22.

Hill, Bridget. *The Republican Virago: The Life and Times of Catharine Macaulay, Historian.* New York: Oxford University Press, 1992.

Hobby, Elaine. *Virtue of Necessity: English Women's Writing 1646–1688.* London: Virago Press, 1988.

Horowitz, Maryanne Cline. "Aristotle and Women." *Journal of the History of Biology* 9 (1976): 183–213.

Hufton, Olwen H. *The Prospect before Her: A History of Women in Western Europe.* Vol. 1, *1500–1800.* New York: HarperCollins, 1996.

Hull, Suzanne W. *Chaste, Silent, and Obedient: English Books for Women, 1475–1640.* San Marino, Calif.: The Huntington Library, 1982.

Hutner, Heidi, ed. *Rereading Aphra Behn: History, Theory, and Criticism.* Charlottesville: University Press of Virginia, 1993.

Hutson, Lorna, ed. *Feminism and Renaissance Studies.* New York: Oxford University Press, 1999.

Jacobs, Fredrika H. *Defining the Renaissance Virtuosa: Women Artists and the Language of Art History and Criticism.* Cambridge: Cambridge University Press, 1997.

James, Susan E. *Kateryn Parr: The Making of a Queen.* Aldershot and Brookfield: Ashgate Publishing, 1999.

Jankowski, Theodora A. *Women in Power in the Early Modern Drama.* Urbana: University of Illinois Press, 1992.

Jed, Stephanie H. *Chaste Thinking: The Rape of Lucretia and the Birth of Humanism.* Bloomington: Indiana University Press, 1989.

Jordan, Constance. *Renaissance Feminism: Literary Texts and Political Models.* Ithaca, N.Y.: Cornell University Press, 1990.

Kamen, Henry. *Philip of Spain.* New Haven, Conn., and London: Yale University Press, 1997.

Kelly, Joan. "Did Women Have a Renaissance?" In her *Women, History and Theory.* Chicago: University of Chicago Press, 1984. Reprinted in *Becoming Visible: Women in European History,* edited by Renate Bridenthal, Claudia Koonz and Susan M. Stuard. 3d ed. Boston: Houghton Mifflin, 1998.

———. "Early Feminist Theory and the *Querelle des Femmes.*" In her *Women, History, and Theory.* Chicago: University of Chicago Press, 1984.

Kelso, Ruth. *Doctrine for the Lady of the Renaissance.* Urbana: University of Illinois Press, 1976.

King, Margaret L. *Women of the Renaissance.* Foreword by Catharine R. Stimpson. Chicago: University of Chicago Press, 1991.

———. "The Woman of the Renaissance." In *Renaissance Characters,* edited by Eugenio Garin; translated by Lydia G. Cochrane, 207–49. Chicago and London: University of Chicago Press, 1991.

Krontiris, Tina. *Oppositional Voices: Women as Writers and Translators of Literature in the English Renaissance.* London and New York: Routledge, 1992.

Kuehn, Thomas. *Law, Family, and Women: Toward a Legal Anthropology of Renaissance Italy.* Chicago: University of Chicago Press, 1991.

Kunze, Bonnelyn Young. *Margaret Fell and the Rise of Quakerism.* Stanford, Calif.: Stanford University Press, 1994.

Labalme, Patricia A., ed. *Beyond Their Sex: Learned Women of the European Past.* New York: New York University Press, 1980.

Laqueur, Thomas. *Making Sex: Body and Gender from the Greeks to Freud.* Cambridge, Mass.: Harvard University Press, 1990.

Larsen, Anne R., and Colette H. Winn, eds. *Renaissance Women Writers: French Texts/American Contexts.* Detroit: Wayne State University Press, 1994.

Lerner, Gerda. *The Creation of Patriarchy.* Women and History, vol. 1. New York: Oxford University Press, 1986.

———. *Creation of Feminist Consciousness, 1000–1870.* Women and History, vol. 2. New York: Oxford University Press, 1994.

Levin, Carole, and Jeanie Watson, eds. *Ambiguous Realities: Women in the Middle Ages and Renaissance.* Detroit: Wayne State University Press, 1987.

Levin, Carole, et al. *Extraordinary Women of the Medieval and Renaissance World: A Biographical Dictionary.* Westport, Conn.: Greenwood Press, 2000.

Lindsey, Karen. *Divorced, Beheaded, Survived: A Feminist Reinterpretation of the Wives of Henry VIII.* Reading, Mass.: Addison-Wesley Publishing, 1995.

Lochrie, Karma. *Margery Kempe and Translations of the Flesh.* Philadelphia: University of Pennsylvania Press, 1992.

Lougee, Carolyn C. *Le Paradis des Femmes: Women, Salons, and Social Stratification in Seventeenth-Century France.* Princeton, N.J.: Princeton University Press, 1976.

MacCarthy, Bridget G. *The Female Pen: Women Writers and Novelists, 1621–1818.* Preface by Janet Todd. Cork: Cork University Press, 1946–47; New York: New York University Press, 1994.

Maclean, Ian. *The Renaissance Notion of Woman: A Study in the Fortunes of Scholasticism and Medical Science in European Intellectual Life.* Cambridge: Cambridge University Press, 1980.

———. *Woman Triumphant: Feminism in French Literature, 1610–1652.* Oxford: Clarendon Press, 1977.

Matter, E. Ann, and John Coakley, eds. *Creative Women in Medieval and Early Modern Italy.* Philadelphia: University of Pennsylvania Press, 1994. This collection is the sequel to the Monson collection, below.

McLeod, Glenda. *Virtue and Venom: Catalogs of Women from Antiquity to the Renaissance.* Ann Arbor: University of Michigan Press, 1991.

Mendelson, Sara, and Patricia Crawford. *Women in Early Modern England, 1550–1720.* Oxford: Clarendon Press, 1998.

Miller, Nancy K. *The Heroine's Text: Readings in the French and English Novel, 1722–1782.* New York: Columbia University Press, 1980.

Monson, Craig A., ed. *The Crannied Wall: Women, Religion, and the Arts in Early Modern Europe.* Ann Arbor: University of Michigan Press, 1992.

Newman, Karen. *Fashioning Femininity and English Renaissance Drama.* Chicago and London: University of Chicago Press, 1991.

Okin, Susan Moller. *Women in Western Political Thought.* Princeton, N.J.: Princeton University Press, 1979.

Ozment, Steven. *The Bürgermeister's Daughter: Scandal in a Sixteenth-Century German Town.* New York: St. Martin's Press, 1995.

Pacheco, Anita, ed. *Early Women Writers: 1600–1720.* New York and London: Longman, 1998. The writers discussed in this collection are all English.

Pagels, Elaine. *Adam, Eve, and the Serpent.* New York: Harper Collins, 1988.

Panizza, Letizia, ed. *Women in Italian Renaissance Culture and Society.* Oxford: European Humanities Research Centre, 2000.

Panizza, Letizia, and Sharon Wood, eds. *A History of Women's Writing in Italy.* Cambridge: Cambridge University Press, 2000.

Perry, Ruth. *The Celebrated Mary Astell: An Early English Feminist.* Chicago: University of Chicago Press, 1986.

Pierson, Peter. *Philip of Spain.* London: Thames & Hudson, 1975.

Pollack, Martha D. *Turin 1564-1680: Urban Design, Military Culture, and the Creation of the Absolutist Capital.* Chicago and London: University of Chicago Press, 1991.

Richardson, Brian. *Printing, Writers and Readers in Renaissance Italy.* Cambridge: Cambridge University Press, 1999.

———. "The Debates on Printing in Renaissance Italy." *La Bibliofilía,* nos. 2–3 (1998), 135–55.

Riddle, John M. *Contraception and Abortion from the Ancient World to the Renaissance.* Cambridge, Mass.: Harvard University Press, 1992.

———. *Eve's Herbs: A History of Contraception and Abortion in the West.* Cambridge, Mass.: Harvard University Press, 1997.

Rose, Mary Beth, ed. *Women in the Middle Ages and the Renaissance: Literary and Historical Perspectives.* Syracuse, N.Y.: Syracuse University Press, 1986.

Rosenthal, Margaret F. *The Honest Courtesan: Veronica Franco, Citizen and Writer in Sixteenth-Century Venice.* Foreword by Catharine R. Stimpson. Chicago: University of Chicago Press, 1992.

Sackville-West, Vita. *Daughter of France: The Life of La Grande Mademoiselle.* Garden City, N.Y.: Doubleday, 1959.

Schiebinger, Londa. *The Mind Has No Sex? Women in the Origins of Modern Science.* Cambridge, Mass.: Harvard University Press, 1991.

———. *Nature's Body: Gender in the Making of Modern Science.* Boston: Beacon Press, 1993.

Shemek, Deanna. *Ladies Errant: Wayward Women and Social Order in Early Modern Italy.* Durham, N.C.: Duke University Press, 1998.

Sobel, Dava. *Galileo's Daughter: A Historical Memoir of Science, Faith, and Love.* New York: Penguin Books, 2000.

Sommerville, Margaret R. *Sex and Subjection: Attitudes to Women in Early-Modern Society.* London: Arnold, 1995.

Spencer, Jane. *The Rise of the Woman Novelist: From Aphra Behn to Jane Austen.* Oxford: Basil Blackwell, 1986.

Spender, Dale. *Mothers of the Novel: 100 Good Women Writers before Jane Austen.* London and New York: Routledge, 1986.

Sperling, Jutta Gisela. *Convents and the Body Politic in Late Renaissance Venice.* Foreword by Catharine R. Stimpson. Chicago: University of Chicago Press, 1999.

Steinbrügge, Lieselotte. *The Moral Sex: Woman's Nature in the French Enlightenment.* Translated by Pamela E. Selwyn. New York: Oxford University Press, 1995.

Stuard, Susan M. "The Dominion of Gender: Women's Fortunes in the High Middle Ages." In *Becoming Visible: Women in European History,* edited by Renate Bridenthal, Claudia Koonz, and Susan M. Stuard. 3d ed. Boston: Houghton Mifflin, 1998.

Summit, Jennifer. *Lost Property: The Woman Writer and English Literary History, 1380–1589.* Chicago: University of Chicago Press, 2000.

Teague, Frances. *Bathsua Makin, Woman of Learning.* Lewisburg, Pa.: Bucknell University Press, 1999.

Todd, Janet. *The Secret Life of Aphra Behn.* London: Pandora, 2000.

———. *The Sign of Angelica: Women, Writing and Fiction, 1660–1800.* New York: Columbia University Press, 1989.

Walsh, William T. *St. Teresa of Avila: A Biography.* Rockford, Ill.: TAN Books & Publications, 1987.

Warner, Marina. *Alone of All Her Sex: The Myth and Cult of the Virgin Mary.* New York: Knopf, 1976.

Warnicke, Retha M. *The Marrying of Anne of Cleves: Royal Protocol in Tudor England.* Cambridge: Cambridge University Press, 2000.

Watt, Diane. *Secretaries of God: Women Prophets in Late Medieval and Early Modern England.* Cambridge, England: D. S. Brewer, 1997.

Welles, Marcia L. *Persephone's Girdle: Narratives of Rape in Seventeenth-Century Spanish Literature.* Nashville: Vanderbilt University Press, 2000.

Whitehead, Barbara J., ed. *Women's Education in Early Modern Europe: A History, 1500–1800.* New York and London: Garland Publishing, 1999.

Wiesner, Merry E. *Women and Gender in Early Modern Europe.* Cambridge: Cambridge University Press, 1993.

Willard, Charity Cannon. *Christine de Pizan: Her Life and Works.* New York: Persea Books, 1984.

Wilson, Katharina, ed. *An Encyclopedia of Continental Women Writers.* New York: Garland, 1991.

Woodbridge, Linda. *Women and the English Renaissance: Literature and the Nature of Womankind, 1540–1620.* Urbana: University of Illinois Press, 1984.

Woods, Susanne. *Lanyer: A Renaissance Woman Poet.* New York: Oxford University Press, 1999.

Woods, Susanne, and Margaret P. Hannay, eds. *Teaching Tudor and Stuart Women Writers.* New York: Modern Language Association, 2000.

INDEX